MARKETING STRATEGIES FOR THE

NEW EUROPE

A NORTH AMERICAN PERSPECTIVE ON 1992

MARKETING
STRATEGIES _{FOR THE}

FOR
THE

NEW
EUROPE

A NORTH AMERICAN
PERSPECTIVE ON 1992

---

by
John K. Ryans Jr.
and
Pradeep A. Rau
Kent State University

Contributors:
James R. Krum
University of Delaware
Cynthia C. Ryans
Kent State University

AMERICAN
MARKETING
ASSOCIATION

President: Jeffrey Heilbrunn
Business Director: Francesca Van Gorp
Jacket Design: Frank Leone

Library of Congress Cataloging-in-Publication Data

Ryans, John K.
   Marketing strategies for the new Europe : a North American perspective on 1992/ by John K. Ryans, Jr., and Pradeep A. Rau; contributors, James R. Krum, Cynthia C. Ryans.
      p.   cm.
   Includes bibliographical references.
   ISBN 0-87757-203-8
   1. European Economic Community countries—Commerce—United States.
   2. United States—Commerce—European Economic Community countries.
   3. Corporations, America—European Economic Community countries.
   I. Rau, Pradeep A. II. Title.
   HF3092.R93 1990
   337.1'42—dc20   89-18279
                                                                                      CIP

Printed in the United States of America

Contents

Vignettes: Benetton, AIG, H. J. Heinz, Northern Telecom, and Buckeye Feeds.
Appendix: Thomas Bennett and Craig S. Hakkio, "Europe 1992: Implications for U.S. Firms," *Economic Review*. (Abridged Version).

LIST OF VIGNETTES

LIST OF ILLUSTRATIONS

Preface

Future historians are likely to rank the developments surrounding European Community-1992 (EC-92) among the most significant events of the Twentieth Century. Further, there is little doubt that EC-92 will have a major impact on the way all U.S. and Canadian firms "do business" for decades to come.

The impact of EC-92 has now been well established through the popular business press and hardly a day passes without another general article on the topic. Therefore, it is not surprising that many U.S./Canadian companies have begun (or are starting) to respond to this opportunity. But, generally their task has not been an easy one.

Part of their problem results from the E.C. Single Market resolution process itself, i.e. nearly 300 major administrative, physical and technical barriers which need to be resolved and many separate commissions which are involved in the overall harmonization effort. One literally needs a "scoreboard" indicating what has been resolved and the nature of the resolution. Then there are the political machinations, the charges and countercharges regarding the U.S.'s role (if any) in the EC-92 outcome, and the rumors that have surrounded much of the deliberations. Stated simply, it has been quite difficult to forecast what the ultimate E.C. rules will be that will affect an individual industry, much less a company.

What has become increasingly clear is that most companies are unlikely to have all the information they wish regarding the new EC-92 rules prior to their making some critical decisions regarding their entry strategy(ies), financial arrangements and marketing structures. The marketplace itself is already changing rapidly due to mergers and aquisitions, alliances, etc., and time is increasingly becoming a concern. "One cannot wait until the last 'i' is dotted on the product standards for our industry before we make our move . . . we know we must have product/presence there regardless . . ." is an attitude we hear more and more frequently expressed.

At this point, no one can do more than make an educated guess as to how many of the harmonization issues will be ultimately resolved or what form the European Community will finally take. However, there are frequently asked questions that can be answered. For example, "to what extent have many of the leading U.S. companies already developed their plans for EC-92 and what are their plans?" or "what alternatives do companies have if they wish to insure a position in the new European marketplace?" Answers to these questions will provide some needed direction for North American firms, as they scramble for a place in Europe in 1993.

Our objectives in this book are actually four-fold. They are to:

1. provide the professional and academic reader with a more in-depth understanding of the problems and opportunities associated with EC-92 than can typically be offered by the business press;
2. present the results of our research that was directed to answering the questions raised in the previous paragraph;
3. offer a complete case-like description of how a few U.S. companies plan to market in the new Europe; and finally,
4. indicate several scenarios regarding EC-92 that should assist a firm plan its overall EC-92 strategy, including its marketing strategy.

Undoubtedly, some of our discussion will have a marketing slant . . . just as some of the public accounting firms' research on EC-92 has emphasized tax planning. However, the very nature of EC-92 mandates that we will look at the bigger picture in most of our presentation. In fact, EC-92 has already caused many firms to take steps ranging from reorganizing on a global or regional basis, or entering into critical alliances they would never have considered a few years ago, to bolstering dramatically their production and distribution skills. In other words, taking steps well beyond just marketing strategies alone.

Finally, it is our goal to attempt to get firms that have been "in-place" in Europe for many years to at least re-examine their post EC-92 position and to see if new strategies might not be appropriate. Recently, a speaker at a national meeting of business executives stated ". . . our company has been in Europe for many years so we will just continue doing what we have so successfully done in the past." Europe will be changing from 12 national markets to one regional marketplace and this alone suggests that this firm needs to reconsider its position. When we add to this, the new competitive milieu in which many industries will become dramatically more concentrated and in which any redundancy of sales, production, etc. cannot be tolerated, such complacency can easily lead to failure.

For many firms, EC-92 will provide substantial rewards, while others will undoubtedly enter too late or otherwise fail to capture the "window of opportunity." Peter Drucker recently challenged European firms to ask "what do we do today to prosper in the Europe of 1993?" A similar challenge can be offered to U.S. and Canadian firms, as well.

We would like to thank Dr. James Krum, Professor of Marketing, University of Delaware, and Professor Cynthia C. Ryans, Resources Editor of the *Journal of Small Business Management* and Chair, Cataloging Department, Kent State University, for contributing special original manuscripts for the monograph. In addition, Dr. Irene Herremans, University of Calgary, and Diana Abdoo, Kent State University, both participated in our original research and wrote vignettes for the monograph. Others who have provided especially valuable assistance are Janet Parkinson, our editor; Brian Rooks, our research assistant; Bernie Messina and Vicki Thompson, our typists; Linda Poje, who prepared the visuals; and Dr. Richard Skinner, Chairman, Department of Marketing, Kent State University. Finally, special thanks are due to Francesca Van Gorp, Business Director, Publications, the American Marketing Association (AMA), and Carolyn Pollard Neal, Editor of *Business*. (The latter was aware of our EC-92 research and suggested that the AMA contact us about preparing the monograph.)

Work on this manuscript began in July 1989 and given the high level of interest currently focussed on EC-92 by business people, the press and others, we wanted to complete the manuscript in the shortest time possible. The assistance of all the people mentioned above helped us to achieve this objective and the manuscript was ready in under three months. We realize that this will not be the first nor necessarily the last book or monograph to be written on the topic, but we do believe that it represents a unique synthesis of research we have done and the collective wisdom of many others who have been studying the market integration process. The responsibility for the views expressed in the monograph and for any errors, of course, remain our own.

Kent, Ohio   John K. Ryans, Jr.
October 15, 1989   Pradeep A. Rau

AN EC-92 CHECKLIST FOR NORTH AMERICAN FIRMS WITH OPERATIONS IN EUROPE

North American firms looking at the market integration process would do well to consider the following questions. It is our opinion that these questions are important not only for firms which have not begun the task of developing their post-1992 European strategy but also for firms who have been doing their homework because for them, these questions will serve as a checklist against which they can compare their own thinking so as to avoid missing important areas in which action may be needed in preparation for 1992. We realize that firms that have no European exposure and have not even been exporting to Europe until now should approach the single market as they would any other individual market in the world. These questions are therefore, primarily for firms that have existing European operations including a physical presence in the form of a sales or manufacturing subsidiary.

1. How is our business organized in Europe? What is the pattern of reporting between the national subsidiaries, the European headquarters, if one exists, and the North American corporate headquarters?
2. What opportunities exist for consolidating our manufacturing activities, if any, in Europe?
3. Related to 2, is our industry marked by significant economies of scale which could render the previously national manufacturing units inefficient?
4. What opportunities exist for rearranging our transportation/logistics/physical distribution activities in the new borderless market? What is the optimal number of warehouses required to serve the European market after integration and where should they be located?
5. What is the likelihood that we can rationalize our product lines including brand names, designs and packaging without losing the ability to respond to regional, linguistic and cultural differences?
6. Can the promotional activities be standardized and what will be the implications for media and agency choice?
7. Where should the R&D activities of our firm be located and is there a need for moving some of the research and development (basic or applied or both) from North America to Europe?
8. Which firms in Europe, North America or elsewhere in the world have complementary strengths (financial, technical or marketing) that may make them attractive candidates for us to explore joint venture, acquisition or other forms of alliance with?

9. What would be the best way for us to inculcate an "European" view among our employees in the various national subsidiary companies and European headquarters?
10. What changes may be necessary in our products as the process of harmonization of product standards across Europe proceeds and what is the best way for us to monitor these developments and possibly even influence them?
11. What level of presence, if any, should we maintain in Brussels both to monitor E.C. legislative and administrative actions and to have our point of view presented to E.C. decision makers?
12. If we have not done any significant preparatory work for 1992, shouldn't we begin by looking at the original E.C. White Paper to understand the scope of the proposals and directives that have been drafted by the E.C. commission so as to identify areas that may impact our business?

Authors' Note

—GE to acquire 50% of Hungarian light bulb manufacturer
—Daihatsu to build cars in Poland
—GM considering investment in Hungary
—Suzuki announces automobile manufacturing plans in Hungary

   This note presents an analysis of some of the events that have occurred since this book went to press in mid-October 1989. Events in Eastern Europe have unfolded in rapid fire succession and as we have pointed out in the book, the whole issue of EC-92 is intimately related to the changes occurring in the East bloc. One by one, democratic reforms and major diminution in the strength of the Communist Party have occurred in each of the Warsaw Pact countries. After Poland and Hungary which had initiated their moves towards reforms quite some time ago, we have seen rapid changes in East Germany, Czechoslovakia, Bulgaria and as 1989 drew to a close, in Romania. Remarkably, in all the countries except the last mentioned, change has come without any major turmoil or loss of life.
   Inevitably, these changes have raised the question of how the newly "reopened" East bloc economies will fit in the overall economic landscape of Europe. Perhaps the most dramatic symbol of the East European opening was the announcement November 9, 1989 by E. Germany that the Berlin Wall would come down and travelers from E. Berlin would be free to travel to W. Berlin. This, of course, led to an immediate reemergence of the question of German reunification. The two Germanys have always considered

xiv

themselves as being part of a single country because they share common origins and the same language. The crumbling of the Iron Curtain and free movement of people between East and West Germany, therefore suggested the inevitable reunification of the two Germanys. The West German Chancellor, Helmut Kohl, traveled to East Germany and in no uncertain terms stated a multipoint plan for reunification. Meanwhile, there was great concern among several other E.C. members about the new developments. The major concern was that West Germany would now become so concerned about the reunification issue and the other aspects of the East bloc opening that its commitment to the single European Market would be reduced. Indeed with the East–West thaw, there was concern that European integration may no longer have a security dimension to it. Now the fears were that if German reunification were to proceed, a unified Germany would so dwarf the next largest E.C. country that there was a danger of it overwhelming the community and perhaps reasserting its power over neighbors as it had done on more than one occasion earlier this century. These fears of a bullying Germany are perhaps quite unfounded in the world of 1989 but the fact that a rush towards German reunification could bog down or even derail the EC-92 process seemed to be a reasonable concern. The French President, Francois Mitterrand, therefore took immediate steps to get a renewed commitment from the Federal Republic of Germany to the EC-92 process. Such a commitment proved easy to obtain and the EC countries affirmed that the best way for them to provide the needed economic support to the East bloc countries was by first strengthening the European Community itself and moving ahead on the EC-92 program.

During this period, between the manuscript going to press and the end of 1989, other developments that have occurred are EC countries' agreement on banking regulation and a renewed call by EC commissioner Jacques Delors and various EC leaders for a complete European Monetary Union. Prime Minister Thatcher of Britain still opposes such a complete union but she has agreed to look into the issue of her country joining the European exchange rate mechanism which is a major first step towards a full monetary union. The E.C. countries have also decided that formal expansion of the community membership should not occur until 1993, at the earliest. This should reassure the poorer Southern countries in the European Community because admission of lower wage countries like Turkey and perhaps even some East bloc countries would have greatly reduced their (Spain, Portugal, etc.) attractiveness as locations for new investment in the EC. Meanwhile, the EC has expanded the scope of its free trade agreement with the EFTA countries which should allow them even easier access to the EC markets than they have previously enjoyed.

So, as 1990 dawns, the best view we can offer of the European market integration process is to repeat what we have said in the original manuscript.

That is to say that no immediate expansion of EC membership is likely to occur and that while there will inevitably be some new interest in the East bloc countries as a result of recent events, major new investment from Western Europe is not likely to occur in E. Europe for at least some time. Most of the East bloc countries continue to suffer from faltering economies and the nonconvertibility of their currencies. For this reason investment, therefore, is unlikely to be very attractive in the short term. However, trade preferences and liberal credit are likely to be offered to the East bloc to help rebuild their economies. All of this, of course, leaves one question of the rival military alliances—NATO and the Warsaw Pact—still unresolved. For the moment, it would appear that both sides would see it in their interest to maintain the two military alliances so as to avoid any destabilizing effects of a sudden realignment. This may also be the best argument against immediate reunification between the two Germanys which are currently part of rival military alliances. Over time, if the East–West relationship continues to evolve as per current trends, a reassessment of the military alliances may be justified and indeed may occur spontaneously if the military forces are no longer needed in a "No Cold War World." The economic alignments on the other hand are likely to evolve slowly. We see a loose federal structure to Europe where there is a central core of countries that cooperate on all economic political matters including having a full monetary union with peripheral bands of countries, possibly including East bloc countries, which have differing levels of linkage with the core. These linkages would range from close economic coordination to just enjoying some of the free trade aspects of the relationship. This is much the same as we have speculated in Chapter 6.

The events in Eastern Europe, during the last few weeks of 1989, no doubt introduce a new dimension to the market integration process currently underway in the European Community but the immediate objectives of 1992 are not likely to be materially affected in any way. If one looks to the longer term, the European Community may countenance a membership of sixteen or eighteen or more members and one may even see a community which more closely resembles the "Common European Home," mentioned by Mikhail Gorbachev, which stretches from the Ural Mountains to the Atlantic Ocean. Such a view is so far in the future that it will require a level of "crystal ball gazing" that is beyond the scope of this book.

January 20, 1990

Charting the European Community's Progress

For the existing "European companies"—the subsidiaries of the American mul-
tinationals first and foremost . . .—a unified European economy . . . is the
only thing that makes any sense at all, the only thing that can possibly work.
—Peter Drucker
"Strategies for Survival in Europe in 1993"
The Wall Street Journal
Tuesday, July 12, 1988

The quote above emphasizes the fact that until now, the only true European companies were from the United States or possibly a handful of giant
European multinationals like Philips, Unilever and Nestle. With the anticipated integration of the European market, even national-only European
companies will come to the same realization that the true European multinationals have always had—the realization, as Drucker says, that a unified
European economy is essential for the future economic and technological
vitality of Europe. This integration process has been in motion for over thirty
years at one pace or the other and in order to understand the present flurry
of activity surrounding the new post-1992 Europe, a historical perspective
is necessary.

HISTORICAL OVERVIEW

It was more than thirty years ago that the idea of integrating the European
market was first mooted in the Treaty of Rome signed in 1957. Initially,
the six members (France, Germany, Italy, Belgium, the Netherlands, and

Luxembourg) concentrated on forming a customs union by abolishing tariffs on trade among themselves and imposing common tariffs on imports from outside the six countries. The full operation of the customs union did not occur until about 1968. At this point, the idea of a true common market was still far away and several more developments had to occur before one could consider a complete integration of the market.

Over the next several years, Denmark, Ireland, the United Kingdom, and Greece joined the European Community (E.C.) and were followed more recently by Spain and Portugal. With twelve members, the community now covered almost all of Western Europe and could begin to focus on additional steps required for the formation of a common market. One step towards that goal was the Common Agricultural Policy which had been adopted by the Community's existing members as early as 1962. But the major move towards a complete integration of the market was to come in 1979 with the creation of the European Monetary System (EMS) which was designed to help coordinate the economies of the E.C. members through controlling exchange rate fluctuations so as to avoid major shocks that may differentially impact some community members.*

In order to hasten the process of forming a common market, the principal executive body of the European Community known as the E.C. Commission issued in June 1985, a document that has come to be known as a White Paper. This document lists some three hundred areas where specific actions would need to be taken before the full integration of the European Community market could be completed. These areas included physical, technical, and fiscal barriers which restricted the free movement of goods, labor, and capital among the twelve member countries. The White Paper also specified 1992 as the date by which the actions needed to remove the barriers had to be completed. The psychological importance of setting a specific date for market integration in the White Paper needs to be underscored. Even though 1992 is not a magic date by which all of the barriers to the movement of labor, capital and products will necessarily be removed, it provides a specific calendar objective which has accelerated the pace of movement towards a common market. In fact, 1992 has come to symbolize in the minds of many, a major watershed in not only the economic dateline of Europe but also in its political and possibly military future which would have implications for all the countries of the world.

One major obstacle to quick action on the directives issued in the White Paper was that all actions suggested by the Commission had to be approved by a unanimous vote of the E.C. Council of Ministers. Given the wide diversity of conditions experienced by the various countries comprising the

---

*The United Kingdom has not yet joined the European Monetary System so the process of economic coordination through the EMS is still incomplete.

European Community, such a unanimity was expectedly difficult to achieve. But in 1987, the European Council, which is the main legislative body of the European Community, passed an act known as the Single European Act making it possible for the Council of Ministers to adopt a regulation or directive (except on some fiscal matters) with a majority vote. This cleared the way for expeditious consideration of the White Paper directives and, to date, about half of them have been acted upon. For example, a major achievement has been the creation of a single administrative document which should make movement of goods across national borders much easier and quicker by abolishing the requirements of separate documents and checks by customs officials in each member country. Other major directives that have been adopted are in the areas of product standards for a number of products—emission standards for small automobiles, for example, which have recently been adopted. Of course, complex areas such as the question of tax harmonization (particularly value added taxes or VAT), rules of origin requirements, etc. still remain unresolved. However, it is reasonable to say that the 1992 process has developed a momentum which makes it unlikely that there will be any backtracking on the basic intent of the process. Part of the reason for the momentum is that business firms throughout the European Community are actively backing the integration process and are convinced that this is the only way for Europe to genuinely compete with the two major economic powers—the United States and Japan. Figure 1.1 provides a chronology of the events leading up to 1992 and the reader is referred to it for an at-a-glance view of the events surrounding the historic market integration process that is now underway in Europe. Figures 1.2 to 1.6 will give the reader details of the 1992 process and a number of vital statistics about countries in the European Community.

PROSPECTS FOR U.S. FIRMS AND THE U.S. ECONOMY

An obvious question that is suggested by the historical overview above is: "What does EC-92 mean for U.S. firms and for the U.S. economy?" In Chapters 2 and 3, we discuss the results of a study of U.S. firms' views of the EC-1992 market integration process. But from a general perspective, we can set down here many implications of the EC-92 process for U.S. firms and the U.S. economy.

Most of the projections made by the European Community would suggest that the successful integration of the European market would lead to the creation of a larger economic pie which should potentially benefit E.C. and non-E.C. firms alike. The European Commission estimates that over five to six years, the Community's GDP could be raised by 4.5 percent, consumer prices reduced by about 6 percent and employment increased by 2 million.[1] Further, the European Community expects the creation of a single market to boost imports by 7 percent and exports by 10 percent.[2] Clearly, the net

4

European Community Dateline

1957	Signing of Treaty of Rome establishing the European Economic Community (EC) with Belgium, France, Italy, Luxembourg, the Netherlands and West Germany as members.
1959	Process of reduction of internal tariffs begins.
1962	Adoption of common Agricultural Policy.
1967	Introduction of Value Added Tax System.
1968	Successful Completion of customs union with no internal tariffs and a common external tariff.
1973	Three new members (United Kingdom, Denmark, and Ireland admitted)
1979	Creation of European Monetary System and election of the first European Parliament.
1981	Greece, the tenth member is admitted.
1985	The European Commission issues a White Paper to eliminate all barriers to the free movement of goods, capital and labor.
1986	The membership in the European Community increases to twelve with the admission of Spain and Portugal.
1987	Passage of the Single European Act improves community-level decision making process and makes it easier to move more quickly on the directives contained in the White Paper.
1990	More than half way to the December 1992 deadline for full integration of the twelve nation market. Problems remain but the process is irreversible and has the broad backing of all community members.
1992	The date set for elimination of all barriers to trade within the European Community.

effect would be a larger economy for the European Community as a whole. Precisely what benefits the U.S. economy and U.S. firms can hope to gain from EC-92 are harder to predict. As stated earlier, the purpose of the single market is to boost the competitiveness of European industry and countries/ firms from outside the community should be fully aware of this and not expect EC-92 to be a unilateral opening of further opportunities for firms from outside the community. However, many U.S. firms which have operated in the Community for decades and have major shares of the E.C. market should be able to seize the opportunity provided by the anticipated growth in the economy that market integration will bring. Already, many U.S. firms are restructuring their organizations to improve their efficiency in the new Europe and many strategic alliances are being forged between both U.S. firms (Maytag and Hoover, for example) and U.S./E.C. firms (AT&T and Italtel, for example). There seems to be a general consensus (supported by the study findings reported in Chapters 2 and 3) that U.S. firms which are already operating within the European Community by 1992 will have additional opportunities provided they have geared themselves to operate in the new environment.

FIGURE 1.2

1992 at a Glance

By 1992, the European Community intends to have implemented 285 regulations to create a single internal market. The following specific changes represent the major part of the 1992 program.

In standards, testing, certification
Harmonization of standards for:
  Simple pressure vessels
  Toys
  Automobiles, trucks, and motorcycles
    and their emissions
  Telecommunications
  Construction products
  Personal protection equipment
  Machine safety
  Measuring instruments
  Medical devices
  Gas appliances
  Agricultural & forestry tractors
  Cosmetics
  Quick frozen foods
  Flavorings
  Food emulsifiers
  Extraction solvents
  Food preservatives
  Infant formula
  Jams
  Modified starches
  Fruit juices
  Food inspection
  Definition of spirited beverages &
    aromatised wines
  Coffee extracts & chicory extracts
  Food additives
  Materials & articles in
    contact with food
  Tower cranes (noise)
  Household appliances (noise)
  Tire pressure gauges
  Hydraulic diggers (noise)
  Detergents
  Liquid fertilizers & secondary fertilizers
  Lawn mowers (noise)
  Medicinal products & medical specialities

Radio interferences
Earthmoving equipment
Lifting and loading equipment

**New rules for harmonizing packing,
labelling and processing requirements**
  Ingredients for food & beverages
  Irradiation
  Extraction solvents
  Nutritional labelling
  Classification, packaging, labelling of
    dangerous preparations
  Food labelling

**Harmonization of regulations for the
health industry (including marketing)**
  Medical specialities
  Pharmaceuticals
  Veterinary medicinal products
  High technology medicines
  Implantable electromedical devices
  Single-use devices (disposable)
  In-vitro diagnostics

**Changes in government procurement
regulations**
  Coordination of procedures on the award
    of public works & supply contracts
  Extension of EC law to
    telecommunications, utilities, transport
  Services

Harmonization of regulation of services
  Banking
  Mutual Funds
  Broadcasting
  Tourism
  Road passenger transport
  Railways
  Information services
  Life & nonlife insurance
  Securities
  Maritime transport
  Air transport
  Electronic payment cards

Figure 1.2 (Cont'd)

Figure 1.2 (Cont'd)

Liberalization of capital movements	Porcine animals and meat
Long-term capital, stocks	Plant health
Short-term capital	Fish & fish products
	Live poultry, poultry meat and hatching
Consumer protection regulations	eggs
Misleading definitions of products	Pesticide residues in fruit & vegetables
Indication of prices	

Liberalization of capital movements
  Long-term capital, stocks
  Short-term capital

Consumer protection regulations
  Misleading definitions of products
  Indication of prices

Harmonization of laws regulating company behavior
  Mergers & acquisitions
  Trademarks
  Copyrights
  Cross border mergers
  Accounting operations across borders
  Bankruptcy
  Protection of computer programs
  Transaction taxes
  Company law

Harmonization of taxation
  Value Added Taxes
  Excise taxes on alcohol, tobacco, and other

Harmonization of veterinary & phytosanitary Controls
Harmonization of an extensive list of rules covering items such as:
  Antibiotic residues
  Bovine animals and meat

Porcine animals and meat
Plant health
Fish & fish products
Live poultry, poultry meat and hatching eggs
Pesticide residues in fruit & vegetables

Elimination and simplification of national transit documents and procedures for intra-EC trade
  Introduction of the Single Administrative Document (SAD)
  Abolition of customs presentation charges
  Elimination of customs formalities & the introduction of common border posts

Harmonization of rules pertaining to the free movement of labor and the professions within the EC
  Mutual recognition of higher educational diplomas
  Comparability of vocational training qualifications
  Specific training in general medical practice
  Training of engineers
  Activities in the field of pharmacy
  Activities related to commercial agents
  Income taxation provisions
  Elimination of burdensome requirements related to residence permits

Source: Business America, August 1, 1988, p. 7.

On the negative side, U.S. firms should also be aware that firms from within the European Community are not sitting still and an unprecedented wave of mergers and acquisitions is already underway in Europe and this can radically transform the competitive terrain not only within Europe but also in the rest of the world. Unilever's attempts to acquire Faberge, Grand Metropolitan PLC's acquisition of Pillsbury and Siemens' joint venture with Westinghouse are just a few examples of such alliances which have either been attempted or already completed. What this would mean for U.S. firms and the U.S. economy is that an increasingly competitive marketplace is likely to result even in the United States as a consequence of EC-92.

On balance, however, both the U.S. government and U.S. firms are sup-

FIGURE 1.3

E.C. Vital Statistics and Comparison with United States and Japan

	Total Area (000 sq. km)	Population 1987 (m)	Unemployment Rate 1988 (%)	1988 GDP at Current Prices ($ Billion)	GDP per Capita at Current Prices ($)
Belgium	30.5	9.83	10.2	147.5	14,071
Denmark	43.1	5.13	5.6	107.2	19,730
France	547.0	55.63	10.3	941.9	15,818
West Germany	248.6	61.20	6.2	1,204.6	18,280
Greece	132.0	9.99	7.4	53.0	4,719
Ireland	70.3	3.54	17.6	31.3	8,297
Italy	301.2	57.33	11.9	826.0	13,224
Luxembourg	2.6	.37	1.7	6.3	16,138
Netherlands	37.3	14.67	9.5	227.2	14,530
Portugal	92.1	10.27	7.0	41.9	3,761
Spain	504.8	38.83	20.1	339.3	7,449
United Kingdom	244.8	56.93	8.3	805.6	11,765
United States	9,372.6	243.92	5.4	4,805.5	18,338
Japan	372.3	122.09	2.5	2,853.0	19,437

Source: OECD –Statistics on the Member Countries—1989 Edition

FIGURE 1.4

Trade Statistics (Goods Only) European Community with U.S., Japan for Comparison

	Imports million $	Imports as % of GDP at current prices	Exports million $	Exports as % of GDP at current prices
Belgium[a]	83,013	59.8	82,848	59.7
Denmark	25,510	25.2	25,661	25.4
France	157,220	17.9	142,849	16.2
W. Germany	227,259	20.3	293,790	26.3
Greece	12,988	27.5	6,505	13.8
Ireland	13,605	46.3	16,000	54.4
Italy	124,682	16.4	116,085	15.3
Luxembourg[a]	83,013	59.8	82,848	59.7
Netherlands	91,068	42.7	92,597	43.4
Portugal	13,424	36.6	9,156	25.0
Spain	48,647	16.8	33,979	11.7
United Kingdom	153,639	22.9	130,492	19.5
United States	405,901	11.1	252,866	5.7
Japan	150,931	6.4	231,332	9.7

[a]—Belgium-Luxembourg Economic Union
Source: OECD Statistics on the Member Countries—1989

8

FIGURE 1.5

Imports of the European Community, 1987

	Extra-EC Imports[1]	Imports from the U.S.
	$US Billions	
EC	$391.16	$65.7
Belgium-Luxembourg	23.0	3.9
Denmark	12.0	1.2
France	53.5	11.3
Germany	103.1	14.2
Greece	5.5	0.3
Ireland	3.8	2.3
Italy	53.9	6.7
Netherlands	36.7	6.6
Portugal	4.9	0.7
Spain	20.8	4.0
U.K.	74.3	15.1
U.S.	405.9[2]	—

[1]Imports from non-EC countries
[2]Total U.S. Imports
Source: Adopted from Business America, August 1, 1988

FIGURE 1.6

U.S. Trade with the European Community 1980–1988

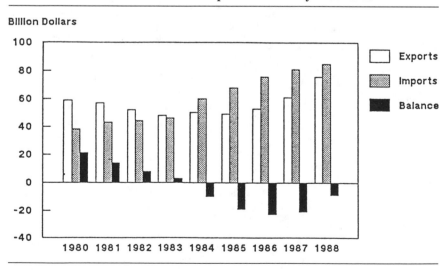

Source: U.S. Foreign Trade Highlights p. 70, 1988
July 1989, U.S. Department of Commerce, Washington, D.C.

portive of and looking forward to EC-92 and it is expected that the net effect on U.S. firms which are positioned to operate in the newly integrated market should be positive. There is some concern about "Fortress Europe" and how the European Community may seek to favor E.C. firms over non-E.C. firms through the product standards setting process or public procurement procedures, but vigilance on the part of U.S. firms and an establishment of their presence within the European Community should forestall any negative effects on them of the market integration. A larger question relates to the role of Japanese firms in EC-92 and the implications for both E.C. and U.S. firms which will be discussed in the next section.

THE ROLE OF JAPANESE FIRMS IN EC-92

Even though Kenichi Ohmae has referred to Japan, Europe, and the U.S. as a triad in the sense that they represent the three most important economies in the world, the European economy until now has been fragmented into twelve separate national economies and for this reason, the Japanese firms seem to have focussed more on the U.S. market as evidenced by their spectacular gains in the U.S. market share across a number of industries. With the integration of the E.C. market now set for 1992, the Japanese firms have become very interested in the potential of Europe as a market and are scrambling to position themselves as major players through a large increase in direct investment within the community. While the industries involved are the same ones that Japan has come to dominate—automobiles, electronic goods, office machines, and the like—the pace of Japanese investment in the European Community is almost as impressive as their earlier investment moves in the United States. In both cases, the main motivation behind the Japanese investment surge is the same—defusing any protectionist sentiments that may result from high levels of imports into the market.

The Japanese firms are clearly concerned about possible protectionist actions that may be taken against them. A considerable amount of the discussion regarding "Fortress Europe" even in the United States is a direct consequence of statements and some actions by E.C. officials which are mainly directed at Japanese firms. Recently, for example, the European Community ruled that Ricoh copiers imported into Europe would be subject to a 20 percent antidumping duty.[3] E.C. officials frequently seem to be at pains to reassure the U.S. that "Fortress Europe" will not result, but it is very difficult for them to take one stance towards one trading partner and a different stance towards another trading partner. Also, the greater interdependence of national economies and the complex sourcing arrangements adopted by firms today make it unlikely that actions taken against one country will not have side effects on other countries. Already, the Ricoh case illustrates the fact that European antidumping duties will also apply to Ricoh copiers assembled in California.[4]

Even in the cases where Japanese firms have made manufacturing investments within the European Community, several uncertainties remain. These uncertainties relate to two main aspects of E.C. policy—local content legislation and country of origin rules—and how these may evolve as the market integration process moves forward. A number of Japanese manufacturing plants in the European Community are what have been called "screwdriver factories" which means that they are largely assembly operations. As the case of Nissan Bluebirds indicates, even cars made within the European Community may face barriers to movement across national boundaries if it is determined that they don't meet the "local content" requirements. In the Nissan case, cars from the United Kingdom were sought to be barred from the French market because they had only 70 percent E.C. content while the community policy requires 80 percent. There is also the related issue of rules of origin. Recently, it was determined that some semiconductor chips made by Japan in the European Community did not qualify as originating in the European Community because the last major manufacturing process they had undergone was not within the European Community. Once again, all of this worries the United States, too, because similar actions may be taken against Japanese automobiles which may be exported from U.S. plants to European markets.

A further question facing Japanese automobile firms, in particular, is that currently both France and Italy have quantitative restrictions on the sales of Japanese cars. While such restrictions will have to be removed over time as part of the market integration process, it is likely that some form of restriction, probably reduced, will be continued for an adjustment period after 1992 to allow the domestic automobile industry in the two countries to cope with the new competitive situation.

Overall, even though one Japanese executive has noted that "Europe is not as open as United States,"[5] Japanese firms should have considerable opportunity in some key European industries after 1992 but for the reasons mentioned above, there is also likely to be considerable uncertainty for them. A word employed frequently in E.C. policy statements is "reciprocity" and Japanese firms will have to recognize that the European Community may very well restrict their access to the European market if similar access is not accorded to E.C. firms in Japan. Of course, the Japanese market has a number of traditional and structural factors which limit the success of some foreign firms and the principle of reciprocity will have to distinguish between "success" and "access" where a particular case is concerned.

THE LINKS BETWEEN THE EUROPEAN FREE TRADE ASSOCIATION AND THE EUROPEAN COMMUNITY

One point that is often missed in discussions of EC-92 is that there is another trade group in Europe which is already highly integrated with the countries of the European Community. The European Free Trade Association (EFTA) countries have a population which if added to the E.C. population would add a further 10 percent to the size of the market. While 10 percent may seem a relatively small addition to the population, the EFTA countries also have some major firms that compete with the largest of the world's multinationals, for example, Electrolux, Volvo, ASEA. Some of these firms from EFTA countries have already started forming alliances with E.C. firms to better position themselves for 1992. Meanwhile, there is also an expectation that some EFTA countries may apply for formal membership in the European Community. Already, Austria has formally applied for membership and while no action is likely to be taken by the European Community in the near term on such applications, it is a distinct possibility that pressure will build from EFTA members who want to join the community in order to participate in the larger market that will result from EC-92.

An interesting aspect of the EFTA-E.C. links is that there is also a political dimension to the relationship. The current EFTA member countries enjoy a neutral status which was part of their agreement with the Soviet Union after the Second World War. This was also the reason that they did not initially join the E.C. which is comprised mainly of NATO members (with the exception of Ireland). So, any application for membership in the European Community from an EFTA country will have a political implication for the map of Europe. Of course, many of the present E.C. members originally belonged to EFTA so it is not inconceivable that more EFTA members could be admitted to the European Community but for the moment the European Commission has made it clear that "internal development takes a priority over enlargement." In this situation "the EFTA countries share most of the fears already listed for America and Japan."[6] Yet, 65 percent of the EFTA exports go to the European Community and these account for 14 percent of their combined GDP.[7] With the EFTA-E.C. tariff free zone which has been in place since 1984, the two economic groups should enjoy a continuing close relationship. A recent survey of managers in one EFTA country (Norway) by KPMG indicates that they are thinking of changing their strategies in the E.C. market in a manner similar to E.C. companies. However, the Norwegian managers viewed EC-92 as a set of constraints to which they have to adapt rather than the important opportunity that E.C. managers thought it to be.[8] This may very well be a general reflection of all managers from outside the European Community looking in.

In summary, the EFTA countries and particularly some large multinational firms located there have to make the most of EC-92 since immediate membership in the community, even if they so desire, is not an option open to them. With their geographical proximity and existing close economic ties with the community, they should be in a position to exploit whatever opportunities come their way as a result of the market integration process. In a larger perspective, given their avowed neutral status, a lot of what will

ILLUSTRATION 1.1

Financial Times (London)

Open Market or Open Warfare?

Get the truth about Europe in the Financial Times.
The voice of authority in a changing Community.

Is 1992 something you should cheer or fear? It depends entirely upon how prepared you are for the battle of the open market.

For instance, do you really know what your foreign rivals are doing right now? Which of your domestic competitors are they talking to? What alliances are they making? And what plans have they for stealing your customers?

Read the Financial Times daily and we'll provide the strategic intelligence you need to defend your markets and expand abroad.

We'll also tell you how the battleground is being prepared in Brussels – analysing how each new directive affects Europe's business – and you.

And, with over 270 European correspondents, we'll explain how businesses like yours are restructuring

management and revising marketing operations to exploit the single marketplace.

It's this kind of authoritative reporting that makes the FT the leading international business newspaper amongst Europe's chief executives.* Indeed, a full 72% of our readers are at board director level.**

Find out why these top decision-makers rely on the FT for insight, analyses and hard business news.

Subscribe now. And be sure to take advantage of this introductory offer. Get your first 12 issues free by simply completing and returning the coupon below to the Financial Times, or by calling: **(02) 513 2816.**

One market. One newspaper.

It's time you tried the Financial Times. 12 issues absolutely Free with your introductory subscription. Delivered to you with our compliments.

To: Financial Times (Benelux) Ltd., Hertogsstraat 39, B-1000 Brussel.
Tel: (02) 5132816. Tx: 64219. Fax No: (02) 512 1404.

YES, I would like to subscribe to the Financial Times, Europe's leading business newspaper and enjoy my first 12 issues free. I will allow up to 21 days before delivery of my first copy. Please enter my subscription for:

(Please Tick) ☐ *6 months at BFR 6040 ☐ *12 months at BFR 10980 ☐ *24 months at BFR 18670 ☐ Bill me

☐ Charge my American Express/Visa/Eurocard/Diners Club Card account.

☐☐☐☐ - ☐☐☐☐ - ☐☐☐☐ ☐☐☐☐

Card Expiry Date ___ / ___ / ___

*Currency rates are only valid for the country in which they are quoted. Subscription prices and promotion are valid until 30th June 1989.

Free hand-delivery services are available in the business centres of Brussel, Antwerpen and their suburbs – and in Brugge, Gent, Kortrijk, Leuven and Liège.

Name___
Title___
Company___
Telephone___
Address to which I would like my Financial Times delivered:
___
___

I understand that I can cancel my Financial Times subscription at any time and that you will refund the price of the undelivered issues.

Signature___ Date___
No order can be accepted without a signature.

FINANCIAL TIMES
EUROPE'S BUSINESS NEWSPAPER

Please reply by 30th June 1989.

3B4V

Note: A number of major U.S., Canadian and European business publications have given significant attention to EC-92. Particularly descriptive of this focus is a promotional advertisement by the *Financial Times* (London) that appeared in its August 24, 1989 issue. Permission to reprint was provided by the *Financial Times*.

happen to EFTA countries (future membership in the European Community, for example) will depend on what happens to East-West relations in Europe which is the topic of the next section in the context of EC-92.

THE EAST BLOC AND ITS INFLUENCE ON EC-92

One prominent educator and thinker has suggested[9] that too much attention is being focussed on EC-92 and not enough on the fact that the success or failure of the European market integration is intimately linked to the success or failure of "perestroika" and "glasnost." Indeed, Mikhail Gorbachev's initiatives in the Soviet Union which have been adopted to a greater or lesser extent by other East bloc countries is mainly designed to improve the competitiveness of the COMECON countries by gaining access to the technology and trade of the West. Recent trade statistics reported by Maier[10] confirm that the volume of East-West trade has gone down and trade within CO-MECON has increased reflecting the "declining innovation force of the socialist countries." So, the East bloc countries have a lot to gain from opening their economies to the goods and technology available only in the West. This desire for greater interchange with the Western economies also prompted Mikhail Gorbachev to write to the Group of Seven leaders meeting in Paris during July 1989 requesting greater participation for the East in the Western economies. More recently, we have seen the historic opening of the Berlin Wall and political/economic changes in Hungary, Poland and other East bloc countries. There is considerable support for such an opening among many Western European countries, and many European banks, particularly those in West Germany, have already extended liberal bank credits to the Soviet Union. But before the East bloc countries can achieve greater integration into the world economy, they will have to deal with their hard currency problems. This will require a change-over to free convertible currency which in turn will require greater integration in the world market. There does not seem to be a simple solution to this problem but if the economic problems in the East bloc have to be solved and demands of their consumers met, some creative solution to their trade and hard currency problems will have to be found and they will be looking to the larger, more confident market in Europe for help after 1992.

PROSPECTS OF EC-92 FOR DEVELOPING COUNTRIES

Many developing countries are former colonies of some of the member countries of the European Community and have therefore historically enjoyed a special trading status with those member countries. There is, therefore, some understandable concern among the developing countries that EC-92 will make it impossible to have such special training relationships with individual E.C. countries and the only effect the market integration can have on the developing countries will be negative. Recently, sixty-six African,

14

Caribbean, and Pacific (ACP) developing countries warned the European Community about any actions that might hamper their ability to export bananas and sugar to the European market after 1992. They sought and received reassurances from the European Commission and some individual E.C. countries that their interests would be protected in the post-1992 market. A number of the ACP countries, as mentioned earlier, have special relationships based on their colonial past with individual E.C. countries and some Latin-American countries can expect to get a sympathetic ear from Spain. Also, under the Lome convention, some countries can receive compensation from the European Community for any shortfalls in hard currency inflows. However, Asian countries including the poorest ones such as Bangladesh, are not eligible for any preferential trade treatment in the European Community and are likely to be most worried about being shut out of the new market. Even some of the newly industrialized countries of South-East Asia are worried and Association of South East Asian Nations (ASEAN) officials have said that "they'll probably have to wait until 1992 before they know whether the unified E.C. market is a blessing or a curse."[11]

Whatever the specific situation of a developing country, there is considerable uncertainty about developing countries' prospects in the EC-92 marketplace. Firms from such countries will face a much larger market and more formidable competitors who have forged strategic alliances within the European Community and therefore, they will have to work much harder and employ more aggressive strategies in order to succeed in post-1992 Europe.

EUROPEAN NATIONALISM AND THE OBSTACLES TO FULL INTEGRATION

While it is true that the EC-92 process has attained a purpose and momentum that is irreversible, there are significant barriers to complete integration of the market. The single most important barrier is the lack of a single currency or central banking system without which the European Community cannot smoothly regulate the overall economy. Also, the symbolic importance of a single currency in an integrated Europe would be a strong force for greater homogenization within the community. However, it is precisely this homogenization and the loss of national sovereignty that a complete monetary union will bring which is opposed by some people in the community. Margaret Thatcher, the British prime minister has often suggested, for example, that already Brussels has developed a large bureaucracy and there was danger of it becoming a "socialist superstate." A brief description of the present situation with regard to the movement towards a European Monetary Union will help to emphasize not only the barriers along the way but also the need for such a Union if EC-92 has to fulfill all of its promise.

In June 1988, at the Hanover Summit, a committee on Economic and

Monetary Union was set up under the chairmanship of E.C. Commission president, Jacques Delors. This committee produced a report which sees a three stage process in the movement towards a complete European Monetary Union.[12] The report also points out that an economic and monetary union will go well beyond a single market and will require changes in economic policy at the European Community level. The three stages outlined in the report can be briefly described as follows:

1) The first stage involves completion of the single market through the removal of all barriers (physical, technical, and fiscal) and stronger economic coordination between member countries which would involve the participation of the various central banks. This stage would also require that all countries join the European Monetary System (EMS) and private use of the ECU (European Currency Unit) would be facilitated.

2) This stage would involve the setting up of a European System of Central Banks which would develop and operate a common monetary policy. The financing of national budget deficits would also be discussed at the Community level. By the end of stage 2, it is expected that no realignments of exchange rates within the EMS would be permitted to individual countries.

3) The final stage would involve complete macroeconomic policy-making for all members at the Community level. The Central Banks created in the previous stage would now be fully responsible for monetary policy. It is also expected that in this stage the transition to a single currency would occur.

The second and third stages above will clearly require radical changes in the political and economic landscape of the community and are therefore several years away at the least. However, the first stage is an integral part of the 1992 process and should be in place by the end of that year. The Madrid Summit of the European Community in June 1989 discussed the Delors Committee report and decided that the first stage should start on July 1, 1990 when all capital controls in most E.C. countries are due to expire. The wording of the Summit agreement was considerably less clear though finance ministers of all twelve countries agreed that work should begin now to lay the groundwork for the second and third stages. No deadlines for the completion of these stages were mentioned.

The discussion above provides a fairly detailed view of the difficulties that remain in achieving a true economic and monetary union in the European Community. The major stumbling blocks seem to be the uncertainties of what will happen in specific member countries when all individual national controls on the economies are removed and decision-making is centralized in the European Community. Already there is some concern about how the capital markets will adjust when the richest E.C. members allow completely free capital movement starting July 1990. On the other hand, centralization of the economic policy-making is essential because currently, countries such as France and Italy do not feel they have commensurate participation in the policy-making of the Community with so much of the power cornered by the German Bundesbank.

Ultimately, the successful integration of the European market will require economic and monetary union, but the question is whether such a union does not also imply a shift of political power to the community level and a true federalist structure to the European Community. Many do not see this as a palatable prospect because of the loss of national sovereignty and identity that it implies.

THE SOCIAL DIMENSION AND ITS EFFECTS ON EC-92

The twelve member nations of the European Community currently present widely different situations in the area of employment laws, management-labor relations and other related matters. The challenge of an integrated market in which labor is supposed to have free movement across national boundaries is to bring the various labor regulations into some kind of parity across the twelve countries. To this end, the European Commission has issued a social charter which lists worker rights and a legislative program that will implement those rights. The charter covers areas such as minimum work age, maximum work hours, worker participation in management, etc., though on matters such as minimum wage and unemployment compensation, it is not specific in wording and leaves a lot of discretion to individual countries.

Expectedly, the social charter has come in for considerable criticism, particularly from the United Kingdom. As in the case of the monetary union, the social charter is viewed as an attempt to interfere in national policies and impose a federalist structure on the Community members. When one considers the fact that some countries in the European Community are avowedly socialist in outlook while others are not, it is not surprising that the initial reaction to the social charter included a comment by Prime Minister Margaret Thatcher that it was "Marxist interventionism."

But whatever the ideological differences among E.C. members on the social charter, it goes without saying that a true common market with full mobility of labor will need some consistency of policies across countries and some protection of rights for citizens of one E.C. country working in another. The language differences and significant cultural variations across the European Community will, of course, make the actual number of people who will migrate in the foreseeable future from one country to another rather small, but in the long term the essence of a homogeneous integrated market would require community-wide labor laws and it is for this purpose that the social charter has been drafted. A related area of concern is the recognition of professional certification and university degrees across the E.C. countries and efforts are currently being made to establish cross-licensing and other procedures to ensure mobility of professionals throughout the European Community.

RESEARCH AND DEVELOPMENT ACTIVITIES IN THE EUROPEAN COMMUNITY

As noted earlier, a primary objective of the single market process has been the improvement of the European competitive position vis-a-vis the United States and Japan. Until now, the differing product standards and regulations across individual member countries made it difficult for countries/firms in the European Community to undertake the high investment, long term research and development efforts needed to match the United States and Japan. With the market integration process now firmly in place, a number of efforts have been initiated at the community level to improve the research and development capability of Europe.

The E.C. Council of Ministers adopted in summer, 1988 five research programs each running for a period of several years and costing a total of over 300 million ECU. These research projects cover a number of areas including plant genetics, road safety, and artificial intelligence.

Perhaps the best known research initiative that the European Community has undertaken in anticipation of EC-92 is ESPRIT (European Strategic Programme for Research and Development in Information Technology). A recent publication of the E.C. Commission provides the rationale for the ESPRIT initiative.[13] Information technology is the fastest growing area of industrial activity with an annual growth rate in excess of 15–25%. With the integration of the European market, a major competitive battleground for information technology will be Europe itself and ESPRIT is designed to ensure that foreign companies will not have a dominant place in the information technology (IT) market. Though ESPRIT was initiated in 1984 before the White Paper and Single European Act, it has assumed increased significance in the light of EC-92. As a matter of conjecture, it may even be said that the ESPRIT and other research and development initiatives in Europe spurred the R&D consortia such as Sematech which have recently been set up in the United States.

The ESPRIT document issued by the European Commission states that while individual approaches to high technology research and development by E.C. nations have proved increasingly inadequate because of the high cost, the twelve countries together have "the resources to stay in the front line of technological advance." The main objectives of ESPRIT are set down in the document as follows:

—to provide European IT industry with the basic technologies to meet the competitive requirements of the 1990s.
—to promote European industrial cooperation in IT
—to contribute to the development of internationally accepted standards.

The major implication of the ESPRIT program is that European information technology firms will no longer be dependent on United States or

Japanese advances in technology and will increasingly be able to develop some of the technology themselves. Besides ESPRIT, the European Commission has adopted programs such as SPRINT (Strategic Program for Innovation and Technology Transfer) and EUREKA which also have technological self reliance as their objective. For the United States, all of this represents a major cause for concern because U.S. industry has already experienced an alleged loss of competitiveness in some areas. If the E.C. initiatives fulfill their promise, the United States will now have to be concerned about the competition in technology on two fronts—Europe and Japan. Meanwhile, there have been some moves to foster cooperation between E.C. and U.S. firms in their joint efforts to meet the Japanese challenge. How all of this will play out remains to be seen but clearly Europe will be a major participant in the research and development game after 1992.[14]

END NOTES TO CHAPTER 1

1. "1992—Getting Into Europe," *South,* December 1988, p. 9.
2. *South,* op cit, p. 9.
3. "Ricoh may face 20% duty on EC-assembled copiers," *Financial Times,* Tuesday, February 7, 1989, p. 20.
4. "EC Photocopier Law Could Target Ricoh for Import Duties," *The Wall Street Journal,* Monday, July 17, 1989.
5. Seiji Sano, deputy managing director Mitsui & Co. Europe quoted in "Storming the World's Biggest Market," *Business Tokyo,* Summer 1989, p. 41.
6. "Other Europeans," Europe's Internal Market-Survey, *The Economist,* July 8, 1989, p. 38.
7. *The Economist,* op cit, p. 38.
8. "1992—Getting Ready," Summary: EC Report, KPMG International Office, 1988, pp. 11–12.
9. Interview with Juan Rada, *The Financial Times,* July 10, 1989.
10. Maier, Harry, "Perestroika and East-West Relations," *European Affairs,* no. 4, 88 winter, p. 30.
11. "Prospect of Rival Trade Blocs Rouses Mistrust between EC and Asean Nations," *The Wall Street Journal,* Wednesday, July 12, 1989.
12. "EC focus," KPMG—EC Centre, Summer 1989, p. 7.
13. *Esprit* (European Strategic Programme for Research and Development in Information Technology) published by the Commission of the European Communities, p. 3.
14. Steven Greenhouse, "Europeans Unite to Compete with Japan and U.S.," *The New York Times,* Monday, August 21, 1989.

VIGNETTES

CHAPTER 1

(Two vignettes that illustrate the rapidly changing environment for the private sector and European consumer marketplace.)

THE CHANNEL TUNNEL: ANOTHER QUESTION MARK AS 1992 APPROACHES*

Shortly after the scheduled completion of the European Community economic integration is the scheduled completion of the Channel Tunnel connecting England and France via a railway system beneath the English Channel. The Channel Tunnel, expected to be completed by summer 1993, will consist of three separate 30 mile tunnels that run about 100 feet below the seabed. Two tunnels will be for rail traffic plus one in between to serve as a maintenance and emergency tunnel. Trains will carry passengers and cargo. The completed system is expected to transport approximately 16 million passengers per year and six million to seven million tons of freight annually. By using the Channel Tunnel, also referred to as the 'Chunnel' or the 'Eurotunnel', passengers will be able to travel from Paris to London in three hours. It is interesting to note that a significant amount of the machinery being used to dig the Channel Tunnel was designed and produced by Robbins Company of Seattle, Washington.

The development and completion of the Eurotunnel will neatly coincide with the economic integration of the European Community. Increased trade potential due to the elimination of tariff and many non-tariff barriers will be further enhanced by the removal of a major physical barrier to growth in European trade, namely, the English Channel. However, the completion of the Channel Tunnel will not in itself be the final link to improved European trade. The Channel Tunnel project includes building a transportation system which includes construction of rail terminals on each side of the Channel Tunnel—one in Folkstone near Dover, England and the other in Sagatte near Calais, France. Also, existing rail lines in both England and France will be extended.

The Eurotunnel project will have a regional, national, and international impact. On a regional level, the cities and towns located near the Channel Tunnel entrances will become important links in distribution networks, therefore, important factors for domestic and foreign firms to consider when choosing new sites for operations. Additionally, centralization decisions for companies already in Europe may be less cumbersome due to the easier access to the whole European Community via this heavy-capacity transport system.

Internationally, the Channel Tunnel project could ultimately change the

---

*Information for this section obtained from: "French/British Plan Underwater Meeting; Eurotunnel Slated for 1993 Completion" by M. Katherine Glover *Business America*, July 3, 1989 and "Channel Tunnel Construction Moves Along" by David Black, *Europe*, May 1989.

shipping routes used and methods of transporting freight to the continent of Europe from North American ports as well as from the Far East.

A project of this magnitude in itself, raises questions of uncertainty as to the probability of on-time completion. Added to this is the manner in which the governments of England and France, have chosen to handle their respective responsibilities. On the French side, the government has chosen to back the project financially and has put money into new high-speed track to help develop the connecting network to the Channel Tunnel.

On England's shore the Channel Tunnel Act, which enables the construction of the Channel Tunnel from the British side, also includes a section which prohibits the British government from investing any public money in the Channel Tunnel itself or in any infrastructure directly serving it. Added to any uncertainty which may be caused by the hands-off approach of the British government are the government imposed restrictions—such as a limit of a seven per cent annual return on investment—on the eventual operator of the Channel Tunnel, British Rail.

As with so many other issues related to EC 1992, the business implications resulting from the construction and eventual completion of the Channel Tunnel are important factors for companies to consider when determining entry strategies or expansion strategies into the European Community.

Diana Abdoo

EURO DISNEYLAND IN 1992

1992 means much more than just the target date for European Community harmonization [or a Single European Market (SEM)] for many Europeans. To the Spanish and the athletes of the world, it is the year that the Summer Olympics come to Barcelona. To others, again including the Spanish, it is the time for a major cultural festival in Seville.

However, to the children throughout Europe, it marks the year that Mickey Mouse and his gang "open in Paris." Whether by design or coincidence, Euro Disneyland will share its 1992 billing with the European Community. And, if it is anything like its predecessors in Anaheim, Orlando and Tokyo, it may even receive "top billing."

The scramble between European countries (and cities) to obtain this unique "direct investment" actually outdid most other similar international or national industry attraction efforts, including the now famous battles waged among the States over V.W., Toyota and Honda plants. To finally win the struggle against its most formidable challenger (Spain), France made available a site just outside Paris that had previously been viewed as "untouchable" and ". . . some of the richest land in France."[1] *Europe* recently described the project site as follows:[2]

> The project site is approximately one fifth the size of the city of Paris. Phase I will open in 1992 on 500 hectares, including 57 hectares in the Magic Kingdom, 33 hectares in service areas, and 41 hectares in parking. Fitzpatrick predicts the park will attract 11 million visitors during its first year—50 percent from France, 40 percent from other Western European nations, and 10 percent from the rest of the world.

Just how Euro Disneyland will affect the mosaic that now is being put together around 1992 is interesting to speculate. To some degree, this most recognized symbol in the world (Mickey Mouse) may assist in cultural homogenization of Europe. To illustrate, some 40 percent of the park's attendees are expected to come from European countries other than France and the Disney Channel is already growing in popularity in Western Europe. Euro Disneyland will soon be another shared experience on the road to a SEM and perhaps even a United States of Europe.

How powerful is the Disney brand name? The *Financial Times* states, "Research by Landor Associates, the San Francisco-based consultants, found that Disney was ranked the seventh most well-known brand name in the

---

[1]Jacques Neher, "Viva Mickey," The *Cleveland Plain Dealer*, February 16, 1986, p. 1-C.
[2]Diana Seimone, "Bonjour, Mickey Mouse," *Europe*, July/August 1989, pp. 46–47.

world . . . and seventh also in consumer esteem. . . .[3] And, it is number one in the entertainment field. However, perhaps even a stronger indicator of the Disney mystique is the fact that France's minister of culture has not attacked President Mitterrand for his "generosity" towards an American firm.[4] Undoubtedly, few politicians question Mickey's clout, much less that of Roger Rabbit or the Muppets, and would not want to carry the burden of being anti-Disney.

From a marketer's perspective, the approach Disney is taking to solidify its position and remain in the forefront of consumer awareness may offer some direction for others building a European marketing strategy. The company is heavily employing television, and satellite tv in particular, to cover the new SEM. France alone is now reported to have 4.5 hours a week of Disney programs.

---

[3]David Churchill, "Mickey Mouse advances on the fair city of Paris," *Financial Times,* September 14, 1989, p. 12.
[4]"Mickey goes to the bank," *The Economist,* September 16, 1989, p. 78.

For the reader who wants a more detailed understanding of the conceptual and practical implications of EC-92, we have included the following article which appeared in the *New England Economic Review*, May–June 1989.

Europe in 1992

by
Norman S. Fieleke
Vice President and Economist, Federal Reserve Bank
of Boston. Valerie Hausman provided research
assistance.

With the approach of the 1990s, the world is witnessing a remarkable conjuncture of movements toward economic integration, movements aimed at tearing down barriers to commerce both within and between nations. Within nations, deregulation or liberalization of markets has been widespread in recent years. Between nations, the recent U.S.-Canada Free Trade Agreement, the emerging European common market, and the Uruguay Round of Multilateral Trade Negotiations seem likely to further the economic integration of vast areas if not the world economy.

The focus of this article is on the European Community internal market. The 12 member nations of the EC (European Community) are now striving to realize the full promise of the 1957 Treaty of Rome (the European Economic Community's founding charter), which called for a Community-wide market free of restrictions over the movement of goods, services, persons, and capital, and for progressively "approximating," or harmonizing, the economic policies of the member states. Much progress toward these goals has been made. By July 1, 1968, a customs union had been established among the original six members of the EC, as France, Germany, Italy, Belgium, the Netherlands, and Luxembourg had abolished tariffs on trade among themselves and had imposed a common tariff schedule on imports from other countries. Subsequently, Denmark, Ireland, the United Kingdom, Greece, Spain, and Portugal have joined the union.

Not only have EC members formed a customs union, but they have taken some noteworthy steps toward approximating their economic policies. For example, a Common Agricultural Policy was adopted in 1962. And the establishment of the European Monetary System in 1979 was a significant move toward monetary integration, as most of the member countries undertook to limit fluctuations in exchange rates between their currencies to rather narrow, publicly announced ranges.

Although the EC states have approximated some of their economic policies and have achieved a customs union, they have yet to complete the next stage of economic integration—the common market. A detailed program for attaining this stage was set forth by the EC Commission (the EC's executive body) in June 1985 in a White Paper entitled, "Completing the Internal Market." The EC Council (the EC's supreme decisionmaking body) promptly committed the EC to carry out the White Paper's program by the end of 1992.

The White Paper lists 300 specific areas (subsequently reduced to 279) for action by 1992. The proposed actions are intended to eliminate the obstacles to an integrated market, which the Paper divides into three kinds of barriers—physical, technical, and fiscal. A genuine European Community, without internal economic frontiers, is the desired result, with freedom of movement for goods, services, persons, and capital.

What has sparked this renewed drive toward economic integration within the EC? What might be the consequences, not only for the EC but for the rest of the world, and particularly for U.S. business?

WHY A COMMON MARKET?

Between the formation of the customs union in 1968 and the adoption of the White Paper in 1985, little progress was made toward a common market in the EC. The hostile economic climate of the 1970s—with the oil shocks of 1973–74 and 1978–79, the high inflation rates, and the recessions—led the member country governments to focus more on protecting their constituencies from external forces than on dismantling economic barriers. *What, then, revitalized the process of economic integration?*

One factor has been the improvement in EC economic conditions during the 1980s. Another stimulus has been mounting frustration with the obstacles to intra-EC transactions. For example (Calingaert 1988, pp. 6–7):

As members of the European Community Youth Orchestra traveled within the Community, they had to carry documentary evidence of their instruments' country of origin and often had to deposit the value of their instruments when leaving their home country to satisfy customs authorities that they had not exported the instruments.

A European television manufacturer had to make seven types of television sets to meet member country standards which required 70 engineers to adjust new models to individual country requirements and cost an additional $20 million per year.

Another motivation for further integration is to rectify the EC's slow growth and high unemployment, a condition partly traceable to structural rigidities that has been labelled "Euro-sclerosis." This particular motivation has been heightened by anxiety that the EC is becoming less competitive in the world economy and is lagging behind Japan and the United States in economic performance. Establishment of a common market is seen as a tonic that will enhance efficiency, largely by promoting competition within the EC and by fostering the development of production facilities large enough to achieve the economies associated with large-scale production.

Establishment of a common market is seen as a tonic that will enhance efficiency in economic performance.

The prospect of substantial gains has fired the imagination of EC officials and of many other Europeans. To convey their enthusiasm, it is worth quoting a few paragraphs from *A Frontier-Free Europe,* a publication of the Commission (1988b, pp. 8–9, 16–17).

This tremendous challenge is galvanizing Europeans as no other has done over the last four decades. Everyone has more or less accepted the ugly truth that continued inertia will lead the member countries of the Community into inexorable international decline. . . .

Yesterday the Twelve were manifestly apathetic, unassertive and disunited. . . . They had failed once again to take the Community's birth certificate—unity is strength—to its logical conclusion. . . . With 'Deadline 1992' the hour of resurgence has come. In an appointment with history, the European Community is gambling on the ability of Europeans to rise to a challenge, on that spirit which, down the centuries, has made them great on the international scene. . . .

. . . the large frontier-free market can make a vital contribution to the recovery and competitiveness of industry and commerce and act as a motive force for European union. . . .

Support for integration . . . is no longer confined to dreamers and old-fashioned romantics. It is coming from pragmatic Europeans, confronted day in day out with the absurdity of 12 national markets every bit as compartmentalized as they were in medieval times. . . .

The need to create a market comparable with that of the United States is obvious. . . . Our present structure of nation-States is costing us enormous sums of money and making it easier for our competitors to divide and rule. Europe is now trailing the U.S. and Japan in key areas of high technology. We must pool our efforts to narrow the gap.

In the same vein, another EC publication prophesies, "After the 'American challenge' of the 1960's and the subsequent emergence of Japan onto the world stage, the 1990's promise to be the decade of a revitalized Europe" (Commission of the European Communities: Spokesman's Service, p. 10).

Is this just empty rhetoric? Or are the potential gains truly large, and is the EC really mobilizing to achieve them? And what barriers must be removed in order to complete the internal market?

COMPLETING THE MARKET: BARRIERS THAT MUST GO

The barriers targeted for removal by the White Paper can be divided into eight categories, some of which overlap.[1]

(1) *Border controls.* At the borders between EC member states are physical controls that regulate the passage of people and goods. Such controls are necessitated by certain differences in laws and regulations between member states. For example, widely differing indirect tax rates (including excise and value-added rates) require tax adjustments at the borders to ensure that goods crossing over are taxed at the rates of the countries they are entering, so as to minimize competitive distortions. Differing health regulations for plant and animal products also require controls to ensure that such products satisfy the regulations of the country the products are entering. These controls impose significant delays and other costs. Harmonization of the differing laws and regulations (including tax rates) would of course be one way to obviate the need for such controls.

(2) *Limitations on movement of people and their right of establishment.* An important illustration of this kind of barrier is that acadeemic degrees and professional qualifications acquired in one EC member country have not, as a rule, been readily recognized in other member countries. Thus, it has been difficult for professionals to transfer the practice of their occupations from one state to an other. In addition, border controls are maintained to combat terrorism, drug trafficking, and illegal immigration by non-EC residents.

---

[1]This is the classification used by Calingaert (1988, pp. 20–27).

(3) *Differing indirect taxation regimes*. As already noted, the existence of differing tax rates and systems is one reason for the maintenance of border controls. Thus, the EC Commission has proposed that the same excise tax rates should be adopted by all EC countries and that value-added tax rates should diverge by no more than 5 to 6 percentage points between countries, a divergence that the Commission believes would be essentially neutral in its effect (Calingaert 1988, pp. 42–43).

(4) *Lack of a common legal framework for business*. The operation of business enterprises in the EC has been governed largely by differing national laws and regulations, introducing complications into cross-border business activity involving mergers, joint ventures, patents, copyrights, and so forth.

(5) *Controls on movement of capital*. Eight of the EC states have maintained some degree of control over capital movements to or from other member states.

(6) *Heavy—and differing—regulation of services*. The service industries, such as transportation and especially finance, have been subjected to regulation that has considerably raised the cost of the services provided and that has also differed significantly from one member state to the next.

(7) *Divergent product regulations and standards*. Often a product has had to meet differing standards in different EC countries.

(8) *Protectionist public procurement policies*. In procuring goods and services, the public authorities in the various EC countries have generally granted preferential treatment to domestic suppliers in a number of ways, including the procedures through which bids are solicited and contracts are awarded.

These eight categories of barriers comprise a formidable phalanx. It is not surprising that substantial gains from their removal are forecasted by a recent study.

THE POTENTIAL GAINS:
SOME QUANTITATIVE ESTIMATES

In order to obtain quantitative estimates of the economic benefits that could flow from the common market, the EC Commission arranged for a major study, the results of which were published only last year. A massive research effort, the study involved 200 people, took two years to complete, and cost about $5 million. It is the only comprehensive analysis available of the potential gains to the EC from completing the internal market. Carried out under the general direction of Paolo Cecchini, a former EC Commission official, the study is summarized in a slim volume widely known as the "Cecchini report" (Cecchini 1988).

In the study the potential gains to the EC from market integration are evaluated using both microeconomic analysis, which focuses on the effects on producers and consumers, and macroeconomic analysis, which focuses on the effects on major components of the gross domestic product (GDP). With both analytical approaches, the starting point is the removal of the market-fragmenting barriers targeted in the White Paper. Their removal will lower the costs of doing business—a favorable supply-side shock—and prices are expected to go down with costs under the pressure of wider competition across the newly unified market. The reduction in prices will stimulate demand and, therefore, output, and the increase in output will lead to further reductions in costs as economies of larger-scale production are realized.

In the microeconomic analysis, two approaches are employed: a price-convergence approach and a welfare-gains approach. The price-convergence approach assumes that the removal of barriers will greatly reduce the substantial price differences often observed for a given product between EC countries. Across countries in 1985, the average before-tax price variation from the EC mean price was 15.2 percent for consumer goods and 12.4 percent for capital equipment. Much greater price dispersion was observed for some individual items, such as glass and crockery (21 percent), boilermaking equipment (22 percent), tea (27 percent), ladies' linen and hosiery (31 percent), and books (49 percent). And glaring price differences (tax inclusive) are reported within the service sector: 28 percent in road and rail transport, 42 percent in electrical repairs, and 50 percent in telephone and telegraph services.

As barriers to arbitrage across countries are relaxed, prices should converge, and intensified competition across frontiers could lower the general average. Thus, the analysis assumes that in sectors where barriers are currently low, any price peaks will be brought down to the EC average, and that in sectors with high barriers, prices will settle at the average of the prices prevailing in the two EC countries with the lowest price levels. On the further assumption that output remains unchanged, this line of analysis concludes that total savings from the drop in prices would be about 4.8 percent of EC gross domestic product—a one-time, once-and-for-all gain.

This gain estimated by the price-convergence approach is conservative in that it takes no account of (1) the increases in output that would accompany the increased demand stimulated by price reductions or (2) the further cost- and price-reducing effects of larger scale production. By contrast, the welfare-gains approach does allow for these ramifications. It is more comprehensive than the price-convergence approach in another respect as well: it takes into account the profit losses that may be suffered by some currently protected producers as well as the gains to consumers and other producers. In the welfare-gains approach, a gain for consumers (or "consumer surplus") stems from lower prices and larger purchases, and this gain is partly offset by a drop in profit for producers subjected to new competition. Another

TABLE 1

Potential Gains in Economic Welfare for the European Community Resulting from Completion of the Internal Market

Source of Gain	Gain as Percentage of GDP
1. Removal of barriers directly affecting intra-EC trade	.2 to .3
2. Removal of barriers to production	2.0 to 2.4
3. Greater economies of scale, and intensified competition reducing inefficiencies and monopoly profits	2.1 to 3.7
Total	4.3 to 6.4

Source: Paolo Cecchini, *The European Challenge: 1992,* p. 84.

gain, with no offsetting losses, results from enhanced operational efficiencies throughout the EC.[2]

Table 1 itemizes the net welfare gains estimated by this approach. "Barriers directly affecting intra-EC trade" are essentially customs formalities and related delays. "Barriers to production" are those that impede entry into a national market by a foreign firm. Among such production barriers are the preferential treatment granted by government purchasing offices to native producers, differing national regulatory practices, and differing national standards for products. The estimated maximum gain, nearly 6.5 percent of GDP, is substantially larger than the 4.8 percent of GDP estimated with the price-convergence approach; but even the 6.5 percent figure might be too low, since it does not allow for the impact of new business strategies and technical innovation that could be stimulated by integration of the market.

Shifting from the microeconomic to the macroeconomic perspective, the study's analysis of potential gains from market integration focuses on the major components of GDP. As can be seen in table 2, the macroeconomic analysis proceeded by quantifying the effects of easing barriers in customs procedures, in public procurement, and in financial services, and by quantifying various supply-side-effects entailing greater business efficiency. The greatest gains are estimated from the liberalization of financial services and from supply-side effects.

The gains from liberalizing financial services stem from the resulting intensification of competition and associated reduction in the prices of financial services. Transmission of lower financial services costs throughout the

---

[2]In a recent theoretical inquiry, Ian Wooton (1988, p. 537) concludes that the welfare of a customs union is enhanced by establishment of a common market as long as the common external tariff structure is set correctly.

TABLE 2

Estimated Medium-Term Macroeconomic Consequences for the European Community from Market Integration Processes

Nature of Consequence	Process				Total	
	Removal of Customs Formalities	Opening of Public Procurement	Liberalization of Financial Services	Supply-side Effects	Average Value	Spread
Change in GDP (%)	.4	.5	1.5	2.1	4.5	3.2 to 5.7
Change in Consumer Prices (%)	−1.0	−1.4	−1.4	−2.3	−6.1	−4.5 to −7.7
Change in Employment (thousands)	200	350	400	850	1,800	1,300 to 2,300
Change in Budgetary Balance (percentage point of GDP)	.2	.3	1.1	.6	2.2	1.5 to 3.0
Change in External Balance (percentage point of GDP)	.2	.1	.3	.4	1.0	.7 to 1.3

Source: Paolo Cecchini, *The European Challenge: 1992*. p. 98.

economy is estimated to reduce prices generally, stimulating demand (both domestic and external) and output. This favorable effect will be amplified by increased investment in response to the lower cost of credit. More general supply-side effects come from the business sector's response to the more competitive environment—from more efficient techniques and greater economies of scale.

In total, the macroeconomic consequences of EC market integration are expected to be very favorable. It is estimated that GDP will be boosted by 4.5 percent, with 1.8 million new jobs, while consumer prices will simultaneously be lowered by 6.1 percent. The aggregate government budget balance is expected to improve by an amount equivalent to 2.2 percentage points of GDP, as government revenues rise with GDP and procurement costs are eased with the opening of public procurement to wider competition. Benefiting from improved competitiveness, the EC's current-account balance with the rest of the world is estimated to improve by the equivalent of 1 percentage point of GDP. Again, these are one-time, or once-and-for-all, gains, and their realization is likely to require 5 or 6 years once the market-integration program is complete.

The nature of these gains—especially the drop in consumer prices and the improvements in public finances and the external balance—suggests that still greater gains might be achieved were EC governments to pursue more expansionary fiscal policies. Thus, policies that reduced the improvement in government budget balances to 0.7 of a percentage point of GDP might boost the medium-term increase in GDP to 7 percent, with 5 million new jobs and no inflation, according to the Cecchini report (pp. 99–102).

As the basic study makes clear, such gains are contingent on removal of all essential barriers to market integration. Retention of only a few key barriers would suffice to restrain competition. In the words of the study, "Implementation of half of the actions proposed in the White Paper will deliver much less than half of the total potential benefits" (Commission of the European Communities 1988a, p. 22).

With such sizable total gains in prospect, the question arises how the gains will be distributed among the EC member countries. The study offers no quantitative estimates of this distribution. Economic theory suggests that proportionately larger gains will accrue to the smaller countries, especially those that have recently joined the EC and have had relatively high protection from external competition. Initially, however, such countries could suffer losses, as could various regions within the EC, until the firms and workers exposed to keener competition made adjustments such as adopting new techniques or acquiring new skills. Should some EC members suffer losses from the integration process, the EC has policy instruments, such as structural funds, that could be used to help them recover (Commission of the European Communities 1988a, p. 21).

POTENTIAL GAINS FOR COUNTRIES
OUTSIDE THE EC

If market integration does yield the growth spurt projected for the EC in the Cecchini report, rising EC income could lead to increased imports and thus to higher levels of economic activity in the rest of the world. The boost to GDP in the rest of the world would be considerably smaller than that inside the EC, however, and like that within the EC, would be a one-time phenomenon. Indeed, the net impact on the rest of the world could be contractionary, since the Cecchini report expects the rest of the world to experience a deterioration in its trade balance with the EC unless EC governments pursue relatively expansionary macroeconomic policies.

EC market integration could lead to higher levels of economic activity in the rest of the world.

Another potentially favorable result for the rest of the world is a lower rate of inflation, induced by the projected deflationary impact of EC market integration. This, in turn, could lead to lower interest rates if inflationary expectations were revised downward. And the rest of the world would experience more favorable terms of trade with the EC, if the real cost of goods purchased from the EC went down. This outcome, too, is far from certain. The expected growth spurt in the EC could generate an investment boom, pushing interest rates upward rather than downward and raising rather than lowering the real cost of goods exported from the EC in the near term. In this case, though, economic growth in the rest of the world could receive a larger boost, as the EC's external trade balance would likely deteriorate.

Still another gain for the rest of the world is possible, although it is even more speculative and imponderable than the preceding gains. As we have noted, one motivation underlying EC market integration is to narrow a perceived lag in EC economic performance behind Japan and the United States. Such competition among nations, if conducted without protectionist devices, can benefit all involved. Perhaps the United States, for example, will be spurred by the European challenge, as it has been by the Japanese challenge, to reconsider and improve some of its ways of doing business.

THE SPECTER OF FORTRESS EUROPE

As the foregoing discussion suggests, the consequences of EC market integration for the rest of the world are highly problematic, even on the assumption that the EC completes its internal market without resorting to intensified protection against the rest of the world. Now suppose that as the

EC allows the winds of competition to blow more freely across its members' frontiers, it simultaneously erects substantially more barriers against competition from the rest of the world, so as to mitigate the overall competitive shock and the degree of internal adjustment that will be required. This outcome, which is rather widely feared, would have damaging consequences for the rest of the world, and perhaps for the EC as well.

Were the EC to turn inward in this way, international economic cooperation in general would surely be undermined. For example, efforts to coordinate macroeconomic policies among the EC, Japan, and the United States would probably suffer. More certainly, the Uruguay Round of Multilateral Trade Negotiations, undertaken to liberalize international trade in both goods and services, would be imperiled if the EC's protectionist course became manifest before the completion of the Round, now scheduled for 1990.

A heightening of the EC's protectionist barriers would tend to negate the benefits that could otherwise accrue to the EC itself from integrating its internal market. After all, realization of those benefits is deemed to depend heavily upon a widening of competition within the market. Insofar as the strengthening of internal competition is offset by the blockage of competition from abroad, the benefits will be choked off near the source.

Were the EC to erect more barriers against outside competition, the consequences could be damaging for the rest of the world and perhaps for the EC as well.

If completion of the internal market in this fashion would yield little benefit for the EC, the rest of the world would benefit even less, and might well be harmed. For example, intensification of EC protectionism would militate against the reduction of costs and inflation within the EC and thus would do little to lower inflation abroad. Other countries might also experience a worsening of the terms on which they traded with the EC, as EC demand for their goods and services was damped by the heightened barriers, although this outcome would depend on the circumstances, including the nature of the barriers and the foreign response to them.

If protectionism were to transform the EC into "Fortress Europe" as it completed its internal market, how might the transformation occur? What measures would work the transformation? Because internal market integration implies removal of barriers between EC member countries but not necessarily between the EC and other countries, EC members might typically agree that all should impose against other countries the harshest of the barriers currently prevailing in any EC member country, while simultaneously eliminating such barriers against movements of goods, services, people, or capital among themselves.

To illustrate, the individual states of the EC currently maintain as many as 1,000 separate quantitative restrictions on imports (including the so-called "voluntary" restraints that some countries impose on their exports to EC countries), mostly on imports from Japan, the Asian newly industrialized countries, and the East European nonmarket economies (Calingaert 1988, p. 83). To prevent imports in excess of any restriction that it has promulgated, each EC country must monitor the flow of the restricted goods that comes to it via other EC members as well as from other sources. However, such border controls over intra-EC trade, with the associated delays and other costs, are inconsistent with EC market integration. To eliminate the border controls and complete the internal market, therefore, EC members must abolish the restrictions or establish a uniform set, to be applied by all the members acting as one, on imports from the rest of the world.

The most important of these restrictions relate to textiles and automobiles. For both of these commodity categories, it is likely that uniform EC restrictions will replace the prevailing individual member restrictions, resulting in no less overall protection than that now in force. Exports from the United States in these two categories are currently exempt from the restrictions, but automobiles from the United States might be covered in the future. Now it is automobiles from Japan that are targeted. If Japanese-brand automobiles manufactured in the United States were to be exported to the EC in sizable volume, the EC surely would consider encompassing them within the restrictions (Calingaert 1988, pp. 83–84).

Of even greater concern for the United States is the possibility of another variety of EC protectionism. This protectionism would take the form of denying "national treatment" for U.S. firms seeking to enter the EC through subsidiaries. The principle of national treatment—meaning government treatment of foreign-owned subsidiaries that is no less favorable than that accorded domestically owned firms—has been endorsed by all 24 member countries of the Organization for Economic Cooperation and Development, including the EC countries. But some EC officials and documents have espoused a different principle, the principle of reciprocity. Under a strict interpretation of reciprocity, subsidiaries to be established in the Community by firms located in a nonmember country would be granted the benefits of the integrated market only if EC subsidiaries in that nonmember country enjoyed similar benefits.

Some measure of reciprocity has been called for in proposed EC directives on financial services, especially with respect to investment services and life insurance, and also to some extent with respect to banking. In regard to banking, it would not be possible for the United States to offer to EC banks opportunities comparable to those that EC banks have in their home markets.

U.S. laws and regulations do not permit banks, either domestically or foreign-owned, to establish branches or subsidiaries nationwide, and banks in the United States are also subjected to other restrictions—for example, on securities activities—that do not apply to banks in the EC. (What the United States can and does offer is national treatment, or equality of competitive opportunity for banks regardless of nationality of ownership.) Thus, a strict interpretation of reciprocity could put U.S. banks at a competitive disadvantage in the Community.

The principle of reciprocity could be applied by the EC within certain sectors such as banking, or could be applied on an overall basis, with the EC granting national treatment in sectors such as banking in return for new opportunities for EC firms abroad in other sectors. The overall approach would be more consistent with the traditional practice in multilateral trade liberalization, in which the negotiating parties generally settle for an overall balance of concessions rather than a balance sector by sector. For the EC to demand sector-by-sector reciprocity as it integrated its internal market would be especially inimical to the achievement of a more libieral international economic order.

Rather than explicitly denying national treatment to foreign firms, the EC might engage in roughly equivalent practices, the effect of which would be protectionist even if the motivation were not. For example, the set of regulations and product standards to be adopted by the EC as part of the integration process could render foreign firms less competitive in the EC market. The purpose of EC regulations and standards is generally to assure some minimum quality, and concerning that general goal there can be little dispute. But if EC authorities refused to recognize product tests administered abroad, foreign manufacturers would face the expense of shipping their products to the EC for testing and sale without the assurance of certification.

Aside from difficulties with the certification process, non-EC firms could be disadvantaged by the EC standards themselves. A good illustration is the controversy between the EC and the United States over U.S. meat produced with the aid of growth hormones. Growth hormones are widely used in meat production in the United States, but not in the EC. The EC recently banned imports of such meat for human consumption on the grounds that it poses a health hazard. Arguing that scientific inquiry reveals no hazard, the United States has retaliated with 100 percent duties on selected U.S. imports of EC food products whose total import value approximates the $100 million of banned U.S. meat exports.

THE LIKELIHOOD OF FORTRESS EUROPE

It is much easier to conjure up the specter of Fortress Europe than to determine whether the Fortress will materialize. What is the likelihood that the EC will become more protectionist as it completes its internal market?

In his classic, *The Customs Union Issue,* Jacob Viner opined that "with respect to most customs union projects the protectionist is right and the free-trader is wrong in regarding the project as something, given his premises, which he can logically support" (Viner 1950, p. 41). Viner believed that the external barriers of the typical customs union would be adjusted so as to offset—indeed, more than offset—any overall decline in protection associated with heightened competition among the members. It would be hard to prove that the EC has followed such a protectionist course from its inception, particularly with respect to tariffs on manufactured goods. With respect to other forms of protection the record is not so good, especially in recent years.

Moreover, some EC documents and official statements are worrisome. In July 1988, Willy de Clercq, then the EC Commissioner for External Relations, asserted that the new common market will "give us the negotiating leverage to obtain . . . overall reciprocity" (de Clercq 1988). Similarly, the Cecchini report warns, "If the fruits of the European home market are to be shared internationally, there must also be a fair shareout of the burdens of global economic responsibility, with market opening measures extended internationally on a firm basis of clear reciprocity" (Cecchini 1988, p. xx). And the White Paper declares that "the commercial identity of the Community must be consolidated so that our trading partners will not be given the benefit of a wider market without themselves making similar concessions" (Commission of the European Communities 1985, para. 19). Not only will the EC seek global reciprocity (an overall balance of concessions), but according to Mr. de Clercq, it will seek sectoral reciprocity in certain sectors not covered by the General Agreement on Tariffs and Trade, particularly the services sector (de Clercq 1988).

Concern is warranted not only by such official pronouncements, but also by EC trade policy, which, as in some other countries, has turned more protectionist and discriminatory over the past two decades. Much of the heightened protection and discrimination has taken the form of various non-tariff interventions. In particular, the EC has made increasing use of selective, quantitative import restrictions (including "voluntary" export restraint agreements), especially to limit manufactured imports from developing countries. In addition, it has subsidized EC exports, notably exports of agricultural goods whose production is also protected by variable import levies, and it has employed countervailing and antidumping duties more vigorously (Henderson 1989, pp. 13–14). In light of this seeming predisposition toward protectionism, it would not be surprising if competitive pressures generated by the removal of barriers to trade within the EC were eased by the elevation, or at least the maintenance, of similar barriers against competition from without. Thus, completion of the EC's internal market may well entail at least the preexisting degree of EC protection against foreign competition.

Any shift toward greater protection by the EC is likely to be slight, however, so that the specter of Fortress Europe will probably remain little more than a specter. As EC authorities are well aware, even minor heightenings of protectionist barriers have provoked retaliation from the injured trading partners, and the prospect of such retaliation is a strong deterrent. To put much the same point more positively, the EC, like most other trading entities, has much more to gain from an open, integrated international economy than from one fragmented by protectionist barriers. Indeed, that conclusion flows from the same line of reasoning that is used to justify the completion of the EC internal market. And the EC has many good logicians.

U.S. BUSINESS AND THE COMMON MARKET

U.S. business has a sizable stake in the E.C. In 1988 the United States exported $130 billion in goods and services to the E.C., one-third more than to Canada, our second largest export markett. Because most export sales are of merchandise and because detailed data are available on the merchandise categories, tables 3 and 4 present statistics for the leading merchandise categories. The data are shown for Canada as well as the EC, not only because Canada is the second largest U.S. export market but because the two nations have recently concluded a free trade agreement.

As shown in the tables, for merchandise alone, total EC and Canadian purchases of U.S. exports were not vastly different in 1988. However, except for automotive vehicles, parts, and engines—in which sectoral free trade between Canada and the United States has contributed to close integration of the national industries—the EC is a much more important export market for the United States in every mechandise category listed in the tables. Especially noteworthy are the EC shares of U.S. worldwide exports in the categories of computers, peripherals, and semiconductors, and of civilian aircraft, parts, and engines (table 4).

Firms invade foreign markets not only by exporting but by acquiring facilities in those markets. Thus, U.S. multinational firms have many affiliates, including branches and subsidiaries, in Canada and the EC, and the sales of these affiliates are much larger than U.S. exports to either area, especially in the case of the EC (table 5). While not all such sales are to Canadian or EC residents, the preponderance surely are.[3] Between 1982 and 1986 (the latest year for which data are available at this writing), the biggest increases in these affiliate sales were in manufacturing industries, although the increase within wholesale trade in the EC also merits mention.

---

[3]See U.S Bureau of Economic Analysis, *U.S. Direct Investment Abroad: 1982 Benchmark Survey Data,* 1985, p. 225, for local as well as total sales by majority-owned nonbank affiliates of nonbank U.S. parents for 1982.

40

TABLE 3

U.S. Exports of Domestic and Foreign Merchandise to Canada and the European Community in Total and by Leading End-Use Categories, 1982 and 1988[a]
Millions of U.S. Dollars

Category	Canada 1982	Canada 1988	European Community 1982	European Community 1988
Grand total	37,799	68,747	51,255	74,679
Total foods, feeds, and beverages	1,966	2,225	8,839	5,689
Agricultural foods, feeds, and beverages	1,801	1,994	8,653	5,561
Total industrial supplies and materials	9,054	12,615	16,650	19,734
Nonagricultural except fuels	6,361	10,043	9,648	14,463
Chemicals, excluding medicinals	1,979	3,170	3,648	6,019
Capital goods except automotive	10,173	16,547	19,628	36,997
Nonelectrical machinery, including parts and attachments	8,194	12,581	14,643	25,581
Industrial and service machinery	3,727	5,055	5,284	7,329
Computers, peripherals, and semi-conductors	1,335	3,853	4,926	12,080
Transportation equipment, except automotive	1,107	2,168	3,588	8,935
Civilian aircraft, parts and engines, excluding special category	925	1,915	3,124	8,434
Automotive vehicles, parts and engines	9,310	19,634	954	2,162
Passenger cars, new and used	2,345	6,266	76	643
Automotive parts, engines and bodies	6,211	10,585	778	1,364
Consumer goods (nonfood), except automotive	2,141	3,452	3,872	7,228
Domestic exports, n.e.c., and reexports	5,156	14,271	1,312	2,680

[a]Special category military-type goods are not included.
[b]Categories shown are those in which total exports to Canada and the EC were $5 billion or more in 1988.
Source: National Institutes of Health, COMPRO data base.

As can be seen in table 6, the EC affiliates of U.S. firms account for almost half of the sales of all foreign affiliates of U.S. companies. In nearly every industry listed the EC is significantly more important for these sales than Canada is. A comparison of the tables 6 and 4 suggests that the EC absorbs a much larger share of these total affiliate sales than of total U.S. merchandise exports.[4] These phenomena may well be heightened by the completion of the EC internal market and the implementation of the free trade agreement between Canada and the United States. The EC internal market will probably serve to raise U.S. direct investment and sales within the market relative to the U.S. exports to it, because market completion plans call for a reduction in barriers to commerce within the EC but not

[4]The same is true if exports are defined to include services as well as merchandise.

TABLE 4

U.S. Merchandise Exports to Canada and the European Community in Total and by Leading End-Use Categories, as a Percentage of U.S. Exports World-wide by Category, 1982 and 1988[a]

Category[b]	Canada		European Community	
	1982	1988	1982	1988
Grand total	17.2	21.5	23.3	23.3
Total foods, feeds, and beverages	6.2	6.8	27.7	17.9
Agricultural foods, feeds, and beverages	5.9	6.6	28.2	18.4
Total industrial supplies and materials	14.6	14.5	26.8	22.7
Nonagricultural except fuels	16.5	15.6	25.1	22.5
Chemicals, excluding medicinals	12.6	12.4	23.3	23.6
Capital goods except automotive	13.5	14.3	26.1	32.0
Nonelectrical machinery, including parts and attachments	14.7	15.2	26.2	31.0
Industrial and service machinery	16.4	17.9	23.2	26.0
Computers, peripherals, and semi-conductors	10.7	12.0	39.5	37.5
Transportation equipment, except automotive	9.2	9.6	29.7	39.7
Civilian aircraft, parts and engines, excluding special category	9.4	9.2	31.8	40.7
Automotive vehicles, parts and engines	58.3	61.2	6.0	7.1
Passenger cars, new and used	74.5	69.3	2.4	7.1
Automotive parts, engines and bodies	60.2	61.2	7.5	7.9
Consumer goods (nonfood), except automotive	13.7	13.4	24.7	28.0
Domestic exports, n.e.c., and reexports	56.6	60.4	14.4	11.3

[a]Special category military-type goods are not included.
[b]Categories shown are those in which total exports to Canada and the EC were $5 billion or more in 1988.
Source: National Institutes of Health, COMPRO data base.

between the EC and other countries. By contrast, the U.S.-Canada free trade agreement mandates the removal or reduction of many barriers to trade between the two nations.

What firms will benefit most from EC market integration? In general, the prime beneficiaries will be those firms that are highly competitive within the EC and that face substantial cross-border and other costs and barriers associated with EC market fragmentation. The lowering of these internal barriers and costs will enable such firms to compete more effectively across the Community. Should the EC maintain or elevate its barriers against external competition, these same firms will become even more profitable, at least in the short or medium term. Thus, it is understandable that the financial press has reported something of a scramble by firms to position themselves advantageously within the EC.

TABLE 5

Sales of Canadian and European Community Affiliates of U.S. Multinational Companies, by Selected Industries, 1982 and 1986
Millions of U.S. Dollars

Industry[a]	Canadian Affiliates		EC Affiliates[b]	
	1982	1986	1982	1986
All industries	120,327	132,594	370,542	430,377
Petroleum	28,642	18,479	104,685	74,118
Oil and gas extraction	d	d	d	12,048
Crude petroleum (no refining) and gas	d	d	9,918	11,233
Petroleum and coal products	19,046	d	63,138	44,228
Integrated refining and extraction	17,233	10,640	35,128	18,841
Refining without extraction	d	d	27,796	25,275
Petroleum wholesale trade	3,645	2,178	23,023	11,553
Manufacturing	56,911	75,521	160,609	226,068
Food and kindred products	5,258	5,655	16,337	23.998
Grain mill and bakery products	1,214	1,465	6,454	9,990
Chemicals and allied products	8,265	10,493	30,451	40,705
Industrial chemicals and synthetics	4,240	24,638	13,791	18,289
Drugs	1,122	1,521	6,583	10,395
Primary and fabricated metals	3,202	3,880	9,284	12,232
Fabricated metal products	2,155	2,575	6,586	7,917
Machinery, except electrical	4,994	5,615	28,416	47.924
Electric and electronic equipment	4,323	4,704	11,928	24,174
Transportation equipment	19,108	34,075	36,867	36,760
Motor vehicles and equipment	18,086	32,383	d	35,036
Other manufacturing	11,761	11,099	27,325	40,274
Tobacco manufactures	d	d	d	10,648
Instruments and related products	1,079	1,024	8,602	10,482
Wholesale trade	9,788	10,984	58,645	75,460
Durable goods	7,001	8,315	36,935	43,013
Nondurable goods	2,788	2,670	21,711	32,447
Finance (except banking), insurance and real estate	6,349	7,499	8,361	11,888
Insurance	4,629	5,600	d	6,410
Services	2,403	2,611	9,413	15,520
Business services	810	966	5,387	9,850
Other industries	16,234	17,499	28,829	27,323
Transportation, communication and public utilities	d	2,349	d	18,884
Retail trade	10,530	12,399	7,189	5,978

[a]Identifiable industries in which Canadian and EC affiliate sales totaled $10 billion or more in 1986.
[b]EC includes 10 countries because data for Spain and Portugal are not available.
d: Data were suppressed for confidentiality reasons.
Source: U.S. Bureau of Economic Analysis, *U.S. Direct Investment Abroad: Preliminary 1986 Estimates,* June 1988, table 7; and *U.S. Direct Investment Abroad: 1982 Benchmark Society Data,* December 1985, p. 112.

TABLE 6

Sales of Canadian and European Community Affiliates of U.S. Multinational Companies as a Percentage of U.S. Foreign Affiliate Sales Worldwide, by Selected Industries, 1982 and 1986

Industry[a]	Percent of Total Sales, All U.S. Foreign Affiliates			
	Canadian Affiliates		EC Affiliates[b]	
	1982	1986	1982	1986
All industries	12.9	14.2	39.6	46.2
Petroleum	8.7	9.2	31.8	37.1
Oil and gas extraction	d	d	d	30.5
Crude petroleum (no refining) and gas	d	d	19.6	32.0
Petroleum and coal products	14.0	d	46.4	52.0
Integrated refining and extraction	30.0	32.4	61.2	57.4
Refining without extraction	d	d	35.7	49.0
Petroleum wholesale trade	3.2	3.6	20.0	18.9
Manufacturing	15.8	16.8	44.7	50.2
Food and kindred products	13.5	12.7	41.9	53.9
Grain mill and bakery products	9.7	9.9	51.8	67.3
Chemicals and allied products	11.9	13.1	43.8	50.7
Industrial chemicals and synthetics	12.8	12.6	41.6	49.8
Drugs	8.6	8.4	50.2	57.5
Primary and fabricated metals	14.0	16.3	40.5	51.4
Fabricated metal products	16.1	18.3	49.1	56.2
Machinery, except electrical	10.8	7.9	61.2	67.3
Electrical and electronic equipment	13.9	10.2	38.3	52.5
Transportation equipment	22.0	30.7	42.4	33.2
Motor vehicles and equipment	21.6	30.2	d	32.7
Other manufacturing	18.6	15.1	43.2	54.9
Tobacco manufactures	d	d	d	79.7
Instruments and related products	8.5	6.4	67.4	65.7
Wholesale trade	8.0	7.3	47.8	50.5
Durable goods	9.6	9.6	50.6	49.7
Nondurable goods	5.6	4.2	43.7	51.5
Finance (except banking), insurance and real estate	22.2	20.5	29.2	32.5
Insurance	27.6	26.6	d	30.4
Services	11.8	10.2	46.4	60.9
Business services	8.0	6.5	53.1	66.6
Other industries	21.4	25.2	38.0	39.4
Transportation, communication and public utilities	d	9.4	d	75.2
Retail trade	38.6	43.1	26.4	20.8

[a]Identifiable industries in which Canadian and EC affiliate sales totaled $10 billion more in 1986.
[b]EC includes 10 countries because data for Spain and Portugal are not available.
d: Data were suppressed for confidentiality reasons.
Source: U.S. Bureau of Economic Analysis, *U.S. Direct Investment Abroad: Preliminary 1986 Estimates,* June 1988, table 7; and *U.S. Direct Investment Abroad: 1982 Benchmark Survey Data,* December 1985, p. 112.

If completion of the EC internal market generates a growth spurt, as forecasted by the Cecchini report, EC demand for U.S. (and other) exports likely will also spurt, even if the EC maintains or slightly intensifies its protection against external competition. On the other hand, the Cecchini report expects EC firms to enjoy lower costs as a result of the market integration. Such enhanced competitiveness on the part of EC producers would enable them to accommodate some of the increase in EC demand that might otherwise generate U.S. exports. Similarly, U.S. firms would encounter stiffer competition from EC firms in other markets, including the U.S. market, not only during the EC growth spurt but over the longer run.

EC officials, however, often argue that U.S. firms will excel in the competitive struggle. One EC publication puts it as follows:[5]

> U.S. businesses are well placed to exploit the benefits of a unified market. First of all, their subsidiaries incorporated in the Community will profit from the removal of barriers to the same extent as purely European companies. American companies are already used to operating in both a global and a large domestic marketplace, so may have less trouble adapting to the new environment than indigenous companies.
>
> U.S. exporters will find themselves selling into a single market with a generally uniform set of norms, standards, and testing and certification procedures. They will no longer have to face 12 different sets of requirements or intra-Community border controls. . . .
>
> In fact, many people of the Community are afraid that the main beneficiaries of the internal market could well prove to be the Japanese and American companies operating in Europe.

PROGRESS IN COMPLETING THE MARKET

It was in June 1985 that the EC Commission released its White Paper detailing a program for completing the internal market by the end of 1992. The undertaking is formidable even at the technical level, and at the political level has encountered opposition from many who would be affected adversely. What progress has been made?

A single quantitative measure is not feasible, but a crude idea of overall progress is conveyed by the percentage of White Paper subject areas that have been acted upon. As of January 30, 1989, the EC Commission had submitted proposals for more than four-fifths of the subjects covered in the White Paper, and the Council of Ministers—the EC's supreme decision-making body—had adopted more than two-fifths of the measures that will eventually be required. Areas in which little progress had been made include

---

[5]"A Europe Without Borders by 1992: Answers to Some Questions," *European Community News,* No. 23/88 (September 15, 1988), p. 4.

freeing the movement of people and reconciling the differences in indirect taxation and in plant and animal health regulation.[6]

Much skepticism exists that the EC nations will resolve all their differences—especially on sensitive matters such as taxation—so as to complete the internal market fully. Certainly it is most unlikely that all of the White Paper's program will be in effect by the end of 1992. But the endeavor should not be labeled a failure on those grounds alone. It has been said more than once that "1992 is a process, not an event." By the end of 1992, that process probably will have made substantial progress in integrating the European market.

CONCLUSION

Motivated largely by frustration with internal economic barriers and by a desire to gain in international economic stature, the EC is well embarked upon a massive effort to establish a Community-wide market free of restrictions over the movement of goods, services, persons, and capital. The potential gains to the EC from such market integration could amount to more than 6 percent of the Community's GDP, with much smaller gains for the rest of the world.

Despite some disturbing omens, it seems unlikely that the EC will transform itself into a protectionist "Fortress Europe" as it unifies its internal market. One deterrent is the threat of retaliation from the rest of the world. Another is the risk that the inefficiencies associated with such protectionism would offset the efficiencies to be reaped from internal market integration.

Viewed as a collectivity, the EC is the largest export market for the United States. Similarly, EC affiliates of U.S. multinational firms account for nearly half of the sales of all foreign affiliates of U.S. companies. The firms to benefit most from EC market integration will be those that are highly competitive within the EC and that have been encumbered by substantial cross-border and other costs and barriers associated with market fragmentation.

Barring a near miracle, the EC internal market will not be completed on schedule by the end of 1992. While there is no guarantee of eventual success, a delay of some years would mean little in such a grand undertaking.

REFERENCES

1. Calingaert, Michael. 1988. *The 1992 Challenge from Europe: Development of the European Community's Internal Market*. Washington, D.C.: National Planning Association.

---

[6]"E.C. Commission Evaluates Progress of 1992 Program," *European Community News*, No. 31/88 (November 10, 1988).

2. Cecchini, Paolo. 1988. *The European Challenge: 1992*. Brookfield, Vt.: Gower Publishing Company.
3. Commission of the European Communities. 1985. "Completing the Internal Market: White Paper from the Commission to the European Council."
4. ———. 1988a. *European Economy*, No. 35, March.
5. ———. 1988b. *A Frontier-Free Europe*.
6. Commission of the European Communities: Spokesman's Service. (no date). *The EC's 1992 Strategy: Market Integration and Economic Growth*.
7. de Clercq, Willy, "1992: The Impact on the Outside World." Speech presented in London, July 12.
8. EC Office of Press and Public Affairs. 1988a. "A Europe Without Borders by 1992: Answers to Some Questions." *European Community News*, No. 23/88, September 15.
9. ———. 1988b. "E.C. Commission Evaluates Progress of 1992 Program." *European Community News*, No. 31/88, November 10.
10. Henderson, David. 1989. *1992: The External Dimension*. New York: Group of Thirty.
11. U.S. Bureau of Economic Analysis. 1985. *U.S. Direct Investment Abroad: 1982 Benchmark Survey Data*. Washington, D.C.
12. Viner, Jacob. 1950. *The Customs Union Issue*. New York: Carnegie Endowment for International Peace.
13. Wooton, Ian. 1988. "Towards a Common Market: Factor Mobility in a Customs Union." *Canadian Journal of Economics*, vol. XXI, August, pp. 525–38.

2

Assessing Executive Views on the Single Market

EC-92 is a popular topic in the North American business community today. Conjecture and speculation is rampant as literally thousands of small and medium-sized firms, as well as a number of larger companies, still are attempting to plot a course for 1993 and beyond.

In response, the trade and popular press, professional journals and even the network news programs have all had their turn at offering an "E.C. overview" or providing background data on the New Europe. Few, however, have offered the type of specificities that firms need or have even suggested the strategic alternatives that may be available to American producers. Further, while the views of several Multinational Corporation (MNC) executives may have been included in such articles, their comments were largely directed to offering broad generalities about "opportunities in the market" or were responses to specific questions dealing with some aspect of harmonization or with product standards.

It is our feeling, however, that an important source of information for the small and medium-sized firm's E.C. planners is the American company that already has a significant presence in Europe. Executives in these U.S. MNC's are watching the E.C. developments "first-hand" and many of these major corporations either have already begun to put their 1992 plans in action or are well on their way to doing so. Further, if one needs evidence of this group's perceived importance (and expertise), he or she needs only to be reminded that many European businessmen feel that the U.S. major, in particular, is well ahead of most of its continental counterparts in EC-92 plan-

47

ning. In fact, many Europeans fear that the U.S. producer will have a distinct "early edge" due to its lengthy experience in marketing throughout (or across) the 12-country marketplace. They recognize that even the larger European firms, except for a few notables such as Nestlé and Philips, have tended to concentrate primarily on their home market, a few neighboring countries and in the United States and other external markets, such as Brazil, Japan and Eastern Europe. (This concern by the typical "national" European company has even manifested itself in the clamor for a "fortressization" of the European Community during the Community's shakedown period.")

We agree with the European assessment that the U.S.-based MNC operating in Europe is particularly knowledgeable about the European Community (and EC-92). Therefore, in this chapter (and the following one), we will present the findings of research conducted among such American companies. We will offer their views on subjects ranging from the "Fortress Europe possibility" to the likelihood of EC-92 spawning new European producers capable of competing in the U.S. itself. And, we will also examine their projected "entry approaches" for EC-92. This chapter (Chapter 2) focuses on multi-company data produced through survey research, while the following chapter (Chapter 3) provides more in-depth case-like insights.

A BIT OF HISTORY

Before considering our 1988–89 findings, however, a brief look at the past is in order. To keep EC-92 in perspective, one needs to be reminded that the European Community was not founded in 1987; many of the *plusses* apparent today were apparent to many American firms two or more decades ago. And, that much of the U.S.-direct investment in Europe in the 1960s and 1970s was made with the Common Market in mind.

To illustrate, one of the co-authors of this book was a co-researcher on a survey project in 1972 that examined ". . . how U.S. firms perceive the Common Market to date."[1] The findings from that 1972 study are most interesting in light of today's attention to EC-92 happenings. First, the survey produced a fifty percent response rate from the top one hundred U.S. MNC's and all those responding said they marketed their products in European (Economic) Community [E.(E.)C.] countries. In fact, ninety percent of those responding said they had direct investment in the then six-country marketplace (1972), and nearly one-third said their investments had occurred prior to 1935.

Second, roughly two-thirds of the respondents in this 1972 survey indicated that their sales had increased as a result of the formulation of the European Economic Community. And finally, their overall image of the European Economic Community was extremely positive. They saw few nationalistic barriers to their developing production subsidiaries and facilities and they chose terms like "competitive," "growth," "profit," "good," "necessary," and "stable" to describe the E.E.C.'s image. The pro-E.E.C. result of this study conflicted with the often reported view of a decade earlier that the signing of the Treaty of Rome and the resulting Common Market would doom the opportunities abroad (Europe) for U.S. corporations.

Clearly, the U.S. MNC has a history that is closely tied to Europe and the original formation and later expansion of the European Community. Now, how do such companies see it today?

EC-92: A MULTI-COMPANY VIEW

The bulk of the U.S. MNC's we have studied are poised to take full advantage of EC-92. Many, in fact, already have in place the type of entry strategy/organizational design that they feel is necessary to make their presence even more prominent in 1993 and beyond than it is to-date.

Our major study of Europe 1992 involved the top 1000 U.S. manufacturers or service organizations;[2] the questionnaire was sent to 250 leading firms chosen from the group. Some fifty-nine (59) firms or nearly 24 percent participated in the survey. A profile of these leading U.S. firms would indicate that they are the types of firms that are at the cutting-edge in terms of EC-92 preparation and the overall results suggest they present the sort of aggressive planning and strategies that many European "national" firms feel is most "threatening."

THE FIRMS

The bulk of the companies in the E.C. study have (a) total annual sales exceeding $3 billion; (b) do between 10 percent and 40 percent of their business overseas; (c) presently operate in six or more of the E.C. countries and (d) were producers of industrial products (Figures 2.1 to 2.4). Further, most employ some form of entry strategy other than exporting to serve their E.C. markets. Among these other entry approaches they employ are overseas subsidiaries, joint ventures or strategic alliances, foreign production (out-sourcing), licensing, third country exporting or some combination of these alternatives. In other words, these firms have the entry characteristics one expects to find in experienced U.S.-based majors. And, as we shall see shortly, this variety of experience and flexibility in adapting to new markets, makes their input especially valuable to those newly engaged in international operations or to the more experienced international organization just beginning to put together its EC-92 strategy.

Finally, most of the companies in our study have focused their initial attention on the larger European markets. In identifying for us their primary

FIGURE 2.1

Total Company Annual Sales ($B) of Majors in the Study N = 59

Annual Sales Category ($B)	Percentage of Firms
1–2	27.1
3–7	42.3
8–15	18.7
Above 15	11.9
	100.0

E.C. market today, the bulk chose countries like the United Kingdom, France, or Germany. As shown in Figure 2.5, The United Kingdom had the largest number of first place rankings and it was ranked either 1, 2 or 3 in importance by over three-fourths of the responding executives. Two other long-term E.C. bulwarks, France and West Germany, were similarly considered to be highly important markets (Figure 2.5). Only Italy, among the Southern-tier countries received sufficiently frequent mentions to be noted separately. And, many of the newer E.C. member countries received no "most important" designation.

Given the level of economic and industrial development, geographic separation, and historic trade patterns of the United Kingdom, France, and West Germany, it is not surprising that they are currently considered so important by the U.S. executives. To illustrate, the three nations were listed as the E.C. countries having the largest number of International 500 companies in the 1989 *Forbes* magazine rankings.[3] Such a pattern of market development, i.e. "attacking" the largest, most competitive markets first, would be consistent with the type of experienced world-wide and European-specific com-

FIGURE 2.2

Overseas Sales as a Percentage of Total Sales

Percentage of Sales	Response Percent
Less than 5	10.2
6 to 10	8.5
11 to 15	8.5
16 to 20	6.8
21 to 30	15.3
31 to 40	27.1
41 to 50	8.5
Above 50	15.3
	100.0

FIGURE 2.3

No. of E.C. Countries with Operations

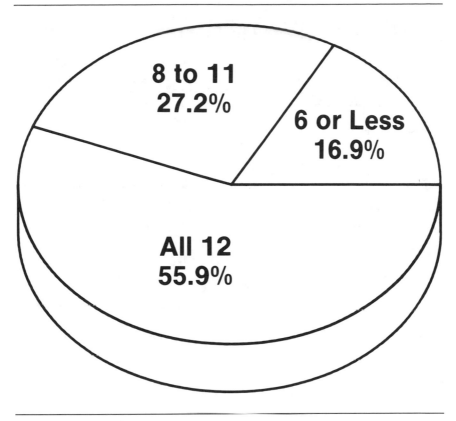

panies reflected in the sample. (And, it again reflects the value of their in-
puts to companies examining their position in relation to EC-92.)

HOW KEY U.S. MNC EXECUTIVES SEE EC-92:
THE ISSUES

There are undoubtedly still more questions than we have answers available
in regard to EC-92. The process of harmonizing the economic, labour, education, etc., rules and regulations of 12 independent countries is well-un-
derway . . . but not complete. The decisions relating to a common currency
(ECU) or a common monetary system will be difficult to resolve, and the
final outcome is difficult to predict.

FIGURE 2.4

Type of Firm

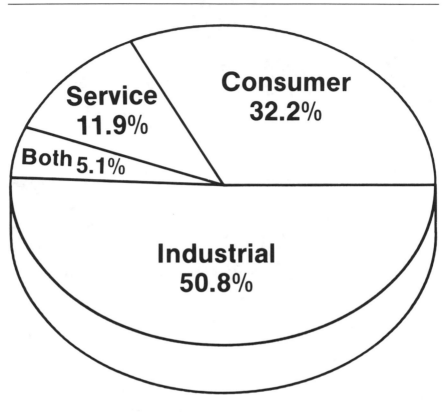

There are a multitude of other differences to resolve and only some of these final results are now apparent. Yet, despite the absence of black and white answers to a whole range of issues that are confounding them, U.S. and Canadian business decision-makers must take actions regarding 1992.

We presented the U.S. executives in our study with 24 critical concerns or issues that strike at the heart of North American involvement in EC-92 and asked them for their opinion on each concern. [Some twelve (12) of the concerns were general and the remainder divided equally between managerial and marketing-specific issues.] Viewed from a position of active involvement in the 12-country market, their perceptions are more than an "educated guess." As we will see later in the chapter, these views have often been translated into company actions by many of these majors.

FIGURE 2.5

Most Important E.C. Market (Current)

Country	Ranked 1st (%)	Ranked 2nd (%)	Ranked 3rd (%)
U.K.	37.3	23.7	15.3
France	28.8	10.2	28.8
West Germany	16.9	39.0	16.9
Italy	3.4	10.2	11.9
Other (OR NR)	7.3	9.3	17.3
	100.0	100.0	100.0

GENERAL OPPORTUNITIES FOR U.S. FIRMS

The MNC executives believe that U.S. firms will have a marked increase in market opportunities as a result of EC-92 (Figure 2.6). Clearly, the overall tone of the respondents is one of high optimism in regard to EC-92. To put their view in perspective, nearly three-fourths (70+ percent) agree that EC-92 will benefit U.S. producers like themselves. And, they undoubtedly should since these firms are by and large well entrenched in the 12-country market.

As further evidence of optimism, the MNC executives believe that the European Community offers them "access to additional markets" and they tend to agree with the widely held opinion that there will be an "increase in E.C. membership" in the future. Such an enlarged membership, e.g. Austria, Norway and Sweden, not only expands the overall market, but provides other national avenues for entry into the European Community. (Given the level of direct investment incentives presently being offered by the European countries, such an increase in membership broadens the entry base alternatives.) On the downside, however, they paint a much less optimistic picture for those firms of all sizes that do not have a physical presence in the European Community today and do not plan to have local (E.C.) production in the future. To illustrate, they predict increased tariff and non-tariff barriers for exporters outside the European Community in the post EC-92 era. And, a few even see non-E.C. producers losing key developing country markets due to their special trading status with the European Community (Figure 2.6).

Especially noteworthy, is the respondents' views on the competitive milieu in the new 12-country market. The three statements that produced the highest degree of agreement dealt with the European competitive marketplace. First, these key executives strongly feel there will be more competition in Europe from E.C.-based firms. As a corollary, they agree that there will be an increase in corporate mergers among E.C. firms. In other words,

54

FIGURE 2.6

U.S. Executives' View on General EC-92 Issues
(scores below 3.5 indicate disagreement and scores above 3.5 agreement)

	Issue	Agree/Disagree	Degree of Agreement
	. . . I feel that EC-92 will result in:		
(1)	increased market opportunities for U.S. firms.	AGREE	3.982
(2)	access to additional markets.	AGREE	3.667
(3)	more interest in the E.C. market by the U.S. exporters.	AGREE	4.203
(4)	an increase in E.C. membership.	AGREE	4.203
(5)	overall, an improvement in U.S. Balance of Trade.	DISAGREE	3.316
(6)	an increase in corporate mergers among E.C. firms.	AGREE	4.644
(7)	increased tariffs for exporters from outside European Community.	AGREE	3.831
(8)	more competition in Europe from E.C. based firms.	AGREE	4.672
(9)	increased non-tariff barriers for U.S. exporters.	AGREE	3.879
(10)	increased European nationalism.	AGREE	3.828
(11)	loss of key developing country markets due to their special trading status with the European Community.	DISAGREE	3.298
(12)	a necessity to establish E.C. production.	AGREE	4.386

a series of inter- and intra-country mergers in a new marketplace will produce stronger transnational competition within the European Community. (Chapter Four describes the evolving competitive mix in several industry sectors where the pattern predicted by the executives is rapidly occurring.) Finally, a large proportion of the executives agree that U.S. companies must establish E.C. production if they are to effectively compete in Europe. To some extent, this view likely reflects a degree of "Fortress Europe" concern. In the main, however, it simply reflects the same sort of realistic assessment they made in predicting more mergers among European producers. The newly "minted" European joint ventures, alliances, or merged companies are seen as being more competitive than the smaller national firms they replace. Couple these highly competitive European firms with a normal level of GATT negotiated tariff and non-tariff barriers and it will be difficult for non-European firms to compete in the European Community via an export-only strategy. In fact, only those U.S. companies with exceptional product quality, R&D leadership, niche advantage or a carefully designed niche strategy are likely to find an export-only approach viable.

MANAGEMENT-RELATED ISSUES

EC-92 will permit some important management/organizational design changes for U.S. firms operating today in the 12-country market, according to the executives. A greater parity in wages across the European Community, a greater flexibility in shifting managers and a consolidation of current European production sites are all seen as quite likely EC-92 outcomes (Figure 2.7). In particular, the consolidation of current production sites by U.S. producers is already well underway and represents the opportunity to take advantage of scale economies under border free distribution. Furthermore, they feel that managers will undoubtedly have a faster learning curve when it comes to assessing intra-European differences in the new marketplace.

From an organizational structure standpoint, the study respondent's assessment is that we will see firms more frequently establishing regional headquarters and more U.S. firms establishing E.C. subsidiaries. Many of these projected management and organizational dynamics can already be seen in the approaches employed by several U.S. MNC's described in Chapter 3.

MARKETING-RELATED ISSUES

The executives are generally as enthusiastic about the immediate marketing advantages of EC-92 as with the management changes that will be produced. On the one hand, they strongly support the notion of EC-92 resulting in greater use of global and regional marketing strategies (Figure 2.8). Trans-E.C. advertising, for example, offers many opportunities to re-

FIGURE 2.7

U.S. Executives' Views on Management-Related EC-92 Issues
(scores below 3.5 indicate disagreement and scores above 3.5 agreement)

Issue	Agree/Disagree	Degree of Agreement
. . . I feel that EC-92 will result in:		
(1) a consolidation of current European production sites.	AGREE	4.345
(2) the establishment of regional headquarters.	AGREE	4.161
(3) faster learning curve for managers about Intra-European differences.	AGREE	4.051
(4) greater flexibility in moving managers from one country to another.	AGREE	4.169
(5) more U.S. firms establishing an E.C. subsidiary.	AGREE	4.288
(6) greater parity in wages across countries.	AGREE	4.138

duce certain promotional expenditures, especially if a somewhat standardized approach can be followed and media redundancy reduced. Earlier research[4] has indicated a growing recognition of the importance of satellite television as a border-crossing promotional medium and similar savings/efficiency can result in the print media, as well. To some extent, a majority agrees that cultural differences in the new E.C. area are on the wane—a necessary condition if true standardization is to be realized (Figure 2.8). This coupled with a perceived "reduced need" for a nation-by-nation approach to the European Community is seen as increasing the possibility for developing Eurobrands. (This point is discussed further in Chapter 5.)

On the downside, several of the study respondents do tend to agree that EC-92 will lead to greater regulation; and in fact, among the twelve countries, the harmonization efforts in some categories have led to the most restrictive national measures being adopted at all. In addition, some regulation has developed in areas previously "untouched" in a few of the member countries. E.C. regulations relating to antitrust activities, price discrimination, advertising, packaging, etc., will all be followed during the early post EC-92 years to determine just what their impact may ultimately be. Finally, the executives envision some greater difficulty in finding E.C.-wide distributors, though a majority give it limited concern. Again, these executives represent MNC's that have a strong presence in the European Community and likely well-formed distribution channels. However, as will be noted in Chapter Five, access to distribution . . . high quality distributors in particular . . . may be a problem for latecomers or small and medium-sized producers.

FIGURE 2.8

U.S. Executives' View on Marketing-Related EC-92 Issues
(scores below 3.5 indicate disagreement and scores above 3.5 agreement)

Issue	Agree/Disagree	Degree of Agreement
. . . I feel that EC-92 will result in:		
(1) fewer cultural differences over time between E.C. countries.	AGREE	3.780
(2) reduced need for a nation-by-nation approach to European Community.	AGREE	3.983
(3) the use of a global/regional marketing strategy including advertising.	AGREE	4.254
(4) the possibility of developing Eurobrands.	AGREE	4.089
(5) stricter regulations.	DISAGREE	3.458
(6) greater difficulty in finding E.C. distributors.	DISAGREE	2.932

CONSUMER VS. INDUSTRIAL MARKETERS

Generally, the consumer and the industrial (business) product companies viewed the various issues in much the same way. There was, however, one interesting (and significant) exception. While both groups agree that there will be more competition in Europe from E.C.-based firms as a result of EC-92, this view was held much more strongly by the industrial (business) firm executives.

Since many of the consumer goods industries have been relatively concentrated for some time and much of the intra-country and inter-country merger activity has taken place in the business-to-business or industrial sectors, this result might be expected. Many of the major industrial markets in Europe depend quite heavily on government procurement and prior to harmonization efforts, these have been primarily protected national markets. (This has led to small national companies dominating the local procurement markets with their primary competition coming from U.S. MNC's and possibly one or two European majors.) With the coming of EC-92 and its more "open access" to government procurement, the increase in mergers, creating more large firms, etc., the industrial producers in our study may well be correct in anticipating a sharper increase in competition.

IMPORTANCE OF OVERSEAS MARKETS

While the executive respondents differed little by broad type of industry category (consumer vs. industrial producers), they did differ more strikingly when classified in terms of their "dependency on foreign sales." Higher Dependence Firms (HDF's), i.e. executives in firms that are most dependent on foreign sales (21 percent or greater share of total sales), feel more strongly that the European Community offers increased market opportunities than do the Lower Dependency Firms (LDF's) (Figure 2.2). Similarly, the executives from firms with greater overseas exposure see a significantly greater opportunity to use a global or regional marketing strategy than do the LDF's. Finally, the HDF's see a stronger potential for more wage parity across Europe than do those with less overseas exposure.

In each instance, the greater (relative) degree of involvement in international markets provides them (HDF's) with a slightly different perspective. In particular, the opportunity to employ a global or regional strategy would mean more to these firms and they would likely be sensitive to any change that might improve that possibility.

CHANGING ENTRY STRATEGY

Do the firms in our survey plan to alter their European Community strategy to accommodate the changes resulting from EC-92? Based on their re-

FIGURE 2.9

Serve E.C. From One (or Few) Key E.C. Production Facilities

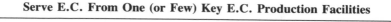

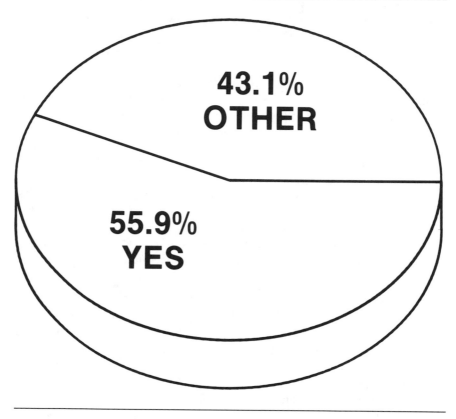

sponses to the various EC-92 issues, it is obvious that the executives in this research put a premium on the events surrounding 1992. And to varying degree, all see it changing the way of "doing business" and specifically, "doing marketing" in Europe. Thus, are they translating this attitude into action? The answer is a resounding yes!

A large percentage of the executives said that their firm plans to alter their primary entry strategy between today and 1993. Clearly, a number of the firms will move away from supplying the 12-country markets through local production in each to serving the European Community from one (or a few) key manufacturing site(s). In fact, over one half of the companies will be using that approach (Figure 2.9) . . . in several instances in combination with some use of licensing, third country exports, etc. In effect, to them

FIGURE 2.10

E.C. Competitive Environment After 1992 (for U.S. companies)

Type of Competition	Percentage
(1) More competition *resulting* from joint venture increase among local or regional E.C. firms.	50.8
(2) More competition primarily from national-only European Co.	37.3
(3) More competition from Japanese and/or other U.S. producers.	5.1
(4) Little or no change in environment (E.C.-92 over-rated).	6.8
	100.0

the European Community will take on much the same type of "production face" found in the United States and they will be fully exploiting the potential of an economically integrated marketplace. Couple this with their earlier views on Eurobranding, the use of regional headquarters, etc., and it becomes evident that Servan-Schreiber was correct in seeing that U.S.-based MNC's are in a good position to compete in (if not dominate) the market. Finally, the overall European competitive environment is seen as shifting in the years after 1992. The types of competitors facing U.S. companies are expected to be European dominated and in fact, they see limited Japanese competition in the market (Figure 2.10).

SUMMARY

The study results tend to bring many of the points mentioned in Chapter One into sharper focus and offer direction to North American producers that are preparing their plans for the new European marketplace. To summarize, their view is:

1. U.S. companies need a physical presence in Europe . . . not just "exporting from the United States";
2. the competitive environment in Europe . . . after EC-92 . . . will dramatically increase;
3. European-wide distribution from a single location in one of the 12-countries will not only be feasible, but an appropriate strategy for many North American companies;
4. EC-92 will set the stage for global/regional marketing strategies . . . immediately . . . and the development of Eurobrands;
5. EC-92 will lead to extensive industry sector (and cross-sector) merger, joint venture and other concentration efforts;
6. EC-92 will produce a defacto "Fortress Europe" resulting from increased non-tariff barriers, standards (common), more regulation and the increased competition from E.C. based companies;

7. EC-92 will lead to heavy competition for distributors; a prime difficulty for late-comers into the new markets;
8. EC-92 will heighten the Europeanization trend that is reducing the real effect of cultural differences;
9. U.S. companies firmly positioned in the European Community will have greater opportunities to exploit labor mobility, management transfer flexibility and the overall "intra-European difference" managerial learning curve;
10. EC-92 will virtually end the need for a nation-by-nation approach to Western Europe.

END NOTES TO CHAPTER 2

1. James Baker and John K. Ryans, "The EEC—As Seen by U.S. Multinational Corporate Executives," *California Management Review*, Fall 1972.
2. *The International Corporate 1000* (New York: Monitor Publishing Company, 1989).
3. "The 500 Largest Foreign Companies," *Forbes*, July 25, 1989, pp. 282–303.
4. Donald G. Howard and John K. Ryans, Jr., "The Probable Effect of Satellite TV on Agency/Client Relationships," *Journal of Advertising Research*, December 1988/January 1989, p. 43.
5. J. J. Servan-Schreiber, *The American Challenge*, (New York: Atheneum, 1968.)

Vignettes

CHAPTER 2

(Two studies that provide additional insights into North American views are presented; one deals with U.S. small business and the other Canadian companies.)

U.S. SMALL AND MEDIUM SIZE EXPORTERS' VIEWS ON E.C.-92 ISSUES

Are U.S. medium and small companies—especially those actively engaged in exporting—sensitive to EC-92 developments? And, do they see a need to "establish a strong presence in the European Community" prior to 1992 as essential?

In late Spring, 1989, we conducted a nation-wide survey among the business (executive) members of the U.S. District Export Council (DEC) to obtain answers to these and other issues. (Each Department of Commerce District office has a Council, whose members are appointed by the Secretary of Commerce.) Essentially, these individuals represent primarily small and medium U.S. companies and serve as an advisory board to the various District Directors on Exporting matters. While their experience level in international business might be somewhat greater than exporters in general, their views represent the thinking of an influential cross-section of industry categories, U.S. geographic areas and firm sizes. Questionnaires were sent to 450 DEC members and 102 (or 22.7%) responded.

What we found was the group is extremely sensitive to E.C. harmonization efforts. And, specifically we found an almost unanimous feeling (nearly 90%) that U.S. companies should have a "strong presence in the E.C." prior to 1992 (Figure 2.11). While this viewpoint could be interpreted in various ways, it is most likely that the executives a) had not "bought" E.C. official assurances regarding the low likelihood of a *Fortress Europe* or b) felt that a presence was needed regardless of the Fortress Europe issue. Equally impressive in terms of E.C. awareness was their general recognition that a united European market would produce more competition for each of them *at home*. In fact, nearly three-fourths saw on the horizon, more competition in the U.S. from European firms.

In light of their overall responses on the European Community and many of the E.C. caveats we have heard, possibly the only surprising finding concerned the question of a harmonized Europe producing greater difficulty in finding distributors. While a number of E.C. watchers, including the authors, have cautioned that EC-92 will result in heavy competition for quality distributor/agency representation, the DEC respondents did not share this view.

In summary, what is clear from these results is the notion that U.S.

FIGURE 2.11

U.S. District Export Council Members' Views on E.C.-92 Issues

		Disagree (%)	Agree (%)
1)	The successful harmonization of the European Community in 1992 will ultimately lead to a reduced need for a nation-by-nation approach to the E.C.	41.0	59.0
2)	The successful harmonization of the European Community in 1992 will ultimately lead to increased market opportunities for U.S. firms.	44.0	56.0
3)	More and more U.S. companies are seeking to formulate a European strategy prior to 1992 due to the belief that "establishing a strong presence" will become more difficult after the European Community "harmonization" is complete.	10.2	89.8
4)	The successful harmonization of the European Community in 1992 will ultimately lead to more interest in the E.C. market by U.S. exporters.	27.0	73.0
5)	For the U.S. to adequately compete with European Community producers, it must adopt a Value-Added Tax, which can, in turn, be rebated to exporters.	64.0	36.0
6)	The successful harmonization of the European Community in 1992 will ultimately lead to an increase in tariffs for exporters from outside the E.C.	34.0	66.0
7)	The successful harmonization of the European Community in 1992 will ultimately lead to greater difficulty in finding E.C. distributors.	66.3	33.7
8)	The successful harmonization of the European Community in 1992 will ultimately lead to more competition in the U.S. from European firms.	27.1	72.9

exporters are carefully watching EC-92 events. The extent to which this is translated into action still must be determifned.

Diana Abdoo
John Ryans
Pradeep Rau

CANADIAN BUSINESS EXECUTIVES' VIEWS ON EC-92

Do Canadian business executives share their U.S. counterparts' views regarding the importance of 1992? And, are the Canadian firms planning to take any special entry/market approaches to this new market?

Just prior to the completion of this manuscript (August, 1989), we initiated a survey among leading Canadian international business executives. (This study paralleled the U.S. research reported in this Chapter.) Essentially, we presented the same EC-92 issues to a sample of 96 Canadian firms chosen from among the largest corporations, by assets, listed on the Canadian stock exchanges. The top 250 companies, ranked by after-tax profits by the *Report on Business Magazine,* served as the initial sample and then banks, investment companies and other non-exporters were eliminated; the remaining 96 firms served as the sample. A preliminary summary of the findings to-date indicate responses have been received from 23 companies (24 percent) and 18 fully completed the questionnaire.

What do these early responses from the Canadian study tell us? First, most felt EC-92 would result in increased market opportunities for Canadian firms; few felt that the enlarged European marketplace would improve the Canadian balance of payments situation or its export position.

Clearly, it was these executives' view that a presence in Europe would be necessary, if Canadian firms were to take advantage of the E.C. market opportunities. To illustrate, a majority of the executives (nearly 60 percent) saw EC-92 leading to "increased tariffs for exporters from outside the E.C." and a similar number said EC-92 would make it necessary ". . . to establish E.C. production."

From a marketing strategy perspective, some three-fourths of the Canadian executives felt EC-92 would result in ". . . the possibility of developing Eurobrands." Further, roughly two-thirds see the harmonized market increasing ". . . the use of global/regional marketing strategies including advertising." Finally, like their U.S. counterparts, most (80 percent) disagreed with the notion that EC-92 would lead to greater difficulty in finding European distributors.

In terms of entry strategy, a number of Canadian firms that now serve their E.C. markets through exports and European distributor network plan to alter their approach after 1992. The number who will serve the entire E.C. marketplace from a single key production site is expected to increase sharply after 1992. This, of course, reinforces the overall view of the executives that the European Community will be a much more competitive market in 1993 and that a physical presence in Europe will be essential for success.

Irene Herremans
Pradeep Rau
John K. Ryans

The following chapter provides results of an in-depth study of twenty-two U.S. multinationals with European headquarters located in the United Kingdom. The study concentrates on the organizational aspects of operating in the Single Market. It is contributed specially for this monograph by Dr. James R. Krum, Professor of Business Administration at the University of Delaware.

Organizing for EC-92

COORDINATION AS A MANAGEMENT PHILOSOPHY: A CASE STUDY

by Dr. James R. Krum

An American multinational manufacturer of both consumer and industrial durable goods is the global market leader in its core product line. The company has had a subsidiary in England since 1925, but did not establish its first subsidiary on the European continent until 1957. Today the company has subsidiaries which employ 10,000 people in all Western European countries except Greece and Luxembourg. All European subsidiaries are fully owned and only two of the 15 resulted from acquisitions. Operations in Europe are quite profitable and represent 40 percent of the firm's business. While most of the remaining business is done in the U.S. today, the firm is placing increasing emphasis on global marketing. Its international group is responsible for Mexico and South America, Australia and Asia, and the Far East.

For marketing and administrative purposes, the firm's European subsidiaries are organized into five regions:

Germany (includes Eastern Europe)
Benelux (includes Scandinavia, Austria, and Switzerland and export sales*)
United Kingdom (Includes Ireland)
France (includes Spain and Portugal)
Italy

*The export group sells to Africa, the Middle East and India.

The company meets 80 percent of its European turnover from manufacturing plants in four EC countries and one EFTA country. Sourcing of im-

67

ports into Europe is split evenly between manufacturing plants in the United States and Asia. Research and development is conducted at design centers in Italy, Germany, and the United Kingdom. Emphasis is on developing panEuropean and global products. One of the firm's most successful new products in the U.S. in the last 15 years was developed and first marketed in England. Many successful products have also been developed by the German company. At one time, the firm reinvented everything on a national basis. It is now sharing R&D skills globally through international coordination-not centralization.

The group vice president Europe heads a European headquarters in England and reports to the head of the core product line in the United States with some dotted line responsibility to the head of a growing consumer business. Reporting to the European group vice president are his headquarters staff and the regional general managers. The European headquarters staff includes a group marketing director that has a dotted line relationship with the sales and marketing directors in the principal subsidiary companies.

Management views the European headquarters as a satellite within the corporate environment with the European subsidiary companies through regional general managers acting as satellites around the European headquarters. The current form of organization in Europe is four years old. Previously, European headquarters with less clout were located successively in two different continental countries.

The major European subsidiary companies in Germany, Italy, France, and the U.K. had great autonomy until about 10 years ago. The process of global branding and designing products for international markets began seven years ago. For the past five years, one advertising agency has been used globally. Five years ago, the firm's product lines in Europe were quite different from the lines in the U.S. Five years from now as the strategy of building global brands builds momentum, 70 to 80 percent of the product lines in the U.S. and Europe will be the same.

European management, which has no Americans in its top ranks, is searching for the proper balance that honors both the strengths of the subsidiary units in Europe and the corporate thrust toward global product lines and marketing. Management is forging its new European structure at a time when the European market is coming together.

The director of European affairs, a senior executive, has been given the assignment of studying the organization in Europe and how it should evolve for the 1990s to fit the new European market environment and the company's global strategy. In describing the relationship between European headquarters and the subsidiary companies, the director makes a distinction between coordination and devolution. If centralization and devolution are the poles, coordination is somewhere between them and describes the system that the company is evolving in Europe and globally. In the process a European group strategy is being developed as part of a global strategy.

The firm defines coordination this way: "The majority of strategic directions, control, and decision-making emanates from the center but with significant local input drawn from the satellite operations." At present, the following are highly *devolved,* i.e. decentralized, to the regional and/or national subsidiary levels in Europe:

Sales
National marketing
Sales promotion
Customer service
Physical distribution
Inventory planning
Manufacturing plant operations
Human resources

On the other hand, there is a greater degree of centralized *coordination* of the following activities:

Group marketing (including advertising)
Product development
Branding and packaging*
Group purchasing
Sourcing
Group asset management
Information technology
*The company uses the same brand and packages in all European countries.

The degree of participation by regional and national management is the key to understanding the difference between coordination (as this firm uses the term) and centralization. Creation of advertising is a good example of coordination. Marketing managers from both the regions and the European headquarters work with the advertising agency in developing an ad. After five years of using the same advertising agency in Europe, the similarities in advertising across Europe tend to be greater than the differences. The same film is likely to be used for a 30 second television commercial that airs throughout Europe with the identical core message taking 20 to 25 seconds. This provides subsidiary companies with 5 to 10 seconds to customize the ad to the local market and culture. Final execution of the ad is highly controlled to make sure that the central theme is being communicated in each market. Thus a combination of centralized strategy and control and decentralized participation and final execution results in ads that are customized to local market conditions while maintaining a common European positioning.

Both the group marketing director at the European headquarters and the regional sales and marketing directors have identical structures of product managers reporting to them. But the regional sales and marketing directors report to their regional general manager and have only dotted line responsibility on functional matters to the group marketing director in this firm. With their input into the advertising process and control over sales (there is no group sales director) and consumer and trade promotions, these regional sales and marketing directors have more autonomy than a regional sales manager in the United States. This autonomy is felt to be necessary because of differences in the national markets.

In recognition of these differences, two other key marketing functions, pricing to customers and physical distribution, are the responsibility of regional and national subsidiary management in this company today. However, these functions are likely to become more centrally coordinated as the creation of the single market presents opportunities for savings resulting from centrally planned logistics operations and also dictates the need to harmonize prices across EC countries.

In summary, this firm has developed coordination as a management philosophy that facilitates corporate leadership in adapting to changing conditions in Europe and the world while providing regional and national management in Europe with a mixture of independence and participation where centralized planning and decision-making is deemed necessary. The group vice president Europe is very much in charge of this process and, in essence, functions as a European C.E.O. in this firm.

A STUDY OF 22 AMERICAN MULTINATIONAL CORPORATIONS

The above case is based on a visit to the firm's European headquarters and a mail questionnaire that was completed by its group v.p. Europe. The firm is one of 22 American multinational corporations that were studied during the first four months of 1989. These firms were selected (1) because they are among the leading U.S. firms in Europe, (2) because they have a European headquarters or central office in England where the research was conducted, and (3) because they represent a cross section of major manufacturing industries as listed in Figure 3.1. Fifteen of the 22 firms are in the top 200 corporations on the *Fortune* industrial list and the remaining seven are in the top 400. In practically all cases, participating firms in the study play a major role in their industries in Europe. In fact, based upon responses to the questionnaire, American firms on average account for 35 percent of the European business in the 15 industries in which these 22 firms compete. This compares with 53 percent for EC based firms and less than five percent for Japanese firms.

The research was conducted to determine how these firms are positioned organizationally to take advantage of the single market in the 12 countries of the European Community that is to be largely completed by the end of 1992. In more than half of the 22 firms, the head of European operations

FIGURE 3.1

Industries Represented

Aerospace
Building Materials
Chemicals
Computers
Food
Forest Products
Industrial and Farm Equipment
Metal Products
Motor Vehicles and Parts
Pharmaceutical
Scientific and Photographic Equipment
Soaps and Cosmetics
Textiles
Tobacco
Toys, Sporting Goods

of a corporation or of a major business was interviewed. The number of interviewees per firm ranged from one to four. Responses to a questionnaire, which was mailed after completion of the interviews, were received from all 22 corporations. In most cases, the questionnaire was completed by an executive who had been interviewed. As it turned out, one of the firms had gone through a reorganization and opened a European office in Switzerland during the course of the study and thus did not meet the second criterion for selection of the sample that is stated above. Information for this firm was supplied by a vice president who had run the European business of the firm from 1970 to 1983. Since firms that participated in the study were guaranteed anonymity, no names are mentioned in this report.

The sample is not completely representative of large American industrial corporations with a major presence in Europe. Omitted are firms that maintain their European headquarters on the continent or manage their European businesses from the United States with no European central office abroad. This latter approach seems to be especially typical of the petroleum and pharmaceutical industries. However, given the diversity of firms and industries represented, the results should provide a good understanding of how U.S. multinationals view the organizational/coordination issues relating to EC-92.

MOST EUROPEAN CENTRAL OFFICES HAVE LINE AUTHORITY

In terms of overall authority, the 22 European central offices that were studied fall into four groups based upon (a) whether the office is part of the operating line, (b) whether it is the only European central office of the firm, and (c) whether it has international responsibilities that go beyond Europe.

1.) **A corporate European line** organization with an executive in charge of all of the firm's business in Europe and in some cases beyond Europe. Twelve firms, a majority, are in this group. One of the firms is atypical in that it is jointly owned by American and European corporations but controlled and managed by the American partner in this joint venture.

2.) **A corporate European staff** or service organization which exists to support decentralized operating businesses in Europe and to compile corporate financial results. Only two firms fit this model. One has four diversified businesses in Europe including a British business that had been acquired. The head of the European region of the other firm is part of an operating support unit which provides services to operating business groups made up of one or more SBUs. Three of the firm's five business groups have European operations. In both cases, heads of the individual European businesses report to their group or division in the United States and not to the head of the European central office.

3.) **A group or divisional European line** organization that is one of two or three businesses that the firm operates in Europe. Management of the six firms that fit this pattern operate independently of the firms' other businesses in Europe.

4.) **A group or divisional line organization that has international responsibilities.** While it is not uncommon to assign responsibility for operations and sales in the Middle East and Africa to the European central office, two firms have established offices in England to manage all businesses outside of the United States, including Canada in both cases. Thus, these are not strictly European central offices.

RESPONSIBILITY FOR BUSINESS ACTIVITIES IN EUROPE

Visits to these firms revealed that there is no typical organization of a European central office and that the functions they perform vary greatly. The titles of the European chief executive range from chairman, _____[1] of Europe, and president, _____ group, Europe through senior vice president, Europe or vice president, Europe to general manager, consumer Europe and general manager, European region. In three cases, heads of a European business had little or no staff. At the other extreme, the European headquarters staff occupies a sizable office building.

---

[1]Names omitted to insure confidentiality.

To get some sense of organizational structures at European central offices, questionnaire results for the 22 firms indicate the following:

19 have a European director of finance.
17 have a European director of marketing*.
13 have a European director of manufacturing.
 6 have a European director of sales.
 5 have a European director of logistics.
 5 have a European director of research and development.

*In one of the firms with no European central staff, the European president functions as a marketing director as well as a chief executive officer.

This list gives a clue concerning the business functions that are centralized and decentralized in Europe. However, as the opening case suggests, organizations in Europe are more complex than they are in the United States because of the existence of legal subsidiary companies, many of which have historically acted with a great degree of autonomy. To more directly assess the roles of the European central office and the subsidiary companies, respondents to the questionnaire assigned responsibility for 24 business functions to: (1) the European central office, (2) subsidiary companies, (3) a regional organization, or (4) the United States. The results of this question can be found in Figure 3.2.

HOW CENTRALIZATION AND DECENTRALIZATION WERE DEFINED

Decentralized responsibility in Figure 3.2 does not differentiate between that which is assigned to subsidiary companies or to a regional level of management that is used in six of the 22 firms. It is important to recognize in reading Figure 3.2 that responsibility is sometimes split among two or even three levels of management. In these cases, .5 was assigned to each level if the split was between two levels and .33 if the split was among three levels. Thus the figure 12.3 for strategic marketing planning understates the number of European central offices that are involved in this activity. In fact, 15 of the 22 central offices participate in strategic marketing planning but only eight of them have sole responsibility for it. Thus strategic marketing planning for Europe tends to be shared with either the subsidiary companies or with the United States. In a few cases it is not being done on a European basis. The item is listed under centralized European responsibility in Figure 3.2 because it received a score of 11 or higher, 50 percent of the 22 firms, the criterion established for sorting out these responsibilities. Where activities are grouped (D, E, and F on Figure 3.2), no one level met the 50 percent criterion. Part G shows that there was no consensus among these firms as to what level of management should be responsible for product

74

FIGURE 3.2

Responsibility on 24 Business Activities

A. Centralized European Responsibility	
Firms	
12.3 Strategic Marketing Planning	n = 22
11.5 Currency Hedging	
11.3 Acquisitions	
11.0 European Advertising	
B. Decentralized Responsibility	
Firms	
21.0 Personal Selling	n = 22
19.5 Customer Service	
19.0 National Advertising	
18.0 Trade Promotions	
17.2 Physical Distribution	
15.5 Pricing to Customers	
13.5 Product Catalogs	
12.5 Purchasing	
11.5 Consumer Promotions (Not applicable: 8.0)	
11.3 Product/Brand Management	
C. U.S. Responsibility	
Firms	
14.8 R&D—Basic	n = 22
D. European Responsibility—Centralized, Decentralized or Split	
Firms	
19.2 Marketing Research	n = 22
17.7 Manufacturing	
16.2 Sourcing	
13.5 Packaging	
E. European Office and/or U.S.	
Firms	
18.2 New Product Development	n = 22
16.8 Transfer pricing	
15.5 Branding	
F. U.S. and/or Decentralized in Europe	
Firms	
19.3 R&D—Applied	n = 22
G. No Consensus on Responsibility	
Product Registration and/or Certification	

registration and/or certification in Europe, i.e. it is done at the subsidiary level in one firm, the European level in another, and by the U.S. level in a third. While this method of assigning numbers to organizational levels may seem arbitrary, it is intuitively appealing and, since it was applied uniformly to all firms, it serves as a basis for comparison and classification.

DECENTRALIZATION OF RESPONSIBILITY VARIES BY FUNCTION

The finding of greater consensus among firms on activities that are decentralized in Europe than on those that are centralized indicates a clearer and quantitatively larger role for the subsidiary companies and regional offices as indicated by the following summations of responsibilities for these 24 activities.

Decentralized in Europe	44%
European central office	28
U.S.A.	21
Not applicable	6
No/other response	1

Most of the functional emphasis in the remainder of this paper will be on marketing, including sales and physical distribution, in Europe, a primary focus of the research. In concluding this section, some brief comments on the level of organizational responsibility for the other key business functions are in order.

FINANCE

While the research did not delve heavily into the finance function, it is clear that with 19 finance directors in 22 firms these American multinationals have centralized financial planning and control in Europe. Even the firm that maintains a small staff to provide services to decentralized divisions in Europe has a European director of finance. The position is missing in only those firms that maintain no European central staff. Three activities with important financial consequences-currency hedging, acquisitions in Europe, and transfer pricing-tend to be either centralized at the European office level, handled by U.S. management, or split between them. A discussion with a group controller indicated that one of his major concerns is taxation and the locations where it is profitable to have operations in Europe. The company's financial strategy is to create less profits in high tax countries. And there is an incentive to shift profits back to the U.S. because of lower tax rates.

MANUFACTURING

All 22 companies have manufacturing plants in Europe and, according to survey results from 21 firms, 78 percent of the European turnover of finished products and services is produced in the 12 EC countries with most of the rest, 16 percent, being imported from the United States. While European manufacturing by these firms tends to be concentrated in the United Kingdom, West Germany, France, and Spain, firms in the sample have plants in all Western European countries except Finland, Greece, Luxembourg, and Norway.

Because of the subsidiary companies, the legal responsibility and management authority for manufacturing are sometimes separated. While some firms have decentralized manufacturing management, others manage, or at least coordinate, manufacturing at the European central office level. Centralized management of manufacturing results in the general manager of a national subsidiary company that has a manufacturing plant having legal responsibility for all of the firm's operations in that country, including manufacturing, but management responsibility only for a sales company.

RESEARCH AND DEVELOPMENT

The European central office is involved in research and development activities in only five of the 22 firms. The most typical pattern is for basic research to be conducted in the United States and for applied research to be split between the United States headquarters and the European subsidiary companies that have manufacturing operations. However, there are three notable exceptions of European companies that are self sufficient in R&D activities with one of the three being the case study at the beginning of the article. Two of the three conduct basic and applied research at the subsidiary company level. The third firm with a European product line that bears little resemblance to the firm's line in the United States has major research centers in Germany and the United Kingdom that are managed as a team from the firm's European headquarters outside of London. According to the executive that was interviewed: "Between Great Britain and Germany, we develop products from scratch. The responsibility for design and development is here with input from the United States headquarters. . . . Our policy is to involve our best suppliers in the R&D process." This company takes pride in producing products with 99 percent European content.

CENTRALIZED RESPONSIBILITY FOR EUROPEAN MARKETING

As noted in the last section, 17 of the 22 firms have a European director of marketing. However, this official has a true line relationship with subsidiary companies in less than one-fourth of these 17 firms. The more typical pattern is to have dotted line authority as shown in the following responses to a question concerning the relationship between the European marketing director and the sales and marketing function in subsidiary or regional operating units.

FIRMS

4 A true line relationship on functional matters.

10 A dotted line relationship with power of review and veto.

2 Largely an advisory relationship.

1 No response.

Although the sales function is largely decentralized with only six firms having a European director, it is not as clear where broader marketing responsibility is located. For example, as noted above, while the European central office participates in setting European marketing strategy in 15 of the 22 firms, it has sole responsibility in only eight firms.

Thus we have two clues (the dotted line relationship and the dispersion of strategic planning responsibility) that marketing decisions are not necessarily made at the European central office level. In some cases they are made in the United States and in others at the subsidiary company level. In addressing the question of the locus of marketing responsibility in Europe, it is, of course, necessary to define marketing. We might simply look at where marketing mix, i.e. product, place, price, and promotion, decisions are being made. If this approach were used, we would find few cases of a European central office that makes all of these decisions. Thus a more limited definition of marketing is needed. For purposes of classifying the locus of marketing responsibility in the 22 corporations, marketing has been defined more narrowly to include only those decision areas that would be handled centrally if Europe were approached as a single market. The seven functions listed in Figure 3.3 are related to creating and managing pan-European marketing strategies for Eurobrands or products. All but three of

FIGURE 3.3

Location of Responsibility for Selected Marketing Functions

Function	Europe		U.S.A.	N.A.
	Centralized	Decentralized		
Branding	8.5	3.5	7.0	3.0
European Advertising	11.0	2.0	3.0	6.0
Marketing Research	9.3	9.8	2.8	
New Prod. Development*	8.2	3.5	10.0	
Packaging	6.5	7.0	4.5	4.0
Product/Brand Mgt.	4.8	11.3	3.8	2.0
Strat. Mktg. Plan.	12.3	6.3	3.3	
Total	60.6	43.4	34.4	15.0
Percent of first three columns	44%	31%	25%	

*.33 other response

the companies reported that their product lines are essentially the same or similar from one European country to another.

In reading Figure 3.3, remember that responsibility frequently is split among two or more levels of management. Summing the columns shows that, on average, the European central office plays a larger role on these functions than do the subsidiary companies or the United States. But averages, of course, can be misleading. In fact, the European central office has the greatest involvement quantitatively in only three of the functions-strategic marketing planning for Europe, European advertising in cases where it is being used, and branding. United States management plays the leading role in new product development and subsidiary companies or regional offices in Europe are most heavily involved in product and brand management, marketing re-

FIGURE 3.4

Classification of Firms on Seven Marketing Functions

Primary Location of Responsibility	Division of Responsibility		
	Europe		
	Centralized	Decentralized	U.S.A.
European Headquarters			
Consumer	100%		
Industrial	100		
Industrial	90		10%
Consumer	71	29%	
Industrial	71	29	
Consumer/Industrial	67	33	
Consumer/Industrial	64	36	
Industrial/Consumer	64	21	14
Industrial	61	14	24
Decentralized			
Consumer		100	
Industrial	21	79	
Consumer	8	67	25
Split in Europe			
Consumer	50	43	7
Industrial	50	33	17
Consumer	43	43	14
Consumer	38	48	13
United States			
Industrial			100
Industrial	7		93
Consumer	21	10	69
Consumer/Industrial	36	14	50
Industrial	40	10	50

Note: The firm with a staff central office that provides services to four diversified businesses in Europe was not included in this analysis.

search, and packaging. The European central office is involved in product and brand management, the hallmark of centralized marketing, in only seven of 20 firms (two responded "not applicable") and has sole responsibility in only three firms.

The data presented in Figure 3.4 moves beyond these averages and classifies 21 of the firms on the basis of where the primary responsibility for these seven marketing functions lies. Percentages are reported because not all seven functions apply to each firm. Four firms stand out in this analysis: two where the European headquarters is responsible for all of the applicable marketing functions; one where the seven functions are decentralized to subsidiary companies; and one where they are all handled in the United States. Beyond these "pure cases" are a variety of hybrid arrangements for assigning responsibility for key European marketing functions. A combination of quantitative analysis and subjective information received in the interviews was used to classify the firms into the four categories in Figure 3.4. With the exception of the first two firms in the "split in Europe" category, the firms were classified on the basis of 50 percent or more of the seven marketing decisions being made at the respective levels of management.

In summary, the marketing role of a European central office varies greatly as these firms prepare to compete in the single European market. In fact, the European central office plays the leading role in performing these seven marketing functions in less than half of the firms. As suggested in the opening case history and discussed in the next section, this diminished role, relative to domestic marketing practice in the United States, is partly attributable to the unique role of the national subsidiary companies and this is not likely to change very soon and certainly not by 1992.

MARKETING ROLE OF EUROPEAN SUBSIDIARY COMPANIES

On average, these 22 firms have subsidiary companies in 11 (10.95) of the 17 Western European countries including 8 (8.18) EC countries and 3 (2.77) EFTA countries. At the extreme are three firms that have subsidiaries in all countries but Luxembourg which tends to be served from Belgium. All 22 firms have subsidiaries in France, West Germany, and the United Kingdom. With the exception of three firms that participate in national joint ventures, generally in one country, the European subsidiaries are wholly owned. And with only four firms using them, licensing agreements as a form of market entry are also relatively unimportant. Where licensing agreements and joint ventures have been used historically to expand into new markets, a number of these American multinationals have bought out their partner or acquired their licensee.

Subsidiary companies are legal entities that operate under the corporation laws of individual countries. While the concept of a European corporation chartered by the EC is being considered by the European Community, it is not part of the 1992 program. Industrial democracy is also being considered in Brussels as an addendum to the changes prescribed in the White Paper on creating the single European market. Current corporation laws range from the extreme of limited worker rights in the United Kingdom to extensive worker rights in Germany, Denmark, the Netherlands, and Belgium. For example, employers of a certain size in Germany are required to have labor representation on supervisory boards and certain decisions cannot be implemented until employees have been consulted. Thus management autonomy would seem to be an issue to these American corporations. However, with only two exceptions, respondents to the questionnaire did not see employee participation, i.e. adopting the German system throughout Europe, as a major concern. One respondent noted that "employee participation will have a minor but beneficial impact on our business."

Executives at the central European office refer to their national units by various names including subsidiary companies, affiliate companies, divisions, or simply "other countries." The marketing role of these units ranges from being simply sales companies to being fully autonomous corporations that receive little direction from above. As indicated in Figure 3.2, the typical subsidiary company in Europe has discretion concerning all marketing mix variables except product. And frequently product must be adapted to the requirements of a country. Two of the three firms (both producers of consumer goods) with the most independent subsidiary companies (Figure 3.4) permit product variation from country to country to take advantage of differences in local tastes and preferences. However, both companies do place emphasis on creating Eurobrands where possible.

For marketing mix variables other than product, Figure 3.2 shows that responsibility is decentralized in at least three-fourth of these firms for:

1. Personal selling and all other promotional activities except pan-European advertising where that is being done.

With national advertising still being important in Europe because of differences in language, culture, and market conditions, there is no clear consensus concerning the value of panEuropean advertising. Its proponents tend to use the same strategy, positioning, and target to develop panEuropean campaigns but vary execution and tone by country. Thus subsidiary company management has some autonomy in customizing the ads to local market conditions.

2. Physical distribution.

Because of national boundaries, physical distribution responsibility has tended to be decentralized in Europe. Only five firms have a European director of logistics. While the need for centralized distribution planning and facilities varies from business to business, this is clearly an area with great potential for savings and better customer service as physical barriers to the movement of goods come down.

3. Pricing.

Competitive conditions in the Europe of the 1980s tend to vary from country to country in many industries. As a result, the majority of firms have decentralized pricing responsibility which has resulted in significant price variations from one market to another in numerous cases. Because customers in some markets have been paying a premium price in some product categories, the inevitable price harmonization that the single market will bring will not be a short run benefit to firms that have profited from these price differentials.

CENTRALIZATION, DECENTRALIZATION, OR BOTH?

Although the 1992 process was set in motion in 1985, many businesses failed to recognize the significance of it until two or three years later. At the time of this research, early 1989, only a few of the 22 firms had made significant organizational changes to prepare for the Europe of the 1990s. (Several firms were studying the situation.) Thus the organizational structures and assignments of responsibility for marketing functions that are being reported here reflect Europe with a large number of markets separated by borders more than they do the single market that is emerging rapidly.

Different corporate philosophies concerning the centralization and decentralization of authority are, of course, one explanation of the differences revealed in Figures 3.2 through 3.4. In some cases, U.S. management refuses to let go of authority. In others, Europe is being managed as part of a broader global marketing program. Interestingly, one consumer goods firm that took the path of global marketing in the 1970s has turned almost 180 degrees in the 1980s. In 1985, the company decided that centralization had not worked and that the growth of the company will come from empowering local people at the individual country level. This process of encouraging entrepreneurship and innovation at the local level was described as "heavy corporate decentralization." The European central office in this firm (the term headquarters is taboo) has an area director with "functional expertise" in marketing rather than a European marketing director.

But the explanation of the high degree of local autonomy in many firms goes beyond corporate management philosophy. According to one European regional vice president, "The strength of the European region is the very solid and capably staffed subsidiary companies." And in an industrial goods firm with a new European central office, each division (subsidiary) is given a tremendous amount of autonomy. This firm sees its ability to be responsive to individual marketplaces as the basis of its success in Europe.

Thus subsidiary units exist for business rather than legal reasons. Customers in individual countries prefer to do business with nationals of their country in the language and currency of the country. For example, there is great advantage in West Germany in having GmbH behind the name of the national affiliate. And it is not likely that this situation will change in the early years of the unified market.

What exists at the end of the 1980s is a mixture of centralization and decentralization with the role of the European central office frequently being ambivalent in many of these firms. On the one hand, in practically all cases, the general managers of the subsidiary companies report to the head of the European central office. Thus we have a direct line relationship at this level. But, as discussed earlier, this direct line tends to break down at the functional level in many firms, i.e. directors of manufacturing and marketing may have limited authority over their counterparts in subsidiary companies. This raises the question of whether these European central offices are true European headquarters and whether a true European C.E.O. exists.

The questionnaire addressed this question by asking respondents to describe the role of the European central office using the following options. Respondents were instructed to select as many of the statements as apply. The numbers in parentheses indicates the number of firms that selected the option out of 21 that answered the question.

A. The office exercises full executive authority over all operations in Europe. (13)
B. The office can exercise veto power over decisions made by national or regional European management. (13)
C. The office is a true European headquarters. (10)
D. The office is here primarily to give advice and provide services to our businesses in Europe. (7)
E. The primary role of the office is to coordinate our European operations and to take advantage of opportunities for synergy and leverage. (5)

While interpretations of the meaning of these terms varied from firm to firm, it is possible to split the firms into two groups.

1. Sixteen of the 21 firms selected A (one firm), C (two firms), or some combination of A, B, and C (13 firms).
2. Five of the 21 firms selected D (one firm), D and E (2 firms), B and D (1 firm), or a combination of B, D and E (1 firm).

Looking at the second category, the breakdown shows that the European central offices in five firms, just under one-fourth, report that they are exercising limited authority over European operations. This result is congruent with the interviews in four of the five firms, one of which is being managed largely from the United States. The case is less clear in the fifth firm where the vice president of European operations carries the second title of managing director of _____[2] Europe Services. This legal entity was created because the firm is sensitive to the British tax laws and does not want to appear to be a European headquarters which would be taxed. Reporting to the vice president and managing director in this firm are three general managers that are responsible for businesses in Europe. While the vice president and managing director clearly has line authority, the general managers do not. Instead of telling people in the national companies what to do, it is necessary for them to negotiate and reach agreement. This causes some frustration especially for one of the general managers that has operated in the United States management environment. He termed the European central office as engaging in a top heavy numbers game that adds excessive administrative expense. His boss, on the other hand, believes that a good balance has been established between his office and the national companies that results in more participative management in which both parties have enough clout for the needs of the individual country to be heard, while an overall European strategy is being followed.

Managing a multinational company in Europe requires more coordination than is typical in the United States. This is true even in those 16 firms that are in the first group above. The case study at the beginning of the article illustrates this point. In another example of a firm that sees its European office as a true headquarters (A, B, and C above), European management views divisional autonomy as a key element of success and believes that leveraging the company's strength in Europe is the European headquarters' role. An executive of the firm described leverage in these terms, "We have the opportunity to bring together the best brains to work on development projects and to use one division as a pilot for a new product." He stressed the point that headquarters management must go back to the divisional general managers to get their support and commitment for any projects that are undertaken.

The general manager or managing director of a national subsidiary company is a key position in Europe with no counterpart in the United States. In some cases European subsidiaries are enormous companies that are larger than many *Fortune* 500 firms in the United States. An interview with the managing director of one U.K. subsidiary was instructive. This managing director has great autonomy in managing the U.K. company. However, he would like a freer hand to take advantage of the strengths of the U.K. company in other countries of the European Community and beyond it. Since

---

[2]Name omitted to insure confidentiality.

the major strength of this firm is in the United Kingdom and Italy, the U.K. managing director views northern Europe and the Union of Soviet Socialist Republics (U.S.S.R.) as natural markets to be supplied from the United Kingdom. His boss, the senior vice president-Europe, is considering the desires of the U.K. company as part of a review of the European organizational structure. As another example of the same issue, the firm discussed above that is committed to leveraging its strength in Europe while maintaining divisional autonomy stops short of permitting the French company to develop the Spanish market. When I posed this hypothetical question, I was told: "This is not their calling."

CONCLUSIONS

This investigation conducted in the European central offices of 22 leading American multinational corporations reveals that U.S. firms account on average for 35 percent of the European business in the 15 industries in which these firms compete. Thus, as 1992 approaches, American firms occupy a strong position in what may become the world's richest market.

To what extent and how rapidly will the national markets that exist in Europe today evolve into a single market in the 12 E.C. countries or the 17 countries of Western Europe as barriers to trade come down? To a great extent this evolution depends on strategies adopted by major European, American, and even Japanese corporations as they respond to opportunities resulting from a single European market. These responses will be affected by the European organization that these firms adopt; i.e. how much autonomy is given to European management and, within Europe, the division of authority between the European central office, if one exists, and the subsidiary companies.

This study was limited to firms with a European central office located in the United Kingdom. From a marketing standpoint—the focus of this study— the role of this European central office varies greatly with key determinants being how much autonomy U.S. management gives to Europe and how much autonomy European subsidiary companies have enjoyed historically. Although each of these 22 European organizations represents the unique outcome of the firm's history including acquisitions in a number of cases, similarities and patterns do exist and have been discussed above. While it is not possible to accurately slot all firms neatly into this scheme, it appears that the role of the European central offices that have been studied fall into one of three models, at least from the standpoint of the marketing function.

1. A strong European headquarters run by a C.E.O.
2. A comparatively weak European central office that exists to support strong national companies.

3. A comparatively weak European central office that exists to implement decisions made in the United States.

The survey and interview results that have been discussed here show that the European C.E.O. model is the most prevalent. Responsibility for European operations has been vested in a single executive with broad authority in a majority of these corporations. However, a philosophy of further decentralization of authority to subsidiary companies and in a few cases to regional management is frequently employed. The case study at the beginning of the article is an excellent example of this approach.

Although important changes are taking place in Europe, differences in culture and language and resulting feelings of nationalism remain. Management of American multinationals must assess the impact of these differences on customers and consumers in determining the proper balance between panEuropean and national or regional marketing programs and thus the degree of autonomy that must be given to local management. And decisions concerning Europe must be made in a larger global context. At this point in time, it is clear that national subsidiary companies in Europe run by general managers will continue to be important well into the 1990s and probably beyond. It is also clear that more and more marketing decisions will be made centrally in Europe as the single market becomes a reality. Thus management in the United States, the European central office, and the national subsidiary companies must work together to evolve the structures and programs that are needed to grow and profit in a rapidly changing Europe. This will require a spirit of cooperation, i.e. an understanding of the perspective of each level of management by the other levels.

Vignettes

CHAPTER 3

(Two vignettes illustrating how specific North American companies are addressing the new European markets from non-E.C. bases. Neither was included in the study reported in this chapter.)

A SMALL CANADIAN "HIGH-TECHER" FEELS A EUROPEAN PRESENCE TO BE ESSENTIAL*

Terry Graham, vice-president of marketing and sales for Westronic Inc., sees EC-92 as a great opportunity for his company but is acutely aware of the necessity of early preparation. Terry explained, "One can't wait until 1992 to do something about one's position (in Europe)." Westronic is a small high-technology company that has expanded its operations into a majority of the states of the U.S., many of the countries of the Pacific Rim, Australia, and several European countries. The company started out as a sales agent for other companies in 1958. In 1980, it began its own manufacturing operations for its remote terminal units. Its major customers are utilities, telecommunications, and energy companies. Westronic's approximately $12 million in sales are geographically distributed in the following manner: 10 percent in Canada; 45 percent in the U.S.; and 45 percent overseas. The company has won numerous awards, both national and provincial, for its exporting and international business activities.

Through its European relationships, the company has been able to take advantage of opportunities in Taiwan and Argentina as well as other countries both inside and outside Europe. It is possible the firm could be closed out of future opportunities if it does not make advance preparation; therefore, Westronic has taken several important steps to be ready for the transitions occurring within the European Community.

The firm has worked hard in learning how to do business in Europe. Several company executives have made extended business trips to Europe to learn the market. Terry feels that there are—and still will be after 1992—major differences between the European countries that the unification will not eliminate. Although the plan looks good on paper, it will take a lot of hard work to actually implement the plan and to get it working smoothly. The firm also has engineering representatives sitting on the relevant E.C. standards committees.

After studying several of the European countries in which it could establish its physical presence, Westronic decided to look for joint venture or acquisition candidates within the United Kingdom. Currently, the United Kingdom is a fairly large market for Westronic's product. And by 1992, Westronic plans to have transferred technology to its U.K. establishment. Terry feels Westronic is well-positioned to take advantage of the opportunities offered in Europe. North American technology is second to none in hardware; however, there is the possibility of reverse technology transfer in software. Europe is very competitive and will probably become even more so as the theory behind 1992 is actually put into practice. Once Westronic

88

is well-established in Europe, Terry feels that this European presence will also provide the firm with an avenue for additional export to southeast Asia and the Middle East.

Other changes in promotion and product have taken place to be able to market successfully in Europe. The company is moving from a product orientation to a corporate orientation in its brochures and advertising. The firm has already tailored its product to meet European standards as well as North American standards. The product is currently acceptable everywhere within the European Community except for West Germany and France. Terry finds both countries are much different from the other European countries in regard to Westronic's product.

West Germany's standards are very stringent, and there are some underlying engineer liability problems associated with West German products that the proposed transportability of standards will, in reality, probably not eliminate. Terry poses the question, "Will an Italian, Spanish, or Greek engineer live by the rules laid down by the German engineering society (regarding liability)?" He sees this liability problem as an area of conflict that will not be easily resolved. Although there will be problems, Westronic will be ready for EC-92 and the opportunities it affords the well-prepared firm.

*Irene M. Herremans
The University of Calgary
September 25, 1989

NATIONAL INSTRUMENTS EMPLOYS AN EXPORT-ONLY EC-92 STRATEGY

National Instruments Company, a high technology firm located in Austin, Texas, plans to continue to serve its expanding European Community markets on an export-only basis in the post-1992 era. However, this successful niche player in the scientific instrumentation field (computer interface) will be altering its sales and distribution tactics in light of the Community's harmonization of product standards. And, it will remain "flexible" on the European production issue, especially if high-value added local content restrictions are imposed. (The latter, for example, could be E.C. produced semiconductors to serve as components.) In this firm's production cost situation, labor accounts for a relatively low percentage of the total and a normal duty would not prove to be an insurmountable concern.

Currently, National Instruments employs an entry strategy that combines strong sales/warehouse, customer service offices in the U.K., France and Italy with a network of national or "country" distributors. This is an approach that permits the company to respond to the product standard and other local market differences that are now present in the 12 countries. As EC-92 unfolds and product standard differences are resolved, the company plans to increase its own branch offices (sales/warehouse/customer service) commitment and phase-out its country-by-country distributor approach. (The firm's target market includes those doing R&D in the field of electronic engineering, i.e. product/process manufacturing, education, etc.)

In our September 1, 1989 interview, Dr. James Truchard, President of National Instruments, made several key points regarding the post-1992 European marketplace that should prove useful to many other high-techers. Regarding sales and distribution, Dr. Truchard noted that the dropping of inter-country barriers will make the use of national distributors obsolete in many industries. "Once the national markets are open, the distributors will have direct access to each other's market; there will be no way to effectively keep them from encroaching on the others' territories." In such an uncontrolled scramble for customers, it is easy to forsee how many pricing and service problems could result. To preclude such concerns, especially those dealing with customer services and support, National Instruments will expand its number of local subsidiaries, as well as reach more customers via its current offices.

Dr. Truchard and his staff are keeping up to date on EC-92. Should it appear necessary to establish some type of production, i.e. component/screwdriver or full production, he feels that the Company will be able to establish such a facility rather quickly. With a large branch office in the

U.K., Dr. Truchard indicates a likely site would be either Ireland or Scotland and both possibilities have been investigated.

Overall, Dr. Truchard sees the positives resulting from E.C.-92 to "far outweigh" the negatives. Besides the major advantage (common product standards), he feels that there will be fewer currency difficulties, especially when/if a common currency develops, and some efforts to reconcile differing labor rules which are all plusses. The only real negative lies in the short-run distribution "shakeout."

Lastly, Dr. Truchard says that there is one very strong plus for U.S. producers that we often ignore when discussing EC-92. Today, not only does each of the 12 countries have separate standards . . . these standards are written in the local language and severe translation problems often occur for "outsiders." When a common set of standards applicable to the whole E.C. is adopted, it will be available in English to their U.K. branch office!

TRACKING CHANGES IN KEY INDUSTRIES

The effects of the market integration process in the European Community will be felt by firms in every industry and in every area of operations. It would, therefore, be impossible to document all the effects in every area of a firm's operations. However, several illustrative sectoral analyses will help to highlight the implications of EC-1992 for firms. Our focus in this chapter will be primarily on marketing related issues though we realize that such compartmentalization simplifies the discussion somewhat and the real effects will be felt in every functional area of business. In each sectoral analysis which follows, we will use examples of individual firms which may be E.C. or non-E.C. based. A number of vignettes have also been included in the chapter to add richness to the discussion and to provide perspective on the diversity of situations facing firms in the different sectors. We realize, of course, that the pace of change in Europe is accelerating as 1992 approaches and that there are several imponderables which may affect some sectors in a way different from what is discussed here, but overall, the following analysis represents the prevailing consensus about the effects EC-92 will have on the various sectors.

RETAILING

One sector that has been particularly fragmented in Europe is retailing and EC-92 is likely to bring to this sector, perhaps the most revolutionary changes of all sectors, and for this reason we are discussing it first.

The existence of national borders and the consequent division of the Eu-

91

ropean Community into twelve separate markets with major restrictions on the movement of goods across borders until now have kept the retailing sector relatively national in scope. Europe does not have many of the large retail chains that one is accustomed to in the United States. In fact, the most visible transnational retail organizations in Europe are frequently U.S. chains, for example, Woolworth, or franchisees of U.S. origin, for example, McDonald's. All of this is, however, likely to change because the major benefits of the market integration will be the free movement of goods across borders and the harmonization of excise and value added taxes across the Community. An immediate consequence of this will be the ability of retail chains to either merge with other chains (within the country or elsewhere in the European Community) or expand on their own beyond national borders. Some of this has already happened as evidenced by the recent merger talks between two Italian retailing groups, Standa and Rinascente[1] with combined sales of over $4.4 billion, and the announcement by three of the largest supermarket chains in Europe (K. Royal Ahold of the Netherlands, Casino of France and Argyll of the United Kingdom) that they will be collaborating in buying and other activities so as to pool their resources for maximum efficiency.

What then are some of the likely effects of E.C.-1992 on retailing?

1. Increased mergers and other forms of purchasing and marketing alliances between retailers within E.C. countries, across countries, and possibly between E.C. and non-E.C. retailers can be expected.

2. A direct consequence of the growth, mergers, and alliances among retailers will be their greater clout in purchasing. For the manufacturers, this will mean pressure on margins and reduced power. Also, as Antoine Riboud, the chairman of France's food manufacturing giant BSN Group has noted, brands which are not in the top three positions in terms of market share in particular markets will find it increasingly difficult to secure shelf space at the retail level. For the consumers, it may mean lower prices because the retailers may pass on to them some of the gains achieved by community-wide buying programs.

3. For both manufacturers and retailers, significant opportunities may lie in reorganizing their warehousing and distribution networks. The removal of border controls will lead to major gains in logistics and transportation efficiency which in turn may mean cost-saving opportunities for both manufacturers and distributors/retailers.

4. Another effect of the changes in retailing will be the different spending patterns of consumers. One study in the United Kingdom has estimated that consumer spending on alcohol will jump by 40 percent while it falls 0.5 percent, 2 percent, and 10 percent on food, newspapers, and children's clothing respectively.[2] This will be directly caused by changes in taxes and retail price levels through distribution and purchasing economies.

5. Continuing barriers to rapid changes in retailing will, however, exist because of the regional differences in culture, taste, and purchasing power across areas in the European Community. Clusters of similar markets may, however, be identified[3] and since these cut across national borders, some retailing and distribution/logistics consolidation should be immediately possible. Also, as the residents of the European Community become more mobile, they may adopt the tastes and attitudes from other parts of the Community which may mean that over time, consumers will become increasingly similar from Aberdeen to Athens.

ADVERTISING AND PROMOTION

Another sector which is likely to experience change as a consequence of EC-92 is advertising and promotion. Major developments are occurring in the European media industry—some are related to EC-92 and some are part of the global trend towards satellite broadcasting and electronic news transmission and retrieval systems. These media changes, combined with the freer movement of goods and people expected after 1992, will open up possibilities for a more standardized approach to advertising products and services across the E.C. countries. Once again, though, cultural differences and the multiplicity of languages will make it unlikely that the level of standardization can reach that of the United States where one finds minimal differences across regions. But major changes can still be expected on the E.C. advertising scene and some of these are as follows:

1. It is certain that television advertising will become much more important across the European Community. Until now, many E.C. countries had stringent restrictions on the amount of commercial TV time. However, with EC-1992 it is expected that such restrictions will have to be relaxed and in fact, this has already begun to occur. This means that advertisers will be able to feature more TV advertising in their media mix. Given the expense and lead time associated with TV commercial production, major changes will be needed in the individual firm's advertising planning and strategy.

2. Satellite TV channels such as Rupert Murdoch's Sky TV and BSB planned to reach 3 million households in the United Kingdom during their first two years of operation. This is a fairly modest goal and perhaps realistic given the general lack of interest in satellite TV subscriptions noted in a recent survey of British households.[4] But longer term, the prospects look good and satellite TV is likely to be a major force throughout the European Community.

3. Overall advertising spending is also likely to grow impressively in the European Community as a consequence of the market integration process. The growth is expected to be greatest in France, Italy, and Spain though spending is going to be strong throughout the Community. Spain, with a

forecast growth of 15 percent in advertising spending during 1989, is going to be the country leading the growth in advertising. This is reflective of the generally backward nature of the advertising industry in Southern Europe until now. Figure 4.1 shows the advertising spending trends in selected E.C. countries.

4. A persistent question about advertising in Europe is the degree to which advertising campaigns can be standardized across the various countries. As frequently noted throughout this monograph, cultural and language differences along with strong traditions and nationalistic feelings make it unlikely that completely standardized approaches to advertising a product will work. On the other hand, many advertisers have not even explored the possibility of standardizing their advertising where it is possible. For example, Braun's advertising was so different from country to country in the European Community that the advertisements may "well be for totally unrelated products."[5] Braun has, therefore, hired Lowe Marschalk, a unit of Interpublic to create a uniform Braun campaign which will be translated into native languages in Europe. Similarly, even in a culturally idiosyncratic area such as food, tastes are converging slowly, with pasta rapidly gaining favor outside Italy. BSN, the French food group, sees "savings in marketing because one advertisement can be beamed to a dozen countries with only the voice-over changed."[6] Gillette is a company which restructured its European operations in 1985 and began a standardized advertising and marketing program which has been very successful. Gillette expected a 50 percent growth in sales and profits by 1988.[7]

5. We may also ask how the European consumers are likely to change in the wake of 1992 and what effects this will have on advertising. Agencies have already started researching this question[8] and have come up with two conclusions. One, there are identifiable geographical clusters of customers based on income, language, etc. that can be selectively targeted for some

FIGURE 4.1

Advertising Spending Trends in Selected E.C. Countries

	Ad Spending Growth Rate	
	1988	1989
Italy	8.5%	11.0%
West Germany	2.5%	2.5%
France	9.3%	9.0%
Spain	20.9%	15.0%
United Kingdom	10.0%	4.0%

Source: Advertising Age, April 10, 1989, p.4.

products. Two, the younger population—mainly teenagers—while quite different in some ways across countries, come close to being true Euroconsumers in terms of their tastes for food, clothes, and drink.[9]

6. The general trend towards consolidation of firms which is already underway in each industry will mean that individual advertising accounts will be larger. This will favor the larger agency[10] and may explain the trend towards greater consolidation in the advertising agency business as well. 3M/Europe has already consolidated its accounts so that it does not have to use the 60 different local advertising agencies it previously employed.[11]

BENETTON: AN ITALIAN RETAILER *WITH A MULTINATIONAL MENTALITY*

Retailing (and cultural) lore would suggest that an Italian specialty shop and textile manufacturer would do well in Italy . . . but, not in Japan and France, etc. *and Italy*. Yet, Luciano Benetton has been the successful forerunner of what E.C.-92 retailing would be like in the decade ahead.

Perhaps, Mr. Bennetton summarized it best himself in an interview for the Italian daily *La Republic* (New York). When asked if there would be any advantages from 1992 for his firm, he replied,

> "No. For the last 10 years, Benetton has considered Europe its true domestic market and looked upon exports as those of its sales to countries outside the Community. For us, nothing will change."[1]

While technically *not* quite correct . . . E.C.-92 will produce changes that can benefit Benetton . . ., Mr. Benetton has offered a credo that can serve other "national" retailers quite well in the new Europe. This Italian retailer/manufacturer simply sees the same view of a single Europe and its opportunities as does a Ford, Philips, Siemens, or any other U.S., European or Japanese major.

For Benetton, this multinational perspective is *not* a recent response to E.C.-92 changes. In fact, the firm had 9 or more retail stores in seven of today's E.C. countries *besides Italy* in 1982.[2] Its operations in Spain, for example, pre-dated the country's entry into the European Community.

Most recent Benetton statistics indicate that Mr. Benetton's company is a "model" for the many post E.C.-92 retail groups that are evolving today. Its annual sales in 1988 were nearly $1.1 billion and the company operates a network of 5000 stores (mostly independently-owned franchises) in 79 countries. And, it has 14 factories to supply them, including seven outside Italy.[3] Although these results are truly impressive for this 24 year old company, one can expect to see many similar successes in the E.C. of the future.

---

[1]Arturo Zampaglione, "A Family Business Takes the World by Storm," *Europe,* June 1989, p. 21.

[2]James L. Heskett and Sergio Signorelli, "Benetton," in Robert D. Buzzell & John A. Quelch, *Multi-national Marketing Management* (Reading, MA; Addison-Wesley Publishing Company, 1988) p. 69.

[3]Alan Friedman, "Clothing loses a little of its lustre," *Financial Times,* June 21, 1989, p. VI. (Special Italian Industry Section).

SERVICES

The E.C. Single Internal Market will have important implications for firms in the service industries. It is estimated[12] that E.C. governments alone spend about $200 billion annually on various services. With the anticipated opening up of public procurement procedures, this will represent a large and increasingly competitive market for all service firms—E.C. and non-E.C. But the service industries are also the area where there is greatest uncertainty for non-E.C. firms because of frequent references by E.C. officials to the concept of "reciprocity." Unlike product manufacturing firms which can prepare for EC-1992 by making investments and establishing a presence within the European Community, providers of service do not have a tangible good. Therefore, they will always seem to be more "outside" rather than "inside" if they are from a non-E.C. country. One may then ask what 1992 means for service firms in general and service firms from United States and other non-E.C. countries, in particular.

Service firms from outside the European Community have to be concerned about the principle of reciprocity. In general, the European Community says it will not discriminate against foreign-owned firms or affiliates as long as the foreign country in question offers equal access to firms from the Community which want to do business there. Financial services firms in the United States are particularly concerned about this aspect because the laws regulating them in the United States differ from those in the European Community; therefore E.C. financial firms can never be expected to do business in the United States the same way they do at home. For example, banks in the United States are not allowed to offer other financial services such as insurance, securities trading, etc., but in Europe they have fewer restric-

AIG
INSURING E.C.-1992

For several years now, American International Group (AIG), the giant U.S. insurance company has been experimenting with some innovative ideas in Europe. It has been handling some of its claims processing work, even for the U.S. market, in Ireland, for example, because of the access to cheap, skilled employees in that country and the fact that modern communication technology allows instant contact between its Irish operation and it offices in the United States. Now, as 1992 approaches, AIG is taking a fresh look at the European market. Financial services firms are particularly interested in the changes going on in the European market as the 1992 process unfolds. For one thing, financial firms in Europe, even the giants—for example, Allianz in Germany—are frequently focussed on the national market. In this respect, Steve A. Schleisman, head of AIG's European subsidiary feels that his company is well placed to take advantage of the opportunities in the New Europe because it has already been operating in several countries and can therefore offer a client firm from one E.C. country services in other E.C. countries which a previously national-only company may find difficult to do. On the other hand, Schleisman is also concerned about the fact that the E.C. market is going to inevitably become a lot more competitive. In order to deal with this more integrated competitive market, AIG has created a Central European headquarters office in Paris with 500 employees. Money management and data processing have also been centralized so as to allow instant monitoring of how AIG's operations are doing throughout Europe at any point of time.

Source: adapted from Business Month, August 1989.

tions. A related issue is whether the European Community will apply reciprocity rules only to firms that enter the Community after 1992. The answers to these questions may not be known for some time yet and will also depend on how the situation develops in Europe with the capital market opening set for next summer.

On the industry structure front, the same trend observed in manufacturing firms is likely to be repeated in the service industries with consolidation, mergers, and alliances being forged in order to gain greater exposure in the unified market. We have already witnessed this in the airline industry with

ILLUSTRATION 4.1

Ogilvy & Mather Europe Advertisement

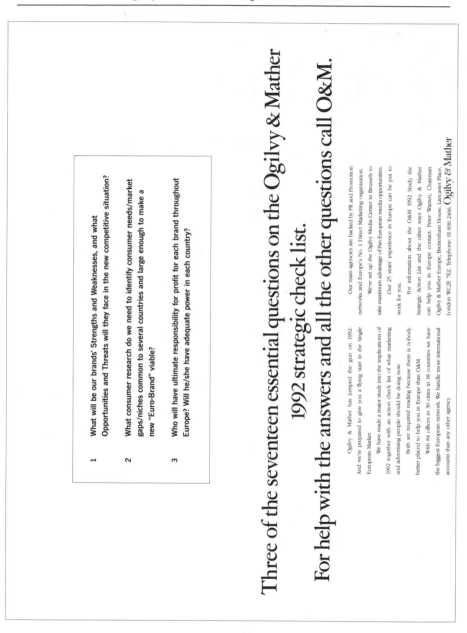

Note: This advertisement appeared in the December 13, 1988 issue of the *Financial Times* (London). It is part of the firm's well-developed campaign emphasizing its ability to provide its clients with needed insights into the new Market. Reprinted with permission.

British Airways entering into an arrangement with Sabena and in accounting with the KPMG-Peat Marwick case, where Peat Marwick and Main Hurdman combined forces in order to serve their corporate clients better. KPMG has stated that its motivation behind the German deal was to provide expanded service to its clients in the European single market. The German insurance giant Allianz has acquired British insurer Cornhill. As noted earlier, the advertising agency industry is also expected to grow through a shakeout and consolidation, and the single major effect of EC-92 on service industries would be to increase the size of individual firms which were formerly protected in their national markets. The European Community has yet to work out fully its competition and merger policy and both service and manufacturing firms will have to follow developments in this area closely to determine which types of alliances, takeovers, and mergers will be allowed and which will not. The services sector is sure to witness important changes as the countdown to 1992 proceeds; and the financial services industry will, in particular, undergo major changes because currently, the costs of some financial services may vary by as much as fifty percent from one country to another.

As this monograph goes to press, Air France and Lufthansa have announced that they will cooperate in a number of areas (computerized reservation system, route planning etc.) and they will even exchange employees so as to achieve collaborative systemwide efficiency in their operations.

AUTOMOBILE

The automobile sector is a sort of bellwether in any economy and the European economy is no exception. The worldwide trend towards globalization of this industry is being observed in Europe as well. However, twelve national markets and strong government protection in some of the markets has meant that the European automobile industry has not experienced the same competitive forces as the U.S. With 1992 on the horizon, the protectionist policies towards the auto industry in some countries (especially Italy and France) will have to be changed and this will ensure a fierce competitive battle in the European marketplace. The main players in this battle will be the larger European manufacturers (Fiat, Volkswagen, etc.), the U.S. manufacturers (Ford in particular), and the Japanese manufacturers. As discussed elsewhere, the Japanese have started concentrating on the E.C. market only recently but in a very short period of time, they have expanded their presence in Europe to an impressive extent. A recent estimate shows Japanese automobile firms increasing their market share in Europe from the current eleven percent to eighteen percent or more in 1995. A large part of the Japanese effort has been concentrated in the United Kingdom because of the liberal incentives provided by the government to attract Japanese automobile

ILLUSTRATION 4.2

Ernst & Whinney Advertisement

Ninety-one per cent of British businessmen believe that 1992 will be good for business.

Good news. Well yes, except that behind this statistic lurks another. Forty-one per cent of those surveyed, revealed they had no game-plan whatsoever.

Frankly that's something that worries the life out of us.

HOW WILL 41% OF BRITISH BUSINESSMEN ENTER 1992?

In 1992, we'll all be fish in a much larger pond. And whilst this means more opportunities, it also naturally means more predators.

For the fact remains that if you can see an opportunity, so can your rivals.

So how can you make sure that as all the rules change, you know how to play the game and win?

Well to start with, you need expert advice. And having worked closely with many clients in Europe, that's something we're well placed to provide.

We'll give you an in-depth analysis of how 1992 will affect not only your business, but that of your clients and suppliers.

And we'll follow this up with a detailed plan of action, telling you what you should be doing about it.

More important, thanks to our extensive network of European offices, we can also give you on-the-spot help as you put your game-plan into practice.

So that, come 1992, when everyone else is waiting for things to change, you're up there making the changes.

E≣Ш Ernst & Whinney
Accountants, Advisers, Consultants

Note: This advertisement appeared in a December 1988 issue of the *Financial Times* (London). Subsequently, the firm merged with Arthur Young and its name is now Ernst & Young. This particularly creative advertisement focuses on the British businessman's need to learn more about 1992 and indicates the firm's ability to provide this service. Reprinted with permission.

companies. Many other E.C. countries were less inclined to attract Japanese investment but this attitude may be softening because as one French official said after seeing the extent of Japanese investment in the U.K.—"Is it better to get some of it or none at all?"

The major effects on the E.C. auto industry after 1992 are likely to be the following:

1. A gradual increase in market share of the Japanese manufacturers. The Italian and French markets have had specific quotas against Japanese vehicles, and while these may not necessarily be fully removed by 1992, the European Community will slowly work to eliminate these barriers. Over time, the Japanese sales in these markets will increase. Meanwhile, the Toyota and Nissan plants in the U.K. will have a capacity of close to a million cars a year and this is sure to make the E.C. market much more competitive for U.S. and E.C. manufacturers.

2. Consolidation of manufacturing facilities and alliances between firms is likely to be another major feature of the European automobile industry. Honda has already acquired part of British Rover and will be producing its Accords at Rover plants. Fiat and Renault will have an unfamiliar situation in Italy and France respectively, because their domestic markets will no longer be protected. Ford has already undertaken a large scale reorganization of its European operations and has set up "centers of excellence" in Europe which will focus on different aspects of automobile design. These centers will together determine the Ford cars of the future in Europe.

3. An interesting question related to the issue of mergers and consolidation is: Which firms are likely to grow stronger in the European auto market and which will have tougher times ahead? It seems certain, as stated before, that Renault and Fiat will have to become much more aggressive. The Japanese companies should collectively do well, though their individual fortunes are difficult to assess. Ford, which is perhaps the most European of all the firms, should do well, but will have to adjust to the new marketplace.

4. Worldwide, an overcapacity has been created in the automobile industry and during the summer of 1989 there is already talk of some manufacturers in the United States having to close down plants and lay off workers. In this situation, there is some concern about how the automobile industry will handle several issues, for example: (a) Will Japanese cars made in the United States be allowed to be exported to Europe? (b) How will the local content and rules of origin policy of the European Community affect U.S. and Japanese manufacturers? (c) What will all this mean to the automobile ancillary and component industry?

In Western Europe there is already a move to reduce multiple sourcing of components to a smaller number or even a single source.[13] This will lead to a consolidation in the component industry as well.

In summary, major changes lie ahead for the European automobile industry and a smaller number of companies are likely to have to fight harder for a share of this market. Currently, the E.C. market has been doing well and it is seen as being of the same size or slightly larger than the U.S. market. Major changes in such a large market cannot but affect the fortunes of all the major world automobile manufacturers.

FOOD

The food sector is one in which national and regional tastes would be expected to differ greatly and therefore, the effects of EC-92 would be of less significance. While the taste differences may indeed be real, a surprising amount of activity has been triggered in the food industry by EC-92. In fact, the industry has seen a flurry of takeover activity and this has involved both firms from within and those from outside the European Community. The primary reasons for these takeovers could come from one or more of the following:

1. The larger integrated European market will mean consolidation in the retailing industry which in turn will reduce the manufacturer's power. One way for food industry firms to compensate for this loss of power would be by growing through acquisitions, possibly even vertical acquisitions.

2. There has been much attention paid lately both in the United States and elsewhere to the equity value of brand names. This attention may not be directly related to EC-92, but the integrated market will be larger than the U.S. market and in such a barrier-free market, there will be many opportunities for leveraging the value of brand names. The quickest way to acquire such brand names is through acquisition. This may explain Nestle's acquisition of Rowntree.

3. Differences in regional tastes notwithstanding, the borderless European market after 1992 should lead to a gradual homogenization of food preferences across countries. Presence in different E.C. countries would then be an imperative for any major player in the food industry.

For the reasons discussed above, a number of alliances have been forged between food companies. Some of them are listed below:

1. Nestle's acquisition of Rowntree which has already been mentioned. Through this acquisition, Nestle obtained ownership of brand names such as *KitKat* and *Smarties* and factories in Britain, France, Germany, and the Netherlands. For a non-E.C. firm, even one with a strong prior presence in the 12 country markets, Rowntree must have seemed like an invaluable acquisition for Nestle.

2. Grand Metropolitan PLC's acquisition of Pillsbury. This is an illustration of an E.C. firm seeking to grow abroad and emphasizes the increased competition that may be expected from E.C. firms in the U.S. market. Once again, Grand Met's strategy was based on the assumption that it was more

HEINZ EMPLOYS EC-92 APPROACH IN THE FOOD INDUSTRY

". . . we at Heinz are ready for 1992." Few heads of U.S. or European food producers can speak with greater confidence (and credibility) regarding the European Community marketplace than Anthony F. J. O'Reilly, the H. J. Heinz Company. One of a handful of European nationals leading a U.S. major, O'Reilly's management background and training was honed in Europe and not surprisingly, Heinz has been an early player in the E.C. game.

The original E.C. architects could be describing Heinz (and O'Reilly's) strategy that is designed to take full advantage of the economies of scale and synergies afforded by the open 12-country market. He has said that ". . . it is not inconceivable to think that in the mega-market of post-1992, all our ketchup in Europe could be sourced from one single location—perhaps Spain or Portugal." Similarly, there would be a single seafood location, a single reciped foods location, etc. (Recent acquisitions in Spain and Portugal, as well as expansion in the firm's Kit Green, U.K., factory, all appear to fit within this rapidly developing Heinz manufacturing centers strategy.)

But, perhaps most interesting to those still coping with age-old European cultural stereotypes is the increased success of Heinz's Weight Watchers brand . . . especially in Italy and West Germany. Weight Watchers, purchased by Heinz in 1979, has reportedly gained a 70 percent awareness among West German consumers and its Weight Watchers' Punto brand is scoring impressive successes with a selection of low calorie dairy products in Italy. O'Reilly sees Weight Watchers as being the next truly global brand at Heinz.

O'Reilly's own history in Heinz and elsewhere has been a story that has been widely chronicled by *Business* (London), *Fortune* and other leading professional publications. A Dublin native and now a spokesman for U.S. industry, O'Reilly told us:

> Heinz has been in Europe for over 100 years and today much of our success results from our careful attention to still-pervasive national tastes. Whereas Heinz sauces and Weight Watchers are pan-European brands many of our products are considered part of the local culture. In Britain, "Heinz means Beanz," in Spain, Heinz means Orlando tomato sauce and in Italy, Heinz means Plasmon baby food. The removal of commercial business barriers in the European Community will allow us to "source regionally" but wise managers will continue to "market locally."

ILLUSTRATION 4.3

H. J. Heinz Company Advertisement

Heinz

SALES BREAK THE $5 BILLION BARRIER

Dr. Anthony J.F. O'Reilly–Chairman President and Chief Executive

For the 24th consecutive year, H.J.Heinz Company surpassed all previous records for financial growth.

Due in large part to the yields of our low cost operator programme, we have invested ample resources in strategies that will expand substantially the scope and size of Heinz enterprise.

The responsibility for our prosperity and our prospects lies with our management, both senior and subsidiary, who share a driving imperative for change. Depth of management skill remains our greatest resource, as Heinz continues its reliance on the initiative and inventiveness of its people.

Fiscal 1988 was a year of juncture, when established programmes matured and new strategies emerged. We transformed the company as we nurtured our existing markets.

Perhaps the most profound transformation of our company has been a transformation of thought. We have generated new methods to capture new markets and reach new consumers.

Heinz has been a particularly acute witness to the growing consumer preference for high nutrition and low calories. We have fashioned a strategy to cultivate this market with an ever-lengthening worldwide parade of new products and services under our Weight Watchers label.

Heinz has gained entry to emerging economies on opposite sides of the globe by purchasing companies of proven performance. We expect to move in step with the rapid pace of growth, particularly in the Pacific Basin countries of Japan, the People's Republic of China and South Korea. The projected 1992 lowering of trade barriers within the European Community opens the doors to a market of more than 320 million people. This change, combined with recent acquisitions in Spain and Portugal, means that the Iberian Peninsula has become a dynamic internal market for our tomato and fish products and a low cost operator base for export to all of Europe and

Sales
$5,244,230,000

Pre-Tax Profits
$622,573,000

After Tax Profits
$386,014,000

Net earnings up: 14%
Earnings per share up: 17.8%

beyond. Fully 70% of our worldwide sales now comes from products that do not bear the Heinz brand, a fact that would have startled management and shareholders alike just 25 years ago.

Our established brands continue to prosper and contribute mightily to our earnings and our growth. We have further increased our marketing effort, devoting $450 million, or 8.6% of sales, more than triple the investment of a decade ago. Most important, half of our consolidated sales comes from products that are the number-one brands in their respective national categories. This is due in no small measure, to our significantly increased expenditures for marketing support coupled with competitive price and profit margin advantages made possible by low cost operator status at home and abroad.

Heinz's gross profits have practically tripled over the past decade. As a percentage of net sales, our gross profit margin this past year stood at 39.5%, an exemplary contrast with the 32.7% recorded in 1978. During this same interval, our market capitalization grew more than eightfold. Within the past five years, investors who held Heinz company stock and reinvested their dividends saw their shares almost quadruple in value.

The rapid pace of change and expansion during Fiscal 1988 makes even the recent past seem almost static by comparison. Furthermore, it has generated a momentum of performance that will carry us vigorously into the future.

H.J. Heinz Company stands as a leader in its industry, rich in resources and progressive in outlook. We have been adventuresome, but not reckless, in extending our reach and expanding our product offerings.

With success as our tradition and our goal, we look upon this productive year with satisfaction and impatience. The past must now serve as prelude to even greater achievement.

Extracts from the statement to shareholders of H.J. Heinz Company by the Chairman, President and Chief Executive, Dr. A.J.F. O'Reilly, for the year to April 27th, 1988.

Note: This advertisement appeared in the September 1988 issue of *Business,* a London monthly magazine. It illustrates one way this company communicates its European Community (and other international) plans to its various European publics. Reprinted with permission.

effective to buy than build good food brands. More recently, Grand Metropolitan has also acquired the British fast food chain, Wimpy's.

3. The French BSN Group's acquisition of HP Foods and Lea and Perrins in the United Kingdom. This is an effort by a French company to try to establish its presence in other E.C. countries in advance of the market integration in 1992.

4. Mitsubishi's purchase of Prince's canned foods and Trex fats and oils which give it an opening to the E.C. market.[14]

The food industry has not seen the last of the consolidations and acquisitions mentioned above. The fact that small national markets are combining to form a large European market represents a major change in a pivotal industry such as food, and more of those changes can be expected in the next few years.

WHITE GOODS

It is a well documented fact that economic integration in the European Community would have significant scale economy effects in certain industries.[15] One such industry is white goods, and predictably, EC-92 has led to an acceleration of takeover and merger activity in this industry. This has occurred in spite of, or perhaps because of, wide differences in the preferences across E.C. countries and between the E.C. countries and the U.S., over sizes and colors of appliances. It would seem that economies of scale are so important in this industry due to its price-sensitivity that in spite of differences in consumer preferences, white good companies feel that it is imperative to grow and establish a community-wide presence. Part of the motivation beyond economies of scale is, of course, access to new E.C. markets. Also, white goods manufacturers may very well see even a homogenizing of consumer preferences in the years ahead.

Europe is the world's largest market for appliances. However, before the EC-92 impetus, there was still the question of how individual firms could target twelve separate markets. Now, those borders have been set for removal and firms, particularly from outside the European Community, have realized that without a quick expansion of their presence in the Community, they may never be able to get a significant share of this new European market. A number of different acquisitions and alliances have therefore been attempted or completed. These include:

1. Whirlpool's acquisition of a share of the $2 billion appliance business of Philip N. V. Whirlpool has long remained focussed on the U.S. market and a large part of its business has been with Sears' Kenmore brand. With the acquisition of Philips N. V.'s appliance business, Whirlpool has become the world's largest major home-appliance company. Philips N. V. and Whirlpool have already combined their purchasing operations giving them

a buying clout which results in lower costs for materials and components.[16]

2. Both G.E.C. of Britain and G.E. of the United States have been looking at Hotpoint which is one of the most profitable white good companies in Europe.[17] Hotpoint has strong links with German companies and should provide an entry to the European market particularly for G.E. of United States which aims to have a strong presence in the world appliance industry.

3. Electrolux of Sweden with its acquisition of White Consolidated in the United States and other European firms has become a formidable player in the world appliance industry.

4. Maytag is another firm similar to Whirlpool, in that it has been content to concentrate on the U.S. market. Recently, however, it acquired another U.S. company, Hoover, which has more than half of its sales outside the United States and a strong presence in Europe. Thus, Maytag's interest became almost immediately global including a strong E.C. presence. The white goods industry has, therefore, undergone a major consolidation in anticipation of EC-1992, and in the future, one should expect a rationalization of product lines and production facilities designed to benefit from the economies of scale inherent to this industry.

TELECOMMUNICATIONS, ELECTRONICS, AND POWER GENERATION EQUIPMENT

While this does not sound like a single sector, and indeed it includes several different products, the players in this group are a handful of the world's largest industrial companies. We have, therefore, chosen to discuss them together as an example of what EC-92 will mean in an industrial product area.

The products of this industry sector are often purchased by government/public agencies and historically, the European Community countries have favored national companies in awarding contracts. A major provision of the White Paper, however, is to make public procurement truly competitive and open to all firms in the E.C. marketplace. Unprecedented changes are, therefore, expected in this industry and already a spate of alliances and acquisitions have been occurring among firms from both within and outside the European Community. The European Community has chosen the telecommunications sector as the "leading industry" of its integration strategy.[18] In Chapter 1, we discussed the Research and Development activities in the European Community, many of which are also geared to making Europe a leader in telecommunications and information technology. In June 1987, the European Community issued a Greenpaper describing its strategy for developing a uniform European telecommunications infrastructure. Both Japanese and U.S. firms should have significant opportunities in this sector provided they have established Research and Development activity within the European Community. There have been suggestions that U.S. companies should participate in the E.C. R&D initiatives and many of them are allowed to do so provided they have a presence in that market.

Some of the major alliances in this industry that have been forged or have been discussed are:

1. American Telephone and Telegraph (AT&T), perhaps one of the few industrial giants to have historically concentrated only on its home market, has decided that not looking abroad can be a major problem in the years ahead and that Europe, in particular, is a market that it cannot afford to ignore. As a first step, it has entered into a partnership with Italtel, the Italian state telecommunications equipment company. AT&T was chosen over strong competition from several European companies and it now can participate in the massive modernization planned in the Italian telecommunication system at a cost of approximately $28 billion.

2. Britain's General Electric Company has explored collaborative deals with Matra, the French electronics group, in order to expand its defense electronics and communications business. In collaboration with Siemens, it has also been engaged in a protracted discussion with Plessey, the U.K. electronics company, in an attempt to gain access to the W. German defence electronics market.

3. Though it is not expected that national barriers will come down completely for power engineering equipment,[19] a number of alliances have occurred in this sector. Some of the major ones include Asea of Sweden and Brown Boveri of Switzerland (ABB). These two non-E.C. companies have pooled their resources, and in addition, have joined hands with Finmeccanica, the Italian State-owned equipment group. Siemens of Germany and ABB have similarly entered into collaborations with Westinghouse Electric of the U.S.

The power engineering industry has witnessed significant changes brought about by alliances. Seven major groups seem to have emerged worldwide. These are ABB, GEC-Alsthom, and Siemens in Europe; GE in the United States; and Mitsubishi, Toshiba, and Hitachi in Japan. Some of the smaller companies that survive, doubt that the large groups can succeed given their size; but for the moment, the giants seem to have decided that bigger is better.

COMPUTERS AND CONTROL EQUIPMENT

One sector that has implications for both the industrial and consumer markets is that of computers and process control equipment. In this sector, as well, the existence of twelve separate national markets has meant that many firms, particularly European ones, have had uneven exposure across countries. For example, Nixdorf Computer A.G. of West Germany sold $1.6

billion worth of minicomputers at home during 1987, but had only $200 million sales in the United Kingdom . . . though the markets are of roughly equal size. EC-92 is quite likely to change all that and make the European market intensely competitive. At the moment, firms from the U.S. have the edge, but this may be difficult to sustain in the face of a concerted charge by both Japanese and European firms. Part of the reason for the U.S. firms' edge is that they have been in the European market from the beginning and many of these U.S. firms have always viewed Europe as a single market. Honeywell, for example, has had a rationalized European production and distribution system including a single warehouse to supply its goods across the region.

A major force for change in the post-1992 E.C. computer market is that national-only firms in industries such as food will suddenly face competition from other E.C. and non-E.C. firms. Their current market share in the home market will look small when measured in E.C. terms. If they want to grow and expand throughout the European Community, these firms will have to adopt modern distribution and inventory planning systems including the use of significant computing power.

Until now, the E.C. market for computers has been characterized by IBM having the preeminent position in each country followed typically by a national company—for example, Groupe Bull in France and Siemens in W. Germany—for mainframe computers. In this fragmented national market situation, standardization has been minimal, but with EC-92 many changes will be sure to occur. Several major computer firms, in fact, have already joined together to form a nonprofit organization to promote computing standards.

One of the effects of standardization and greater competition will be a shake-out in the European computer industry. Already, major alliances are being forged. Honeywell has joined with Groupe Bull and NEC, for example. In the personal computer market, a number of companies have started selling low-priced Asian-produced clones and these should provide strong competition to IBM. In the mainframe area, IBM is preeminent, and European firms on their own will find it difficult to challenge "Big Blue." One attempt to counter IBM has been launched by Siemens which has joined BASF in a joint venture called Comparex which is selling Hitachi-made clones of IBM mainframes. Comparex president Rolf Brillinger is quoted as saying: "We have only two options—accept an IBM monopoly or go with the Japanese."

Research and development programs such as ESPRIT mentioned earlier, may hold the key for the European computer-makers' future. However, U.S. firms with a slow domestic market are sure to aggressively market themselves in Europe. In addition, Japanese firms are certain to make an all out effort to get a piece of Europe's expanded pie. As a result, the European computer market is sure to be extremely competitive after 1992 creating a level of aggression that is certain to have a fallout impact in North America as well.

NORTHERN TELECOM: A CANADIAN MAJOR BATTLING FOR POSITION IN EUROPE'S TELECOMMUNICATIONS STRUGGLE

Northern Telecom is one of eight Canadian companies listed in *Fortune's* 1989 ranking of the top 200 industrial corporations outside the U.S.[1] Its current sales of $5.4 billion place it at the 147th position in this ranking. Yet, perhaps even more important to anyone assessing Northern Telecom's future, was the recent *Financial Times* (London) special survey of the Telecommunications Industry, which showed the company positioned in 5th place in terms of overall world market share[2].

Certainly, this position might be viewed as "heady stuff" for this erstwhile equipment manufacturer, but the world telecommunication industry is going in a direction that permits no overconfidence. "Ten years ago, there were about 30 major telecommunications equipment manufacturers in the developed world. Today there are 15. . . ." And, ". . . Ten years from now, it's likely that only five of those 15 companies will still be around, and they'll all be globe-spanning giants."[3] Given these sobering predictions, it is a small wonder that Northern Telecom's new CEO, Paul Stern, is taking the company along a global path. (A path, incidentally, which had already been started by his predecessor, Edmund Fitzgerald, when he took advantage of deregulation to carve an important niche for Northern Telecom in the vast U.S. marketplace.)

Today, Northern Telecom owns 27.5 percent of STC, a United Kingdom electronics company, and is opening a plant in Verdun, France, which will be its second European facility. But, this is seen as just the "tip of its future iceberg" as it explores new avenues in the European Community and elsewhere, as the accompanying advertisement sug-

---

[1]"The International 500: the Biggest Industrial Corporations Outside the U.S." *Fortune,* July 31, 1989, p. 294.

[2]Terry Dodsworth, "Pace of Change Quickens," International Telecommunications Section III, *Financial Times,* July 19, 1989, p. I.

[3]Michael Salter, "Shoot the Moon," *The Globe and Mail Report on Business Magazine,* August 1989, p. 30.

gests. As with other majors, a significant manufacturing presence in the European Community was viewed as essential by the company.

Recently, we asked Stephen N. Bowen, Senior Vice President for Public Affairs, Northern Telecom Limited, to comment on EC-92. He told us:

> "Northern Telecom views 1992 as a major opportunity for major growth. In addition to our manufacturing plants in Ireland and France, we've established research and development "centers of excellence" in the U.K. and France to ensure that we maintain our role as one of the global leaders in telecommunications equipment. Over the next decade major changes will be occurring in the telecommunications industry as industrialized nations come to understand fully the strategic role telecommunications plays in maintaining a highly competitive and efficient industrial organization. A number of years ago we put forth the idea of the "Intelligent Universe" wherein the worldwide transmission of voice, data, text, and video communications would be as effortless as calling across town is today. The establishment of Europe 1992 will create a market where that concept will flourish."

AGRICULTURE

The European Community has had a Common Agricultural Policy (CAP) since 1962 which predates the White Paper by almost a quarter century. 1992 is therefore independent of CAP but the White Paper does call for changes in some areas of agricultural policy to permit the dismantling of border controls. These two areas are the harmonization of veterinary standards and the elimination of some monetary compensation programs so that common support price levels can be reestablished. In the first area, standard rules on hormone and antibiotic use in cattle production are due to take effect in 1989. From a North American perspective, U.S. and Canadian agricultural exporters will have to comply with these rules. The recent flap between the United States and the European Community on growth hormone treated beef exported by the United States is only the first incident in what is likely to be a series of disputes regarding the trade of agricultural products between the two markets. On the monetary compensation issue, the effort to stabilize price supports will lead to farmers in some countries not taking income cuts which they have been taking so far. Ultimately, the "central question for Community farmers is how to adjust to the fact that there is land to spare"[20] and some form of control has to be employed to limit overproduction and protect farm incomes. As the 1992 process unfolds, it is certain that the E.C. Agricultural Commissioner will have to address these issues and U.S./ Canadian agricultural product exporters will have to monitor the developments closely.

ILLUSTRATION 4.4

Northern Telecom Limited Advertisement

Note: This advertisement appeared in the September 4, 1989 issue of the *Financial Times* (London). It indicates the role this Canadian company is playing in various world markets and particularly, in the European Community. The advertisement demonstrates that the company has gone well beyond a national focus. Reprinted with permission.

ILLUSTRATION 4.5

NCR Corporation Advertisement

Note: This advertisement appeared in the September 7, 1989 issue of the *Financial Times* (London). One of its major strengths lies in its effectively portraying the importance of seeing the European Community as a single market. Reprinted with permission.

BUCKEYE FEEDS TARGETS AN E.C. NICHE THROUGH LICENSING IN THE U.K.

Shipping costs, high import duty on starches, and variations in national nutritional standards have historically been among the factors limiting the export potential for North American firms seeking to serve the large European animal feeds market. However, Buckeye Feed Mills, Inc., is one specialty agri-business company that is positioning itself to take full advantage of the 1992 removal of inter-country barriers, including national standards variations. According to Ted Stults II, Buckeye's President, the company's E.C.-92 entry strategy calls for employing a combination of licensing and distribution, that will utilize its technical expertise as a means to penetrate the U.K. and Continental Europe.

As a first step, Buckeye Feeds entered into a licensing and distribution agreement with G.R. Bailey Ltd. of Braintree, England, in mid-1989. Under this arrangement, Bailey will produce and market Buckeye's high quality horse feed brand, which will have leading U.K. breeders as its target market. Founded in 1910, Buckeye has a strong brand recognition and reputation among leading breeders in the U.S. equine market in such locales as Lexington, Kentucky, and Ocala, Florida, and will build on this image base in the E.C.

Initially, Buckeye's goal will be to establish its presence in the United Kingdom through its well-recognized skills in nutritional ration balancing, i.e. differences in available grains and forages require the altering of vitamin and mineral mixes in order to provide a set level of nutrition. Buckeye has the equine nutritionist talent and computer capabilities to offer an "instantaneous" mix alteration formula and thus, to insure the level of nutrients that thoroughbred breeders must have at their disposal.

Such a horse feed niche in the United Kingdom and Europe, which have long been world-class racing centers, is analogous to a designer targeting the most affluent consumer market in the U.S. apparel marketplace.

Once the firm's English market role is established, the Braintree base will be used to serve the important Continental horse feed market. And, according to Mr. Stults II, it will be France and the remainder of the E.C. marketplace that will offer the level of sales potential that will ultimately determine the program's success. Later, when Buckeye's name is well-established in Europe, and the various feed standards are fully harmonized, he sees the Company exploring additional animal feed markets similar to those it serves in the U.S., including the dairy cattle, dog, rabbit, poultry, etc. markets.

TIRE INDUSTRY[21]

The tire industry is dominated in Europe as in the rest of the world, by a few major players. For this reason executives in this industry feel that 1992 will not make a major difference to them because they have already been approaching the European Community as a single market. Alliances between tire companies such as Bridgestone-Firestone and Continental-General have not necessarily been motivated by 1992 and the tire industry is clearly not going to be as affected by the market integration process as say, the automobile industry in Europe. The major tire companies—Goodyear, Michelin, Pirelli, for example, already operate several manufacturing plants in most of the major E.C. countries. Economies of scale in this industry are also unlikely to favor manufacturing plants above a particular size so consolidation of manufacturing facilities will not be a major goal in the integrated market. A major worry over the longer term, though, is the likely competition from low cost imports because all the industry majors, including the European ones, have been increasing their investment in the Pacific Rim countries. This will mean that the smaller European producers will see a shakeout and many of them may disappear. There is also speculation that Pirelli of Italy and Continental of Germany may explore a merger or some similar alliance. The tire industry is also one of the few industries in Europe where there is a significant presence of E. European companies though their share is only about 5 percent and is mostly restricted to the commodity end of the business which should be a situation that will continue after 1992. Overall, the industry is marked by a rough balance between demand and supply and with no significant growth forecast for the automobile industry, no major new investment would be expected. About the only thing one is likely to see is the shakeout mentioned earlier and as this monograph goes to press, one indication of this shakeout is the takeover just announced by Michelin of Uniroyal-Goodrich further consolidating the industry in the hands of a few major players.

END NOTES TO CHAPTER 4

1. "Two Leading Italian retailing groups explore possible merger," *Financial Times,* April 24, 1989, p. 1.
2. Eric Salama, "Europe's New Shop Window," *1992 Now,* Quarterly Review published by IBM Europe, March 1989, p. 5.
3. Sandra Vandermerwe and Marc-Andre L'Huillier, "Euro-Consumers in 1992," *Business Horizons,* January–February 1989, p. 37–39.
4. "Advertising: Healthy Long Term Outlook," *Financial Times* Survey on Satellite Broadcasting, March 14, 1989, p. V.

5. "Lowe Marschalk will Create Braun's World-Wide Campaign," *The Wall Street Journal*, March 8, 1989, p. B8.

6. "1992 whets BSN's big appetite: French food giant in a flurry of deals," *The New York Times*, July 25, 1989, p. C1.

7. "How '92 will change things," *Ad Week*, June 6, 1988, P. G6–G9.

8. "Looking to 1992, Agencies Rush to Define New Euro-Consumer," *The Wall Street Journal*, Tuesday, June 27, 1989.

9. "Now Comes the Hard Part: Marketing," *The Wall Street Journal Special Supplement*, Friday, September 22, 1989, p. R 10.

10. *Ad Week*, op cit, p. G6–G9.

11. *Ad Week*, op cit, p. G6–G9.

12. Brant W. Free, "The EC Single Internal Market: Implications for U.S. Service Industries," *Business America*, August 1, 1989, p. 11.

13. World Automobile Components, *Financial Times* Survey, June 8, 1989.

14. "Mitsubishi buys UK food groups from Nestle," *Financial Times*, February 9, 1989, p. 21.

15. Jacques Pelkmans, *Market Integration in the European Community*, The Hague: Martinus Nijhoff Publishers, 1984, p. 82.

16. "Whirlpool is Gathering a Global Momentum," *The New York Times*, Sunday, April 23, 1989, p. 10F.

17. "Hotpoint represents a tempting target," *Financial Times*, January 11, 1989, p. 29.

18. Alfred L. Thimm, "Europe 1992—Opportunity or Threat for U.S. Business: The Case of Telecommunications," *California Management Review*, Winter 1989, p. 57.

19. "The Hectic Scramble for Partners," *Financial Times*, January 20, 1989, p. 18.

20. Bridget Bloom, "Brave New World on the Land," *Financial Times*, January 30, 1989.

21. adapted from John Griffiths, "Europeans have conflicting views of market growth," Survey of World Tire Industry, *Financial Times*, Thursday, December 15, 1988, p. VI.

Banking is an area in which there has been special concern because of frequent mention by E.C. officials of the concept of "reciprocity" as it applies to this sector. The following article presents a detailed analysis of how EC-92 will affect the banking sector. It is excerpted with permission from Bennett, Thomas and Craig S. Hakkio "Europe 1992: Implications for U.S. Firms," *Economic Review* (a publication of the Federal Reserve Bank of Kansas City), April 1989.

Europe 1992: Implications for U.S. Firms

By Thomas Bennett and Craig S. Hakkio

This article examines the implications of Europe 1992 for U.S. firms doing business with Europe, focusing on nonfinancial firms and banks. The article concludes that U.S. firms will benefit from Europe 1992 unless the EC members raise external trade barriers or adopt discriminatory financial regulations.

Financial market integration. Just as the EC hopes to create a single European market for goods, it also hopes to create a single market for financial services. Market forces, such as the globalization of capital markets and financial innovations, are moving the world toward a single capital market. To complement these market forces, the EC under Europe 1992 will work to streamline financial operations within member countries. Capital controls will be eliminated, and banks that are licensed in one country will automatically be allowed to establish branches in any other EC country.

Many kinds of capital market controls will be eliminated in an integrated Europe. Firms in one EC member country will be permitted to issue bonds denominated in the currency of another EC country without obtaining approval from that country's central bank. EC citizens will be allowed to hold bank accounts and tap into credit markets throughout the EC. All restrictions on short-term capital flows will be removed, and capital flows between EC countries and non-EC countries will be liberalized.[1] Three countries—the

---

[1] As long as some EC country does not restrict capital movements from non-EC countries, restricting capital movements between an EC country and a non-EC country would be pointless. The reason is simple: If, for example, U.S. funds can flow freely into the United Kingdom, and if U.K. funds can flow freely into Italy, then there is no reason to prohibit U.S. funds from flowing freely into Italy.

117

United Kingdom, Germany, and the Netherlands—have already liberalized capital movements, and an EC directive adopted in June 1988 requires the other member countries to remove all remaining capital controls by 1990.[2]

Moreover, banks will be allowed to operate throughout the EC under a single banking license. The same principle that is applied to technical standards for goods—mutual recognition—will govern EC banking. In other words, a bank established in one EC country will be allowed to branch into any other member country without obtaining permission from authorities in that country.

The EC has proposed a list of activities permissible to European banking. The list adopts the universal banking principle; that is, EC banks will be allowed to provide securities-related and advisory services in addition to commercial banking services (Table 2). As long as the country in which a bank is domiciled (the home country) permits its banks to engage in one of the essential activities, then those banks may engage in that activity in another country (the host country), even if the activity is prohibited to domestic banks in the host country.

Bank supervision under Europe 1992 will generally be the responsibility of the home country. Bank regulators in the home country can impose restrictions to ensure the safety and soundness of banks domiciled in their country. In three areas, however, banks will be subject to host-country supervision. First, branches will be subject to host-country rules imposed for monetary policy purposes. For example, reserve requirements on various assets will be set by the host country. Second, the host country will supervise the securities activities of banks. And third, the host country will retain primary responsibility for supervision of liquidity.

Eventually, a common set of banking regulations will likely emerge within the EC. Because banks domiciled in different countries will initially face different regulations, banks located in countries with stringent regulations will be at a competitive disadvantage. Over time, one would expect political pressures to remove regulatory disparities. To keep these political pressures from leading to regulatory anarchy, however, the EC plans to adopt some essential requirements for safety and soundness. For example, minimum standards will be set for capital adequacy, and minimum levels for deposit insurance will be established.[3] Moreover, procedures will be established for handling bank failures.

---

[2] Four countries that are heavily reliant on capital controls have an extended deadline: Spain and Ireland, 1992; Greece and Portugal, mid-1990s.

[3] Capital adequacy standards will be based on the work of the Basel Committee on Banking Regulations and Supervisory Practices. The Basel Committee is made up of representatives from the G-10 countries (Belgium, Canada, France, West Germany, Italy, Japan, the Netherlands, Sweden, the United Kingdom, and the United States), plus Switzerland and Luxembourg. For additional information on the Committee's proposal, see "Fed Staff Summary and Recommendations on Risk-Based Capital Plan," *BNA's Banking Report,* vol. 51 (Washington, D.C.: The Bureau of National Affairs, Inc., 1988).

TABLE 2

Permissible Banking Activities Under Europe 1992

---

(1) Deposit-taking and other forms of borrowing;
(2) lending (including consumer credit, mortgage lending, factoring and invoice discounting, and trade finance);
(3) financial leasing;
(4) money transmission services;
(5) issuing and administering means of payment (credit cards, travelers' checks, and bankers' drafts);
(6) guarantees and commitments;
(7) trading for the institution's own account or for the account of its customers in (a) money market instruments (such as checks, bills, and CDs), (b) foreign exchange, (c) financial futures and options, (d) exchange and interest rate instruments, and (e) securities;
(8) participation in share issues and the provision of services related to such issues;
(9) money brokering;
(10) portfolio management and advice;
(11) safekeeping of securities;
(12) credit reference services; and
(13) safe custody services.

Source: Annex to the Second Banking Coordination Directive.

Thus, like goods market integration, financial market integration is moving ahead. Europe 1992, if fully integrated, would reduce burdensome financial regulations.

POTENTIAL BENEFITS OF EUROPE 1992 FOR U.S. FIRMS

Europe 1992 will replace 12 separate national markets with a single EC market. The EC comprises 320 million people, a third more than live in the United States. The EC's gross domestic product is $4.6 trillion, nearly equal to that in the United States. As long as the EC market remains open to outsiders, increased uniformity brought about by the Europe 1992 initiative will prove advantageous to U.S. firms. As restrictions are removed, nonfinancial U.S. firms will be able to operate more freely throughout the EC, thereby reducing their production and distribution costs. And U.S. banks will be able to branch throughout the EC while providing a greater range of financial services.

POTENTIAL BENEFITS FOR U.S. BANKS

If the Europe 1992 proposals are adopted by the EC, banks will be able to operate in all 12 member countries under a single banking license and under a universal banking concept. The single license will enable all banks in Europe, including banks from the United States, to realize a number of cost benefits. The universal banking concept will expand the powers of U.S. banks providing services in Europe.

A single banking license will directly lower bank costs by enabling banks to operate throughout the EC using common distribution networks, managers, and support staffs. Additional cost savings could be realized by centralizing funding of loans. Moreover, operating under a single banking license will enable banks to reduce risk by diversifying the geographic distribution of their loans. For example, if a bank's portfolio includes loans to farmers in one country, the risk to the bank may be very high due to the possibility of drought. However, a portfolio with loans to farmers in all EC countries may be much less risky, since crop damage is less likely across all EC countries than within a single country.

A single banking license and home-country supervision of banks will also indirectly lower bank costs in Europe. Currently, to operate in all 12 EC countries, a bank must meet the standards set by each country's regulators. However, with a single banking license and home-country supervision, a bank need meet only one set of regulations—those set by the home country. If overlapping or conflicting standards and regulatory procedures are eliminated, the cost of banking in Europe will decline. Furthermore, whereas in the past a bank might have chosen to locate and operate in only the larger European markets, it will now be able to establish itself in one market and then branch into all the other markets of the EC.

U.S. banks, like others, will have an incentive to expand into new countries because the prices of banking services vary greatly from one country to another. Chart 1 shows that the prices of two banking services, commercial loans and credit cards, differ considerably among EC countries.[4] To the extent these differences persist, at least temporarily, countries with high prices will attract new entrants. Some U.S. banks may also attempt to gain presence in the EC market by merging with existing European banks.

As noted earlier, under the Europe 1992 program universal banking will become the norm for European banking. Subsidiaries of U.S. banks operating in the EC will be able to engage in capital market activities, such as underwriting securities—unlike their parent banks operating in the United States, which are prohibited from underwriting securities by the Glass-Steagall Act. These expanded powers will give U.S. banks the opportunity to use their expertise to earn additional income in European capital markets. Furthermore, with U.S. banks underwriting securities in Europe, the U.S. Congress may be more inclined to repeal the Glass-Steagall Act and thus increase the international competitiveness of U.S. banks.

---

[4] For more detail on the calculations shown in Chart 1, see "The Economics of 1992," *European Economy*, (Brussels: Commission of the European Communities, March 1988), pp. 86–94.

CHART 1

Prices of Banking Services in Selected European Countries

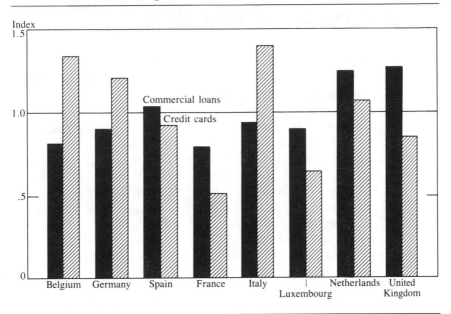

Note: Prices for each country are expressed as a fraction of the average price in the eight countries. The price for a commercial loan is the annual cost (including commissions and charges) to a midsized firm of a 250,000 ECU commercial loan; the price for credit cards is the difference between the interest rate on a 500 ECU debit and money market rates.
Source: "The Economics of 1992," *European Economy* (Brussels: Commission of the European Communities, March 1988), p. 91.

Thus, if adopted, Europe 1992 will enable both nonfinancial U.S. firms and U.S. banks to operate more efficiently in Europe. Non-financial U.S. firms, unhampered by costly overlapping standards and regulations, will be able to reduce both production and distribution costs. And U.S. banks will benefit from both expanded powers and the ability to operate in all 12 EC countries.

U.S. APPREHENSIONS OF EUROPE 1992

Europe 1992 presents U.S. firms not only with opportunities but also with potential dangers. Access to a barrier-free market with a population that is one-third larger than the United States opens up lucrative possibilities. However, these possibilities will be realized only if the EC's markets remain open. If the EC becomes a Fortress Europe by raising trade barriers against foreign competition or by adopting financial regulations that discriminate against foreign banks, U.S. firms will be harmed.

WILL DISCRIMINATORY FINANCIAL REGULATIONS BE ADOPTED?

Apprehensions that U.S. banks might be discriminated against arise because the EC has not made it clear how it will treat foreign banks. The EC has indicated that access to a single European financial market will be limited to banks from those countries outside the EC that provide reciprocal treatment to banks from all EC countries.[5] Unfortunately, the EC's definition of reciprocity is unclear—both in its meaning and its implications. Reciprocity may mean either "national" treatment or "mirror-image" treatment. National treatment would strengthen U.S. banks; but mirror-image treatment would severely limit the powers of U.S. banks operating in the EC.

As a matter of policy, the United States accords national treatment to foreign banks. Under national treatment, all powers granted to U.S. banks are also granted to foreign banks operating in the United States. By allowing domestic and foreign firms to compete on an equal footing, national treatment is nondiscriminatory.

U.S. policymakers have urged the EC to provide national treatment to U.S. banks operating in the EC. An official of the U.S. Treasury Department has argued, for example, that national treatment is consistent with our treaties with European nations, with the codes and instruments of the Organization for Economic Cooperation and Development, and with U.S. federal law.[6] U.S. officials further argue that since the United States provides national treatment to foreign banks, the EC should provide national treatment to U.S. banks.

If the EC adopts national treatment as its definition of reciprocity, U.S. banking in the EC will not be unduly restricted. Since EC banks can branch throughout Europe and underwrite securities, national treatment will allow U.S. banks operating in Europe to do likewise.

On the other hand, if the EC adopts a mirror-image definition of reciprocity, U.S. banking activity in the EC will be severely restricted. Under mirror-image reciprocity, treatment of U.S. banks in the EC will mirror the treatment of EC banks in the United States. Since the United States prevents EC banks (and U.S. banks) from branching throughout the United States

---

[5]While reciprocity provisions could be applied to any product or firm, they have been incorporated only into directives on banking, investment services, and public procurement.

[6]U.S. Deputy Secretary of the Treasury M. Peter McPherson, "The European Community's Internal Market Program: An American Perspective," remarks before the Institute for International Economics, Washington, D.C., August 4, 1988, p. 6.

and from underwriting securities, mirroring that treatment in the EC will prevent U.S. banks from branching throughout Europe and underwriting securities. Thus, U.S. banks would be unable to compete effectively against European banks, which would have much wider powers.

The October 1988 document on the external aspects of Europe 1992 has allayed some of the apprehensions about the reciprocity provisions. Lord Cockfield, Internal Market Commissioner of the EC, assured foreign bankers that the reciprocity provisions will not be applied retroactively.[7] As a result, U.S. banks already established in the EC will be treated the same as European banks, regardless of the definition of reciprocity.

Lord Cockfield also asserted, however, that reciprocity provisions will be applied to "newcomers." In the event that reciprocity is defined as mirror-image, Lord Cockfield's assertion raises several questions. Suppose, for instance, a nonfinancial company already established in the EC establishes a new financial services subsidiary. Is the firm a newcomer? Alternatively, suppose a U.S. bank becomes established in the EC between 1990 and 1992. Is it a newcomer? Or suppose a U.S. bank, already established in the EC, reorganizes or adds another subsidiary. Is the reorganized bank a newcomer? Is the new subsidiary a newcomer?

As debate has continued within the EC over the treatment of foreign banks, U.S. policymakers have emphasized the importance of adopting the national treatment definition of reciprocity. For example, Governor Heller of the Federal Reserve System stressed that anything other than national treatment "would be detrimental not only in that it would harm the ability of U.S. banks to compete in the European market for financial services, but it could lead to further protectionist pressures that would be harmful to all."[8] And Mr. McPherson, then Deputy Secretary of the Treasury, argued that mirror-image reciprocity "could be applied in a manner that would discriminate against firms in the United States seeking entry to the EC," concluding that the U.S. government finds this reciprocity concept "particularly troubling."[9]

SUMMARY

Complete integration of Europe 1992, as envisioned by the White Paper, may not become full reality by 1992. Disagreement on such central issues as tax rates, banking control, and national sovereignty may take years to unravel. Yet there is little doubt that Europe 1992 is moving strongly toward implementation—and that it will have significant ramifications for U.S. firms.

---

[7]"EC Allays Freeze-Out Fears," *American Banker*, October 24, 1988, p. 6.
[8]*Daily Report for Executives*, November 3, 1988, p. A-12.
[9]M. Peter McPherson, "The European Community's Internal Market Program . . . ," pp. 4–6

Identifying Entry and Marketing Strategies

In the previous chapters, we have provided an overview of the changes occurring in the European Community as the Single Market program proceeds, and we have also looked at specific sectors and how they will be affected. Along the way, we have presented the results of two studies detailing how U.S. firms are viewing the developments and strategy changes they are planning for the new European Community market. In this chapter, we present a somewhat prescriptive framework for analyzing the strategic options that will confront firms as they approach EC-92. We will take the perspective of firms in general, though our specific emphasis will be on North American firms. It is worth noting that the strategic options will differ based on the type of industry and size of firm that is involved. Our discussion will, therefore, include such contingencies, and we hope that the framework will help executives charged with strategic planning responsibility for the European market as they begin the task of formulating new approaches to a marketplace that will move from twelve fragmented parts to a single integrated one.

The first aspect of the Single Market process that firms should recognize is that it requires them to respond on three levels.[1] The first level involves dealing with the changes in product standards, customs procedures and other legal/fiscal ramifications of EC-92, but this level has more of a tactical than strategic dimension to it and will require day-to-day attention on the part of management. Our focus will, therefore, be more on the two levels of macro–environmental changes in as far as they affect (1) business in general, and (2) marketing in particular.

Before we proceed to the framework itself, we may add that the global competitors from outside the European Community such as IBM and Ford are better positioned strategically, because in a sense, they have always viewed Europe as one market. This was also borne out in our study findings discussed in Chapter 2. To that extent, they may have less to worry about, but even they will have to recognize that EC-92 represents a realization on the part of E.C. firms that they, too, have to expand their horizons to include the entire twelve-country market. Although, they may find this difficult to do initially because they are so steeped in their compartmentalized view of the European Community. With the numerous alliances being forged between firms from both the European Community and outside, the competitive structure of the European market is sure to change, and this will call for a whole new look at competitor analysis and competitive intelligence by all firms, large and small, established in the European Community or new to the European Community. The following questions could help in conducting such a competitive analysis[2]:

1. Who is the competition now and who will be in the future?
2. What are the competitors' strategies, objectives and goals?
3. How important is a specific market to the competitors and are they committed enough to continue to invest?
4. What unique strengths do the competitors have?
5. Do they have any weaknesses that make them vulnerable?
6. What changes are likely in the competitors' future strategies?
7. What are the implications of competitors' strategies on the market, industry and one's own company?

FRAMEWORK FOR ANALYZING STRATEGIC OPTIONS

GENERAL FRAMEWORK

Figure 5.1 provides a simple two-by-two matrix that firms can employ in evaluating their strategic options vis-a-vis Europe-1992. The matrix recognizes that small and large firms are likely to experience very different options and will have to choose an appropriate strategy based on the level of commitment they desire in the European marketplace.

As the matrix shows, some companies that are large may undertake relatively small investments through the setting up of simple assembly operations. What have been termed Japanese "screwdriver factories" are examples of this, where Japanese automobile and electronic manufacturers have initially chosen to undertake primarily assembly of component parts rather than fully integrated manufacturing plants. In cell 2, we have large companies which have made a significant commitment through setting up major

FIGURE 5.1

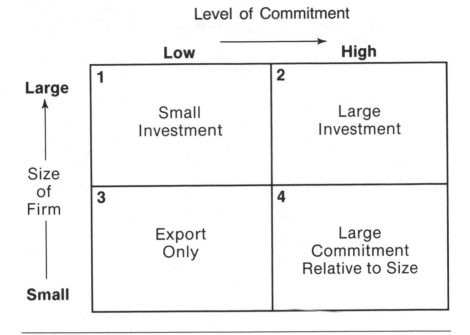

Level of Commitment

manufacturing and marketing subsidiaries or through the acquisition of companies already operating in Europe. Ford is perhaps the best example of this, though their commitment to the European market predates the recent interest in the EC-92 market integration process. Ford's level of commitment is emphasized by the fact that at their European plants they expect to develop future models of their automobiles that are not only intended for sale in the E.C. market, but also in other markets around the world, including the home market. Another example of a major commitment is the acquisition of Hoover's operations in Europe by Maytag, which immediately gives them a Community-wide presence where previously they had none.

In cell 3, we recognize the possibility that a small firm located outside the European Community or in a single E.C. country may choose to export its products to the entire E.C. market because it occupies a specialized niche that protects it from competitive inroads being made by other firms. Business Week reports that exports from small firms with less than $400 million in sales was a major reason for the recent surge in U.S. exports to Europe.[3] Such firms may not have the resources to make a major investment in the E.C. market but because of their unique product niches, they can still successfully reach the European market. An example of such a firm would be

Gerber Scientific Inc, a manufacturer of high tech equipment for the apparel and electronics industries which has 24 percent of its sales in Europe, but all of it from exports. H. Joseph Gerber, its chief executive is quoted by Business Week as saying that "we can easily pay a tariff and still come out ahead."[4]

Finally, in Cell 4, we consider the possibility of a small firm that makes a major commitment to the E.C. market relative to its size because it sees the market as crucial to its success. In many cases, such firms may have a high percentage of their sales and profits coming from the European market. Several small technology firms are examples of cell 4. Filament Fiber Technology Inc. is a case in point because though it has less than $100 million in sales, it has plans for a $5 million polypropylene factory in France. Business Week has called such firms "plungers."[5]

In figure 5.2 we have presented the matrix again with some examples of firms indicated in the different cells.

In addition to the above kind of analysis, which is very general, firms considering their strategy towards the post-1992 European market will also have to take into account some factors that are industry and firm-specific. Two of the most important ones are (1) competitive structure—some industries, such as the automobile industry, are by their very nature, likely to

FIGURE 5.2

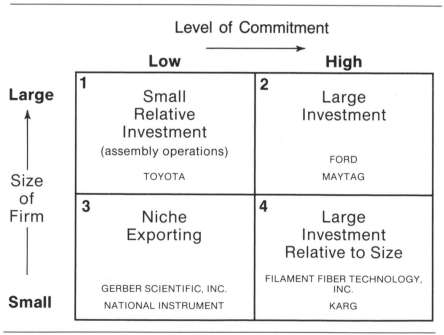

be quite concentrated with a few major players. Any major change resulting from new entrants in such an industry will mean a radical transformation of the strategic environment for all firms, and indeed, the automobile industry in the European Community will face precisely this situation with the inevitable growth of the Japanese firms' market share and production capacity in the European market. The pharmaceutical and chemical industries are also relatively concentrated, but here the European companies have often been dominant; therefore, U.S. firms are likely to face a stronger competitive challenge. (2) Economies of scale—a second, though not unrelated issue deals with the economies of scale inherent to an industry. If such economies are important, a larger integrated market will inevitably force out the inefficient and smaller firms that may previously have been protected in their national markets. The white goods industry represents a good example of this phenomenon with major U.S. and European players (Whirlpool, Electrolux, Maytag) likely to dominate the market. Besides economies of scale in production, there could also be economies of scale in marketing made possible by reduced distribution costs, consolidation of brands, standardized advertising, etc., and this may explain the feverish merger and takeover activity in the European food industry.

STRATEGY FORMULATION: A LOOK AT ALTERNATIVES

In order to more fully examine the entry options available to North American manufacturers, the matrix suggested in the previous section can be expanded. Depending upon the firm's desired level of commitment (or presence), there are a number of possible entry strategies that can be employed, and in fact, companies may employ a combination of strategies.

Further, companies that do not exactly fit the suggested categories (Figures 5.1 and 5.2) tend to fall "in between" on a nine-cell matrix (Figure 5.3). To illustrate, a number of companies that really are not small, may prefer to continue to serve the new European market from the U.S. (or a non-E.C. third country) and still move to employing a more aggressive distribution stance. In this instance, the company would more comfortably "fit" in cell 4 (Figure 5.3). Another company, this one large, might choose to produce certain key products or components in one of the E.C. countries . . . often the components are those that are frequent consumables or replacement parts . . . and rely on exporting from the States for other products/components.* Here, the company would more appropriately fit into cell 2 (Figure 5.3). To allow for such "flexibility," the nine-cell matrix will be employed in this discussion.

---

*As a point of clarification, a non-E.C. company is not automatically considered to have E.C. status for *all* of its products if it manufactures one (or a few) of its products in a member country. Just as in the U.S., all products coming from the "outside" are subject to appropriate duties or quotas and only those actually produced *in* the E.C. are afforded E.C. status, i.e. can move freely throughout the 12 countries.

130

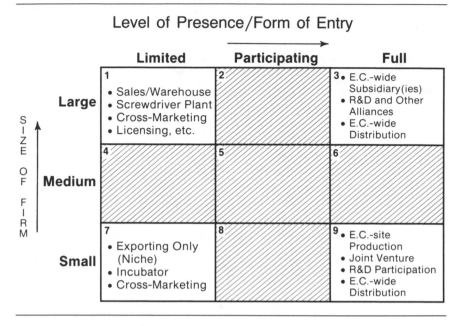

FIGURE 5.3

Level of Presence/Form of Entry

LIMITED ENTRY (AND/PRESENCE) ALTERNATIVES

At first glance, limited entry strategy appears to be most appropriate for North American companies that either lack the necessary capital for a more directly competitive stance or have such a quality image (or play such a niche leadership role) that the appropriate duties (or non-tariff barriers) are unimportant. (For years, Rubbermaid products brought a healthy premium in the Japanese market and were unaffected by the local tariffs.)

However, there are, of course, many other reasons why a company may choose a limited presence, including the fact that it may lack prior experience in Europe and wish to take a conservative approach until it has fully assessed these opportunities. A further reason that we have often heard in our discussions with executives is that their company is waiting to learn what type of standard(s) will ultimately be determined for their product. If the European standard is quite similar to their domestic product, they may be able to compete on an export-only basis even with the added burden of the E.C. duty [and any non-tariff restriction(s)].

Having chosen to follow a limited entry/presence strategy, the company may choose from a variety of options. To illustrate, Ireland has developed an interesting alternative for the small firm wishing to do some local assembly, packaging, or even minor production, etc. in order to get its "feet wet" in the European Community. The Irish Industrial Development Authority established this variation of the industrial incubator concept that has been widely used by cities, universities and the like in the United States to assist "international start-ups." Or, a small to medium company may find a national manufacturer of complementary products in one of the 12-countries and enter into a cross-marketing or co-distribution arrangement. Simply put, each carries all or part of their cross-marketing partner's product-line and perhaps, even provides warehouse, delivery and service assistance. While the North American company is still serving the European Community on an export-only basis and is not avoiding the tariff and non-tariff barriers, it still has assured distribution, and if the partner is chosen properly, a good marketing force operating in its behalf in Europe. Under such an arrangement (cross-marketing) a firm can get a better picture of its product-line potential in the E.C. and increase its own offering to the U.S. customers at home.

In addition to the other limited entry alternatives, larger firms may be more likely to consider licensing, contract manufacturing and/or screwdriver plants, as well. When compared with exporting, each of these limited entry approaches offers slightly more E.C. presence; and when coupled with European sales offices/warehouse facilities places them on potentially firmer competitive ground in the market. As cited earlier, the Japanese auto producers found the screwdriver factory to be an attractive way to initially enter the European Community, especially when coupled with a strong distribution network. Subsequent "local content" problems faced by the Nissan Bluebird and the Sterling do not diminish the original attractiveness of this approach.

FULL ENTRY (AND PRESENCE) ALTERNATIVES

Large companies seeking to follow a full-scale E.C. presence strategy have a seemingly endless number of alternatives they may employ. However, those firms wishing to enter via acquisition (full or partial) or through solid joint venture arrangements will undoubtedly find their possibilities reduced as increasing consolidation occurs. Among the many examples that might be cited are AT&T's partnership with Italtel and Motorola's acquisition of Storno (Denmark).[6] The former places that U.S. producer in a key position in the modernization of the Italian telephone industry, while the latter makes another U.S. major a strong player in Scandinavian mobile telecommunications.

Another popular possibility in Europe will be R&D alliances that are designed to better position the European Community in those high-tech races that have been dominated by external producers. In some instances, combined U.S. and European private sector efforts can be expected to forestall Japanese domination of important future markets. And, the European Community can be expected to continue to provide grants to stimulate some of these consortium efforts.

The complexity of many of the alliances that are now unfolding seems to defy the simple organizational constructs of the past. Multi-company production and/or cross-licensing agreements, joint research, complementary distribution arrangements, etc., seem to all be possible within the realities of a well-developed body of E.C. anti-trust law and the E.C. mergers and acquisition review procedures. In fact, there are those who predict that the final "sort-out" in post-E.C.-92 will find a number of industries consolidated into as few as a half-dozen majors or less, plus some additional niche players.

For the smaller companies, there are also a number of entry alternatives that offer full participation in the new 12-country market. For example, there are several bio-tech and medical instrumentation companies that have acquired or formed alliances with similar sized European companies. Similarly, the Karg Corporation, an Ohio manufacturer of steel braiding equipment, has established a joint venture in Britain in order to be able to serve the European Community after 1992.

These are not isolated examples. The key is often to find national-level counterparts that either need the technology or capital offered by the North American partner or who have chosen to withdraw from the market and sell to the U.S. producer. In either instance, the small U.S. or Canadian producer achieves at least a degree of access to the European Community by its joint venture or acquisition. Frankly, there are a number of smaller E.C. companies that have been "protected" due to their national laws, especially those dealing with government procurement. They may well be more intimidated by an "open 12-country marketplace" than smaller U.S. companies galvanized by competing in the United States. (A word of caution or a caveat is important here; large-scale market experience in the United States does not transfer easily or directly to the European Community regardless of what one may hear.)

Finally, of course, a small U.S. producer may find an advantage merely by establishing a production facility (subsidiary) in the European Community; one that does not involve a joint venture or acquisition. In fact, it can usually obtain the same local government investment incentives, such as tax relief and plant construction costs, as would a larger company. This decision can be made essentially on the basis of a market opportunity assessment of the European Community or the opportunity in one or a few of the 12-countries. Political and other risks inherent in the E.C. member states are quite similar to those a Cleveland company faces when it decides to construct a plant in Enid, Oklahoma to serve the Southwest U.S. In other words, these risks are often minimal.

IMPLICATIONS FOR MARKETING STRATEGIES

The Single Market program will have a number of major implications for the marketing strategies of firms. We will discuss these implications by focussing on the principal marketing decision areas, i.e. marketing research and the choice of the target market with associated marketing mix (product, price, place and promotion).

Marketing research: Traditionally, marketing research has been much less well developed outside the United States and Europe is no exception. The existence of twelve different markets and the diversity of languages and cultures may have been partly responsible for the situation, but it is likely to change after 1992. Besides the efforts by advertising agencies to understand Euro-consumers mentioned in Chapter 2, several other changes are currently underway on the European marketing research scene. The consolidation/mergers/alliances occurring in many industries would point to the need for marketing research studies in many different countries simultaneously. This will demand marketing research suppliers who have full service capabilities in all the E.C. countries. Already, Nielsen is moving ahead with plans to expand its retail audit services across the European Community.[7] Along with the need for suppliers who have the ability to perform research in several countries, many firms will also need to establish fresh estimates of their European market share. The concept of European market share may seem new to some firms, but increasingly, it will be the measure of a particular firm's clout in the E.C. marketplace. Finally, the anticipated freer mobility of people across borders, though it is not expected to occur widely at first, will mean a need for continuing marketing research to see if tastes, particularly for food and other consumer products/services, are indeed becoming homogenized over time.

Product: We have already mentioned the issue of economies of scale several times in our discussion. Until now there were twelve distinct countries with barriers which protected firms through subsidies and high prices. In this situation, the need for and likelihood of developing pan European products/brands was small. With the removal of barriers, however, wholesale and retail businesses will, theoretically, be able to purchase a product anywhere in the European Community and therefore, product quality and price will become more and more exacting. Greater effort is likely to go into product development and in order to gain the production and marketing economies, firms are likely to try and develop pan European products/brands. The net effect will most probably be a smaller total number of new products introduced in the twelve countries, but each one will potentially have more riding on it because it will be targeted at a wider population. This will mean a much tougher assignment for the product development/testing people. The patenting and branding of the products will also take on greater significance because each successful product will potentially have a much larger market than before.

On the positive side, the task of product development should become easier because of the adoption of community-wide standards in a number of product categories. The idiosyncratic differences in product standards that previously existed may have forced smaller, less profitable production runs on manufacturers and this will no longer be the case. Over time, the greater mobility of Europeans, the wider availability of media and the resulting homogenization of tastes/preference should also make for easier product development decisions.

Pricing: No other element of the marketing mix will perhaps be as dramatically affected by Europe-92 as pricing. Overall, the decision is going to become much more difficult with fewer choices for manufacturers. Some of the reasons are as follows:

1. A company which ships products across national borders previously had the advantage of using transfer prices to get around the widely differing tax burdens it experienced in different countries. With the harmonization of excise, value added and other taxes, the company will have fewer degrees of freedom in this regard.
2. We have already mentioned the likely effects of the consolidation of retailing and wholesaling organizations on manufacturers. The locus of power is definitely apt to shift in the direction of retailers and wholesalers, and this will mean pressure on manufacturers' prices and margins.
3. On the positive side, the opportunities for savings in distribution and warehousing costs once border controls are removed, will provide manufacturers with some cost cutting possibilities that they can either use to improve their margins or more likely, pass on to consumers in the increasingly competitive post-1992 marketplace.
4. Consolidation of production sites and the moving of some of the production to lower cost locations such as Ireland and Southern Europe will also provide cost savings that may be reflected in the pricing decision.

Place: A variety of changes are likely to occur both in channel institutions and the distribution/logistics systems of companies and in many respects, this marketing mix decision may represent the major challenge to a firm after 1992. Indeed, some of the changes in the other elements of the marketing mix that we have discussed flow directly from changes in the "place" part of the mix. Besides the mergers/alliances between E.C. retailers, reduction of transportation time because of elimination of multiple border check points, and the consolidation of warehousing facilities, which has already been mentioned, other factors that need to be considered include cross border purchasing by consumers, Europe-wide sourcing by industrial customers, a relaxation of restrictions on the hours retailers can stay open in some countries etc. In Germany, for example, stores have not been allowed to stay open late in the evenings, but already there are signs that these laws are likely to change. For the consumer, this will mean a much wider degree of choice, but for the manufacturer, it will mean much opportunity/threat depending on how he manages the "place" part of the mix.

Promotion: Both in advertising and sales promotion, major new developments are occurring or are likely to occur as a consequence of EC-92. The laws governing forms of sales promotion allowed in different markets, the restrictions on both availability of media and types of advertising, the fragmented nature of the advertising agency industry and other such factors have made Europe a very difficult place historically for promotional executives to operate in, particularly if they are from outside the European Community. All of this is going to change and while this will not necessarily make the promotional executive's job easier, major new opportunities and challenges lie ahead for those in charge of a company's promotional mix. These opportunities and challenges may be summarized as follows:

1. Media choice—The lack of availability of media (restricted TV advertising in many E.C. countries, for example) has until now been a major problem. With the anticipated homogenization of laws relating to advertising across E.C. countries after 1992, the overall availability of media should increase. The most dramatic changes will occur in television because of the addition of new channels as in Britain and the penetration of satellite and cable TV across the European Community. Of course, more options mean a more exacting decision process for the media planner.
2. Message choice—There are two issues involved here. One relates to the degree of standardization of the theme/message/creative aspects of advertising and the other to the language differences across countries. The latter is not likely to disappear overnight but already many companies are experimenting with commercials that are used across countries with only the voice over changed. In fact, some of the satellite networks have even experimented with programming in a single language—English and it is likely that over time, one language (possibly English) will emerge as a link language across the E.C. countries.
3. Agency choice—Consolidation of accounts by clients is proceeding apace in the European Community. Besides the example of 3M which was mentioned earlier, Sara Lee and several other consumer product companies have announced that they will consolidate their accounts. On the agency side, there will therefore be a consolidation as well, and many

smaller national agencies will either fold or will have to establish alliances with other agencies. This trend is, of course, not restricted to Europe and the major implication for advertisers is how they will make sure that conflicts of interest will not occur with a single agency handling two competing products.

The above discussion provides a general idea of what changes in marketing strategy will be necessary in the Single European Market (SEM). The discussion was not designed to be exhaustive given the extent and pace of change occurring in the European Community during the past couple of years. On a more general level, we may note that the key to a successful marketing strategy in Europe will be the level of skills/knowledge of the European marketing/sales managers.

In fact, we could speculate that companies will increasingly move executives identified for senior management and coordination roles from one country to another so they may develop the cultural, linguistic, and broader market sensitivity that will be essential after 1992. Therefore, in addition to pan European brands and pan European Marketing Strategies, we will also need to be concerned with the development of a cadre of pan European managers whose task it will be to coordinate the marketing strategies of firms in post-1992 Europe.

CONCLUSION

Planning an appropriate EC-92 strategy is likely to be the biggest challenge that many U.S./Canadian corporate decision-makers will face in their career. In one of the best pieces written about EC-92, John Magee calls the changes occurring in Europe ". . . to be as potentially profound-economically-as any in European history."[8] And, some might even call that vision an understatement.

What is perhaps most vexing to the decision-makers, however, is the fact that this new Europe will be a totally unique marketplace. Experiences gained in the U.S. or Japan . . . or even the old, fragmented Western Europe will help; but a company could well make a major blunder by relying too heavily on such experience alone. Recently, at a meeting on EC-92, one of the authors heard a speaker from a U.S.-based MNC state confidently that his company would watch the changes with interest, but was highly unlikely to alter its proven national (nation-by-nation) market approach of the past. Such confidence in past successes can have unfortunate consequences for a firm, since no one knows exactly what to expect from EC-92.

Stated simply, there has never been a comparable amalgamation of highly-developed countries . . . whatever this exact amalgamation turns out to be. Thus, given the caveat that any EC-92 decisions today will be made in the gray, rather than black and white, U.S. and other non-European companies need to recognize that there is still an enormous downside to waiting until the new market is fully-formed and all the answers are in. Changes are already fully underway in most industry sectors; alliances are being formed, dealerships and distributor arrangements being made, R&D linkages put in place, etc. As time progresses toward 1992, the alternatives become increasingly limited. Further, there are still doubts as to whether some form of "Fortress-Europe" can be avoided. Openness to the outside is good, but as America's own experience suggests, it is difficult for governments to hold firm to openness in the face of short-term national-level problems, such as wide company closings or inflationary trends. To illustrate, when Ireland initially entered the European Community, it experienced massive industrial layoffs. Ultimately, only 25% of the firms that were existing at the time of Ireland's entry were able to survive the long haul. In fact, Percy Barneick, Chairman of Asea Brown Boveri, recently was quoted as predicting that ". . . only one-third of the companies now operating in the E.C. . . ." will survive EC-92. Any similar economic turbulence in the United States or Japan would be met with some national-level response, therefore, some "fortressing" of Europe could well happen.

What sort of "fortressing" might we see? In deference to GATT and the European Community's on-going dialogue with the United States, Japan, EFTA members and the Eastern bloc countries, there is little likelihood of higher tariffs. Rather, any new (or continuing) barriers would be more subtle and "non-discriminatory." Such non-tariff barriers would probably be directed to individual industries or sectors instead of across-the-board. We are most likely to find the European Community emphasizing equal access to the outsider's market or reciprocity. (This flag, in fact, has already been raised regarding the U.S. banking industry.) Much discussion has also been generated regarding the nature and potential for local content requirements, especially the quality of the local content that may be mandated. The Europeans, quite naturally, want to be on the cutting-edge of research and development, especially in high-tech industries, and may establish a *quid pro quo* stipulation in some of their final directives. To illustrate, a directive could stipulate that an outsider (company) may only have completely "open access" to the European Community if a certain proportion of its R&D efforts and its higher value production takes place in a member country. One could go on and on identifying a whole litany of non-tariff barriers including product and packaging standards that could be employed.

The biggest downside concern, however, may not relate to "Fortress Europe" at all. Some North American firms will ultimately decide they want access to the strongest distribution network (top agents and/or distribution reps), to establish the most viable alliance possible, or to build on a key acquisition. For such firms, time alone may be the biggest downside concern

138

and their own delays their biggest barriers. While varying greatly by industry, the current level of private sector activity is staggering and prolonged hesitation may simply leave some firms waiting in the wings. As our study (Chapter 2) indicates, the executives in the U.S. majors feel that a physical presence in Europe including some production, is essential for most companies. A few firms do have such a unique product or service, dominance in a narrow niche, or a particularly strong image (quality, etc.) that might permit them to continue to compete on a U.S. or third-country export-only basis. Such firms will, however, become increasingly rare in the post EC-92 era and the desirability of an E.C. presence will undoubtedly take on even greater significance in the mid-1990's.

END NOTES TO CHAPTER 5

1. David Mitchell, "1992—The Implications for Management," *Long Range Planning,* vol. 22, No. 1, 1989, p. 32.
2. William E. Rothschild, "Competitor Analysis; The Missing Link in Strategy," *Management Review,* July 1979.
3. "Should small U.S. Exporters take the Big Plunge?," *Business Week,* December 12, 1988, p. 68.
4. *Business Week,* op cit, p. 68.
5. *Business Week,* op cit, p. 64.
6. Terry Dodsworth, "Quest for more consolidation," *Financial Times,* July 19, 1989, p. 11.
7. Keven Cote and Julie Skur Hill, "As world shrinks, Nielsen expands," *Advertising Age,* June 5, 1989, p. 52.
8. John Magee, "1992: Moves Americans Must Make," *Harvard Business Review,* May–June 1989, p. 78.

KARG CORPORATION: A FLEXIBLE
E.C. ENTRY STRATEGY

Can a relatively small, high quality industrial marketer develop an effective strategy to cope with 1992? If the company is Karg Corporation, Tallmadge, Ohio, the answer is a resounding yes.

The Karg Corporation's initial involvement in international markets occurred in 1963, when the firm received an order from a U.S. customer's European subsidiary. Two years later, James Karg, the firm's president (now CEO), decided that the European potential for this company's equipment created the need for a stronger involvement in Europe. As a result of a European-wide personal visit, he entered an agreement with a West German manufacturer of braiding machines who used the Karg product as original equipment and served as an agent for Western and Eastern Europe. This worked well for a number of years. Then due to a few problems in 1980, he changed agents. After a brief trial and error period with several agents, the Karg Corporation, a manufacturer of a line of steel braiding machines, wire and yard carriers, and related industrial products, selected National Standard Company Limited (U.K.) as its European-wide agent in 1986. This British firm is an overseas subsidiary of Niles, Michigan—based National Standards Company and it carries a number of products that completed Karg's target markets. (Among the latter are the world's major tire manufacturers.) Further, to balance the European effort, Karg had earlier (1980) established an agreement with a Japanese trading company to cover that key marketplace.

Last year (1988), the Karg Corporation took its first steps to insure a *manufacturing presence* in the E.C.; it entered into a joint venture agreement with Hi-Draw Engineering Ltd. (U.K.) to design, engineer and produce a cable braiding machine. This joint venture, named Karg, Ltd., has a license to use select Karg Corporation patents and will have as its target market a different European-wide product sector from its Ohio parent. (Hi-Draw will sell the new cable braiding machines, while National Standards will continue to sell the full Karg (U.S.) line.)

In our discussion with Jim Karg, he stressed the flexibility that the new joint venture arrangement will give his company. "If the E.C. decides to impose local content restrictions, we can move the production of various components (or the assembly of complete machines) to the British joint venture operations." Otherwise, the company is able to be most cost competitive (worldwide) exporting from its U.S. plant.

As for the future, Mr. Karg sees the forging of other new European alliances, an expansion of its cross-marketing efforts and other new

industrial machine products on the horizon. "To exploit these opportunities, the company must be sufficiently flexible to consider all potential entry/marketing strategies including European production for
some of our products sold in the U.S. and greater home-office marketing support for our foreign distribution." For example, the firm sent
several of its home office executives to the K-89 Duesseldorf (West
Germany) Fair to support National Standards' promotion/selling
program.

In summary, Karg Corporation finds itself today with a joint venture
operation in England, cross-licensing (and cross-marketing) agreements, a broader distribution network for Europe, sales in some 22
countries, and a flexible approach to the global business scene. Not bad
for a company, that received its first non-North American order some
25 years ago.

COUNTRY DIRECT INVESTMENT INCENTIVES
AND U.S. CORPORATE E.C.-92
ENTRY DECISIONS

Recently, *Business Month* featured an article dealing with the aggressive competition being conducted in the United States by "nearly
every state in the union" to attract industry, including investment from
overseas. However, what appears to have gone relatively unnoticed is
the battle for foreign investment being waged by European Community
countries (and their cities, regions, etc.). And, their primary objective
tends to be U.S. companies that are entering Europe (or increasing
their presence in Europe) in response to EC-92.

While not directly playing to the possibility of a "Fortress Europe"
as a result of E.C.-92, most of the promotional efforts do point to the
advantages of "being there." To illustrate, the Scottish Development
Agency has a campaign theme that states, "The Scottish Development
Agency is committed to assisting U.S. companies to tackle the Eu-
ropean Market from a Scottish base." Besides Scotland, it appears that
Ireland, the Netherlands, Belgium, and the United Kingdom, including
Northern Ireland, are among the most active E.C. locations seeking
U.S. direct investment. Further, cities/regions, such as Cheshire County
(U.K.), have been attempting to entice corporations to their locale once
the firms have made their *country decision*. At each level, i.e. country

and then locale in their country, there are many incentives ranging from tax abatement to worker training and site preparation available to the U.S. producer. Most direct investment incentives are only available to firms that are building *new* plants, either through wholly-owned subsidiaries or joint ventures. (They are typically not available to those merely entering their country or city/region via acquisition). However, once a U.S. producer has decided to enter Europe or expand its European operations as a result of E.C.-92, such foreign direct investment incentives should become one of the factors it includes in its site-specific decisions.

In late summer, 1989, we asked Peter Ahern, Vice President of the Irish Government's Shannon Development Company, to comment on the effect EC-92 has had on the level of interest U.S. companies have been showing in Ireland. (Ireland offers a particularly strong incentive package for U.S. manufacturers.) He says: "The level of interest from US companies in Ireland is high at present—probably higher than it has been at any time in this decade. Intel, Motorola, Pratt and Whitney are among a large number of companies—of all sizes—which have committed to new projects this year, selecting Ireland as much for our educated workforce as for our incentives. Obviously, this upsurge is linked to EC-92, and the publicity about "Fortress Europe" may have had an influence. However, it is our perception that the investment surge is primarily and simply due to the EC being seen as an attractive investment opportunity, just as it was in the 1970's."

ILLUSTRATION 5.1

Scottish Development Agency Advertisement

You have three years to prepare your company for the most important European battle in business history.

Because by 1992, barriers to trade between European countries will be coming down. Strategic alliances will quickly form. Costs of doing business within Europe may be significantly lower.

Compaq chose Scotland for their first European manufacturing base. Today, they are marching successfully across Europe.

Some of the world's most successful high-technology companies have discovered this. Companies such as IBM, Digital, Unisys, Compaq, Motorola, NCR, Hewlett-Packard and Honeywell, just to name a few, are already strategically settled in Silicon Glen.

Which means that a well-developed supplier base is already in place. So whatever you need is probably available just down the road.

Scotland also offers some of the best-educated, highly skilled people in Europe.

With so many high-technology companies already manufacturing in Scotland, you'll find the supplies you need.

If yours is an uncompromising company, perhaps you should be talking to us.

We can help you with everything from selecting the right site to hiring the right people. And we will help you do it all quickly.

For more information, please call 1-800-THE SCOT. Or write to the Scottish Development Agency, a UK govern-

Direct satellite telecommunications systems instantly link Scotland with North America and Europe.

The fastest way to conquer Europe is through Scotland.

And the result will be the creation of the largest, fastest-growing developed market in the world for high-tech products. A united European Community. With over 320 million consumers.

A large, well-educated workforce is ready to help you plan your attack.

The competition for this huge market will be fierce. Quite possibly unlike anything your company has ever experienced.

Now, more than ever, you need to choose powerful, dependable allies. We suggest that Scotland would be an excellent place to start.

So there is an abundance of qualified workers to quickly turn out quality products. And give you quality service.

And since our telecommunications and transportation capabilities are both modern and dependable, you can rapidly get products out the door and to that important market.

The bottom line is, those companies wishing to win the battle of 1992 cannot afford to wait.

And they cannot afford to compromise. When they come to Scotland, they do not have to.

Scottish Development Agency

When you locate in Scotland, every European country is within easy striking distance.

ment body, at the address below.

Because how fast and far you get in the new Europe depends greatly upon where you start.

Scotland. Where high technology is going

SCOTTISH DEVELOPMENT AGENCY, 1 LANDMARK SQUARE, SUITE 345, STAMFORD, CT 06901   SDA OFFICES ALSO IN HOUSTON, CHICAGO AND SAN MATEO.

This material is prepared by Clarke Goward Fitts Matteson, 580 Stuart Street, Boston, MA 02116 which is registered with the Department of Justice, Washington, D.C. under the Foreign Agents Registration Act as an agent of the Scottish Development Agency, Glasgow, Scotland. This material is filed with the Department of Justice where the required registration statement is available for public inspection. Registration does not indicate approval of the contents of the material by the United States Government.

Note: This classic economic development advertisement appeared in a recent issue of the *Wall Street Journal*. It illustrates how the Scottish Development Agency is using the opportunities offered by the enlarged European Market as well as its country's own particular strengths as a way to attract direct investment. Reprinted with permission.

ILLUSTRATION 5.2

Nixdorf Computer Ltd. Advertisement

Your company is about to be unceremoniously excluded from the world's richest market.

In 1992, United Europe will represent a $4.1 trillion market, with a consumer population almost as large as that of the U.S. and Japan combined.

American companies, yours included, will be excluded.

Trade barriers within the EEC will come crashing down, giving European companies an "unfair" advantage over U.S. competitors. (It will be almost as easy for Europeans to trade with each other as it is for us to trade goods between states here.)

Most American companies will be unprepared to play on the uneven field. Some, however, are taking advantage of Nixdorf COMET®, one of the world's largest business software libraries. COMET is now available on UNIX®. It is installed in 65,000 systems serving over 250,000 workstations around the globe,

and everywhere in Europe. So Nixdorf customers with COMET and subsidiaries producing goods in Europe can reap the benefits of '92 like Europeans.

Our new Targon Open System now works with COMET. It makes it even easier to tie in the head office with subsidiaries around the globe, while maintaining maximum hardware and software freedom.

Nixdorf is one of the largest and most respected computer companies in Europe. Our commitment to customer support has won us a reputation for service which is second to none. Our experience and know-how extends to hundreds of vertical industries, especially retail and banking, where we are world leaders, and where we have enjoyed a solid and rapidly growing share of market in the United States.

So if your company would like to pass for a European, give us a call. Pick our brains. We'll make you an insider.

We'd like more information on the Best of Both Worlds.
Name: ....
Title: ....
Company: ....
Street: ....
City/State: ....
Telephone: ....
Nixdorf Computer Corporation
80 Main Street, North Reading, MA 01864
Telephone: (508) 664-5781

American ingenuity
and German precision engineering.
The Best of Both Worlds.

NIXDORF
COMPUTER

Note: This advertisement appeared in the May 3, 1989 issue of *Financial Times* (London). It illustrates how this firm is targeting the specific needs of companies operating throughout the European Community. Reprinted with permission.

A. C. NIELSEN
RESEARCH SUPPORT FOR E.C.-1992

The lowering of geographical barriers between member countries within the European Community will have profound implications for the marketing function within firms as has been pointed out throughout this monograph. Demand for pan European marketing support services is also likely to grow as a result. A. C. Nielsen, a major research firm best known for its TV ratings service in the United States, is gearing up to provide precisely the pan European research services that marketers will be looking for in the integrated market. The twelve countries of the European Community have had wide differences in even the way they classify products—for example, lemon flavored Perrier could be classified as a mineral water in France but a soft drink in Italy. (Ad Age, June 5, 1989). Until now, Nielsen subsidiaries in individual E.C. countries would set up their studies according to such country differences and the specific client's needs in a particular country. But with E.C.-1992, Nielsen will seek to provide Europe-wide comparable data to their clients. They will also provide information regarding a client's European market share, which is likely to be increasingly the yardstick of choice to evaluate how well a particular company is doing in the New Europe. Nielsen with 16 offices in Europe is the most international of research firms and is determined to be at the head of the European market research industry which is set for major growth in the years ahead. We asked Bert Kretch, President of Nielsen Worldwide to comment on the marketing research industry in Europe as 1992 approaches and he said, "Nielsen's strength in Europe has traditionally been our responsiveness to the needs of our customers in local country markets. We don't see this going away in the Europe of 1992. Rather, we see this traditional local need particularly with the sales and marketing constituencies being supplemented by additional customer needs for transnational information to support their new emerging management infrastructures. We intend to deliver comprehensive integrated information on both a country-by-country basis as well as on a total European or regional basis."

Adapted from "As world shrinks, Nielsen expands," Advertising Age, June 5, 1989.

ILLUSTRATION 5.3

JWT Europe Advertisement

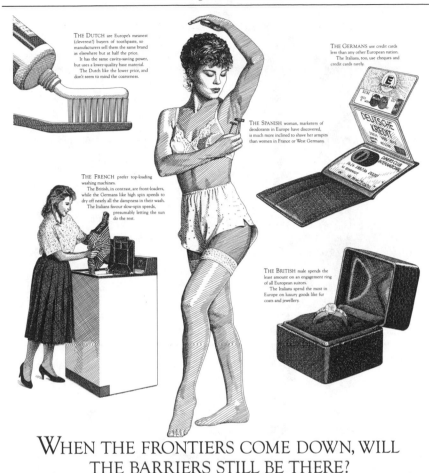

THE DUTCH are Europe's meanest (cleverest?) buyers of toothpaste, so manufacturers sell them the same brand as elsewhere but at half the price.
It has the same cavity-saving power, but uses a lower-quality base material. The Dutch like the lower price, and don't seem to mind the coarseness.

THE GERMANS use credit cards less than any other European nation. The Italians, too, use cheques and credit cards rarely.

THE SPANISH woman, marketers of deodorants in Europe have discovered, is much more inclined to shave her armpits than women in France or West Germany.

THE FRENCH prefer top-loading washing machines.
The British, in contrast, are front-loaders, while the Germans like high spin speeds to dry off nearly all the dampness in their wash. The Italians favour slow-spin speeds, presumably letting the sun do the rest.

THE BRITISH male spends the least amount on an engagement ring of all European suitors.
The Italians spend the most in Europe on luxury goods like fur coats and jewellery.

WHEN THE FRONTIERS COME DOWN, WILL THE BARRIERS STILL BE THERE?

The 'single' European market is going to be a very rich one indeed.

It is estimated it will be worth twice as much as either the US or the Japanese markets.

But it will also be a complex one to sell to for a considerable time to come.

320 million consumers from twelve countries, speaking nine languages, won't suddenly become Europeans on 1st January, 1993.

They will still have their fascinating cultural and psychological differences as peoples (and long may they continue to do so!).

To build successful brands across Europe has always demanded enormous experience and local knowledge. In these 'Jeux sans frontières,' advertisers will really have to know the rules.

It's much easier, for example, to produce pan-European advertising for soft drinks, jeans or a personal stereo – you are often selling a life-style.

Food or cars can be more difficult. Differences in cuisine or climate demand different solutions.

Commercials with too much national humour or dialogue may not travel well.

It will take real skill to know when to translate an advertisement word for word. Or translate the idea or strategy, and allow local executions.

Allow a different campaign for each country. Or even, as technology now permits, to transmit a single commercial across Europe with simultaneous soundtracks in several languages.

Only the best advertising agencies will be able to create strong enough ideas to win through in the 'Eurovision Ad Contest.'

Whether in 1993 or 2093, in order for an advertisement to persuade successfully, it will have to be captivating, disarming, engaging and utterly believable too.

For, when all is said and done, 320 million consumers are still 320 million human beings.

JWT
EUROPE

CONTACT BRIAN JOHNSON, EUROPEAN NEW BUSINESS DIRECTOR, JWT EUROPE, 40 BERKELEY SQUARE, LONDON W1X 6AD. TELEPHONE: 01-629 9496.

Note: This advertisement appeared in the June 1989 issue of *EuroBusiness*. It effectively raises some potential pitfalls for those companies seeking to employ a pan-European advertising approach and suggests how this agency might assist clients in solving the problems. Reprinted with permission.

ILLUSTRATION 5.4

Nielsen Marketing Research Advertisement

Can your product line handle the lure of foreign markets?

The global marketplace is a world of tempting opportunities. And potential snags.

Because in many cases, the line between marketing success and marketing failure is an international border.

Customs, tastes, retail structures and economic conditions vary widely from country to country. Which means that much of what you know to be true may not be true.

That's why you need to know Nielsen. We have offices in 27 countries, each with a native genius for foreign intelligence.

We can tell you which countries hold opportunities for your product.

If you're already there, we can tell you how you're doing, how your competition is doing in each market and much more.

And armed with that information, there's no reason on earth why you can't succeed.

For more information, write Carolyn Huey at Nielsen Marketing Research, Nielsen Plaza, Northbrook, IL 60062, or call 312/498-6300.

We'll show you how to land the big ones.

Nielsen

Nielsen Marketing Research

Note: This advertisement appeared in the June 5, 1989 special section of *Advertising Age* on the European Community. It focuses on this research firm's ability to provide the services it offers in the United States to clients with European Community and other overseas information needs. Reprinted with permission.

Vignettes

CHAPTER 5

CATERPILLAR, INC.: UNIQUELY POSITIONED FOR EC-92

While many U.S. companies, including a few majors, are struggling to choose their best entry strategy for EC-92, one U.S. MNC finds itself with a regional headquarters in Europe and yet, still a bit "outside." When Caterpillar, Inc., the U.S. competitor in the tightly concentrated world earthmoving industry picked Geneva, Switzerland as its European headquarters site, the real importance of EC-92 was only a dream in a few European minds.

Today, Caterpillar could have found itself just as "outside the European Community" as it would have been from its Peoria home, had not it provided itself with a true E.C. presence. To illustrate, the company now has manufacturing facilities in France, Belgium and the U.K., as well as a trans-Europe network of national dealerships. As EC-92 unfolds, the company reportedly plans to consider the desirability of such changes as (1) selling from a single site and (2) some consolidation within its distributor network.

Currently, Caterpillar is accelerating its pace of preparations for EC-92 and has a task force set up to insure that all opportunities related to this new 12-country market are considered. According to Mr. Lawrence Williams, Vice President for European Operations, . . . "we're already very pan European and 1992 will help because of the standardization of products, etc." In particular, Mr. Williams feels that from a marketing perspective the company will need to look at its dealer structure "by region and not by country," and will seek to ". . . optimize its distribution systems." Finally he told us that the company will also be looking for . . . "synergies that relate to manufacturing and especially to common services." While the firm's EC-92 plans are not fully in place, it is evident that this important U.S. capital goods producer is moving aggressively to maintain (and expand) its role in Europe.

L. Williams
Chairman of the Board
Caterpillar Overseas S.A.

TUPPERWARE ESTABLISHES TRADING COMPANY IN *ANTICIPATION OF E.C.-92*

In 1988, Tupperware, a familiar name to both European and U.S. housewives, took steps to better position itself for E.C.-92. First, it created a trading company that allows it to market and plan on a European-wide, rather than on a national basis. Second, this new trading company concept permitted it to restructure its European manufacturing operations, so that its production facilities were specialized by *product* not *national* boundaries.

As noted in its 1988 Annual Report (March 6, 1989):

> Manufacturing operations in Europe also were strengthened during the year with the creation of a trading company. Under the trading company structure, European manufacturing operations have been reorganized so that facilities are specialized by product rather than geographic boundaries. This new organization enables operations to take advantage of longer manufacturing runs and centralized purchasing. It also provides greater product sourcing opportunities worldwide, which will enable Tupperware to benefit from different labor rates in various geographic regions. The trading company will improve the company's competitive position for the advent of a single European market in 1992. Tupperware is currently expanding the trading company to other geographic regions including the Pacific and Latin America.

As an up-date (September 18, 1989), we asked Charles L. Dunlap, Associate General Counsel, Tupperware International, to comment on the use of a trading company approach. He told us:

> "We are of the opinion that our trading company is enabling us to be in the best position as the anticipated changes occur when 1992 becomes a reality in Europe. The European market is very important and U.S. companies must continue to be willing to make changes if they are serious about playing any role in Europe. Operating in Europe is different from operating in other areas of the world. If companies intend to benefit from the anticipated advantages of 1992, the companies must be willing to be responsive to the requirements promulgated by the Europeans and not expect to force the Europeans to accept the ways a company operates in the U.S.
>
> It is anticipated that the impact of our trading company will enable us to respond to three major concerns: first, to effectively deal with local cultural differences in different countries; second, to effectively operate in different areas of the world, such as in the Pan-European arena; and third, to be effective in a global operation as a multi-national operating throughout the world, and not just in Europe.
>
> Europe is a tremendous challenge; however, the benefits make the efforts worthwhile."

Considerable interest has been focused on the extent of demographic and cultural differences/similarities across regions in the European Community. For consumer product marketers, in particular, these differences/similarities will be crucial to their EC-92 entry and marketing strategies. The following article discusses how consumers in the European Community may be clustered along demographic/cultural/geographic/economic dimensions. The article first appeared in the January–February 1989 issue of *Business Horizons* and is included here with permission.

Euro-Consumers in 1992

Sandra Vandermerwe and Marc-André L'Huillier*

The removal of internal trade barriers in the European Community is just three years away, and managers need information so they can begin planning. This article provides it.

Managers worldwide have their eyes on 1992—the year the European Community (EC) will create a single internal market. This important event will affect businesses from East to West. American, Japanese, and European multinationals, with their global marketing and clout, will be able to muscle in on the unified market. Smaller companies will be able to target one Pan-European economy instead of many separate economies, helping to improve their international competitive positions.

To assist managers in understanding the risks and opportunities of a new Europe and the impact the unified market may have on their business strategies, this article takes an analytical look at some key demographics. What emerges is a picture of Euro-Consumers—a potential new market, in a new geographic and economic space, that could grow faster, be more lucrative,

*Sandra Vandermerwe is director of the MBA program and a senior faculty member in international marketing and services at the International Management Institute, Geneva. Marc-André L'Huillier is the president of CartaGen DemoGraphics SA, also in Geneva.

and possibly become more stable in some respects than the United States and Japan.

We say "could" because there are at least three possible scenarios for the EC, depending on the actions of the European Free Trade Association (EFTA) in the next decade. In our analysis we've tried to accommodate all of these possibilities:

The EC's size could remain at 12 member countries: Belgium, Denmark, France, Germany, Greece, Italy, Ireland, Luxembourg, the Netherlands, Portugal, Spain, and the UK (EC-12).

The EC could expand, probably by 1995 at the earliest, with the inclusion of Austria, Norway, and Sweden (EC-15).

By the year 2000 Iceland, Finland, and Switzerland could join, expanding the market still further (EC-18).

THE MARKET: LARGE AND DYNAMIC

Size is one important indicator of market potential, and with the scrapping of physical, technical, and fiscal barriers, the whole EC picture will change in this respect. From a market in which each country consists of relatively small numbers of customers, Europe will convert itself into a single market, the largest in the industrialized world. In fact, by 1990 this new market will be 30 percent larger than the U.S. and almost three times the size of Japan. As Figure 1 indicates, in 1990 the 12-member EC will consist of 325 million Euro-Consumers; the U.S. will have 249 million people and Japan 123 million.

If the EC remains at 12 countries, it will be the largest of the three markets in terms of consumer numbers. But the growth in population will be slower than in the U.S. or Japan. Half a million Euro-Consumers will be added to the market each year until 2000, an increase of 1.6 percent over the decade. By contrast, the U.S. market will grow at a 5.5 percent rate and the Japanese market will grow at a 4 percent rate.

If, as our second scenario suggests, the EC has grown from 12 to 15 countries by 1995, the number of potential consumers would rise to 348 million, compared to only 256 million in the U.S. and 126 million in Japan. This scenario shows that over the next decade consumer growth in the EC would go from a 1.6 percent rate to one of 7.8 percent. A jump to 18 countries, the third scenario, would make the market 362 million strong in 2000, compared to 262 million people in America and 129 million in Japan, and force a growth rate of 11.5 percent. In this scenario, by the year 2000 there will be 100 million more consumers in the EC than in the U.S.

AGE: EVENLY DISTRIBUTED

With or without EFTA, age groups will be more evenly distributed in the EC than in Japan or the U.S. In other words, gaps between generations will

FIGURE 1

The Population of the European Community, the United States and Japan in 1990, 1995 and 2000

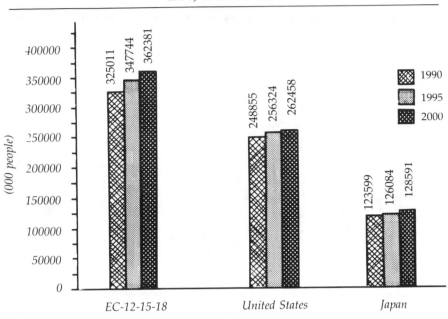

Source: World Bank. 1987–88 World Population Projections (000 people).

be smaller (see Figure 2). The difference between two generations of Americans will vary by as much as 91.5 percent in 1990. In Japan this difference will be as high as 82.4 percent. In the EC, however, the largest difference will be only 31.8 percent.

This even distribution of age groups makes the EC a more stable market than the U.S. and Japan. Between 1990 and 2000, as Euro-Consumers get older and move from one age group to another, the total number and proportion of people in each age category will change less dramatically than in the U.S. and Japan. Thus corporations aiming at Euro-Consumers will have to do considerably less adapting to an aging population than they may need to for the U.S. or Japan.

Companies will, however, be faced with the same opportunities and challenges an older population brings. The EC is no exception to the industrialized world's aging market phenomenon. In line with trends in the U.S. and Japan, more than 30 percent of the market will be 50 or older. Another 30 percent will be in their thirties and forties, around 15 percent will be in their

154

FIGURE 2

Population by Age Group, 1990–2000

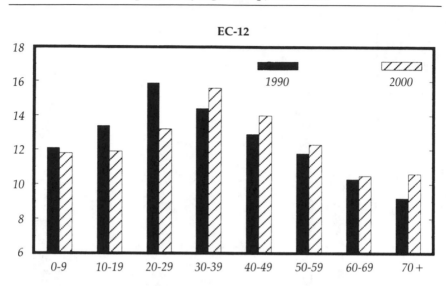

EC-12

The percentages for the EC-18 scenario are almost exactly the same as those for the EC-12 scenario.

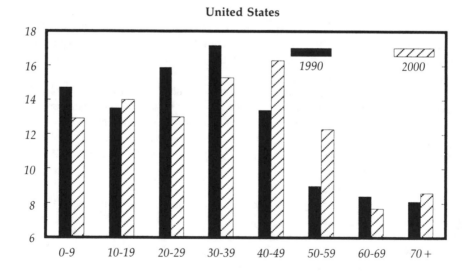

United States

FIGURE 2 (Cont'd)

Japan

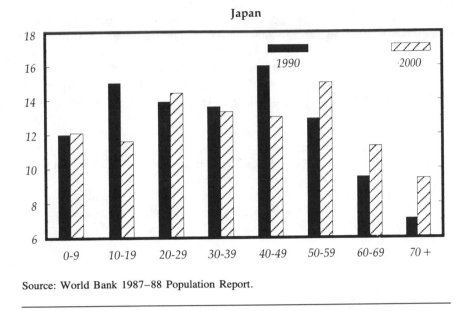

Source: World Bank 1987–88 Population Report.

twenties, 14 percent will be 10–19, and 13 percent will be under 9 years old.

THE RICHEST MARKET

A big market in itself is not as attractive as one that is large and wealthy. Indeed, one of the most interesting aspects of marketing in the EC is that the market will be both large *and* rich.

The latest 1987 estimate for the 12-member European Community is a GDP[1] of $4,263.7 billion at current prices and exchange rates. This figure is four times the GDP for Germany, Europe's richest country. It is slightly below the $4,436.2 billion GDP of the United States and well above Japan's $2,379.3 billion.

If the U.S. dollar stays as low as predicted, in 1988 the EC will be a richer market than the United States. If Austria, Norway, and Sweden join the EC, its GDP will be 11 percent higher than that of the U.S. and nearly twice that of Japan. Add Iceland, Finland, and Switzerland to the equation and Euro-Consumers wind up with 17 percent more wealth than Americans and twice as much as the Japanese.

156

This is the macro picture. The average Euro-Consumer's purchasing power is, however, less than that of the average American or Japanese consumer. GDP per capita in the EC averaged $13,208 in 1987, as opposed to $18,225 in the U.S. and $19,510 in Japan. And Euro-Consumers spent 40 percent and 30 percent less on average than did American and Japanese consumers. All of this may change, of course, if after 1992 Europe indeed becomes more prosperous, and consumers begin to earn and spend more.

Let's examine in more detail what age groups will own the wealth. Figure 3 shows the expected distribution of income in 1990 for the various Euro-Consumer age groups. As the generations move on, the proportion of income they own is likely to move with them. Because of their population size, the American and European markets will continue to be twice as rich in overall dollar terms as the Japanese market up to the year 2000. But their wealth will be distributed somewhat differently.

The 30–50 age group in both the U.S. and the EC will have more money. In the U.S. these people will own 55 percent of total income; in the EC their share will be 43 percent. People 60 and over in the EC will have more

FIGURE 3

Population and Income by Age Group in 1990

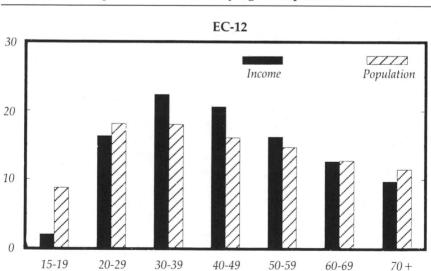

Percentages refer to those aged 15 and older and do no correspond to those in Figure 2. Percentages for EC-15 and EC-18 scenarios are almost exactly the same as those for the EC-12 scenario.

FIGURE 3 (Cont'd)

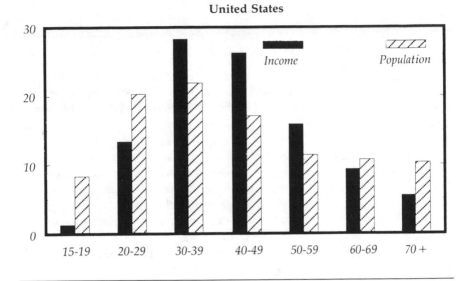

United States

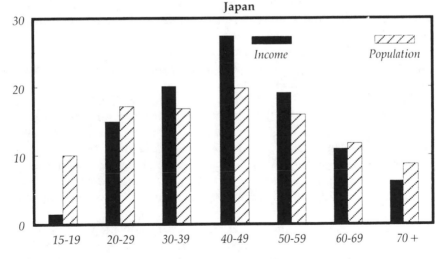

Japan

Source: CartaGen DemoGraphics, Geneva, Switzerland.
Percentages refer to those aged 15 and older and do not correspond to those in Figure 2.
Percentages for EC-15 and EC-18 scenarios are amost exactly the same as those for the EC-12 scenario.

to spend than their counterparts in America. In Japan, the richest group will be those consumers 40–49, whereas in the U.S. and the EC it will be those between 30–39. Looking at per capita incomes, in all three markets consumers between 40–49 will be the richest.

A SINGLE BUT COMPLEX MARKET

As large as it will be, and as wealthy, the EC market only begins to make sense to marketers as a single and unified concept if we can assume that sufficient numbers of Euro-Consumers will be reasonably homogeneous in their purchasing behavior.

It is almost impossible to make a blanket statement about this behavior, as so much will depend on the product and market segment. But what we can say is that, like every other group in the world, Euro-Consumers are likely to become more similar in their needs for products and services. The blending of tastes, lifestyles, and purchasing behavior will inevitably accelerate, especially if we consider trends in electronic media and information technology.

As a result, we expect an increased attraction to global brands and products. Euro-Consumers are also likely to show preference for Pan-European goods and services over local alternatives. More mobile in their purchasing, they will shop in different countries rather than being locally bound. With growing economies, increased competition, and the consequent downward pressure on prices, Euro-Consumers will expect and get better quality at lower and uniform Europe-wide prices.

But the arrival of 1992 will *not* erase all the national aspects of purchasing behavior. In fact, if we coldly consider the statistics, there are quite significant disparities among the EC countries—especially compared to the disparities among the 50 American States and among the 47 Japanese prefectures. For example, in 1985 the population of Germany—Europe's largest country—was 165 times larger than that of Luxembourg—Europe's smallest country. Its most-populated region, southeastern England, was 151 times larger than Italy's Valle d'Aosta, the least-populated region. In contrast, the least populous state in America, Wyoming, was 52 times smaller than California, the most populous state. In Japan, the ratio between Tokyo, the largest prefecture, and Tottori, the smallest, was 19 to 1.

Income disparities highlight the degree of regional diversity. The per capita GDP of the EC's richest members, the Danes, in 1986 was 5.4 times that of the Portuguese. In that year per capita income in Connecticut was only 75 percent higher than that in West Virginia; in 1983 Tokyo, Japan's richest prefecture, had a GDP per capita 2.8 times larger than did Okinawa, the poorest.

The intriguing question about the EC, then, is this: to what extent will it be a "common," homogeneous mass market? How many of its diverse individual and complex characteristics will it retain?

NEW EURO-CONSUMER CLUSTERS

Instead of one homogeneous mass market or a collection of small specialized markets, the most likely outcome is that new Euro-Consumer clusters will emerge, formed by consumers close to each other geographically but not necessarily living in the same country. These new clusters will have similar demographic and economic characteristics cutting across cultural and national boundaries, and they will display similar needs and purchasing behavior.

There are several ways to cluster Euro-Consumers, depending on the market or product. Each company will have to take its own circumstances into consideration. In Figure 4 we have used the basic cultural, geographic, demographic, and economic variables to define six main Euro-Consumer clusters.[2] This map serves as a good starting point, although managers may need or want a more sophisticated approach. The clusters and their characteristics are as follows:

Cluster 1: UK and Ireland

- Northeastern Europe
- Average income ($11,450)
- Age profile average of EC
- Common language (English)

Cluster 2: Central and Northern France, Southern Belgium, Central Germany, and Luxembourg

- Central Europe
- Average income ($15,470)
- Low proportion of middle-aged people and high proportion of older people
- French and German languages

Cluster 3: Spain and Portugal

- Southwestern Europe
- Young population
- Lower than average income ($6,530)
- Spanish and Portuguese languages

Cluster 4: Southern Germany, Northern Italy, Southeastern France (and Austria if it joins)

- Central Europe
- High proportion of middle-aged people

FIGURE 4

The Six Clusters and their Population (1990, in 000's of people)

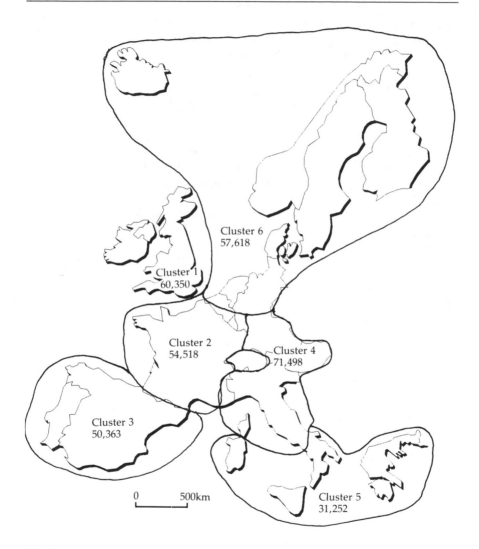

If Switzerland were to join the EC, she would be included in Cluster 6.

Source: World Bank and CartaGen DemoGraphics

- Higher than average income ($16,740)
- German, French, and Italian languages

Cluster 5: Greece and Southern Italy

- Southeastern Europe
- Lower than average income ($7,610)
- Young population
- Greek and Italian languages

Cluster 6: Denmark, Northern Germany, The Netherlands, and Northern Belgium (and Switzerland, Iceland, Sweden, Norway, Finland if they join)

- Northern Europe and Switzerland
- Very high income ($19,420)
- High proportion of middle-aged people
- Multilingual: Scandinavian, French, Italian, and German Languages

All six consumer clusters transcend national boundaries, reinforcing the claim that consumers living in different countries have similar characteristics. In some cases—Cluster 4, for example—consumers from different countries are closer in profile to each other than they are to consumers in their own country.

These clusters are only a starting point. Within each there are segments that share life-styles and specific psychographic needs. The clusters do indicate, however, an important change in market configuration. Managers working in those markets will need a fresh marketing approach. Rather than tackling each country or market separately, they will be able to tap large cross-cultural Euro-Consumer clusters. This will necessitate an adjustment in their marketing and operating strategies, from market segmentation and product planning to distribution and logistic network decisions.

NEW GEOGRAPHIC, DEMOGRAPHIC, AND ECONOMIC CENTERS

Until now each European country's capital and economic centers were the gateways to its markets. For example, Milan and Rome were the keys to Italian business and customers. With doors now open between member countries, the official key to individual markets will become less relevant and less obvious.

The market will be contained in a very different geographic and economic space. This could, as figure 5 shows, create new geographic, demographic, and economic centers and influence how and where companies do business in Europe.[3]

FIGURE 5

Europe's new centers

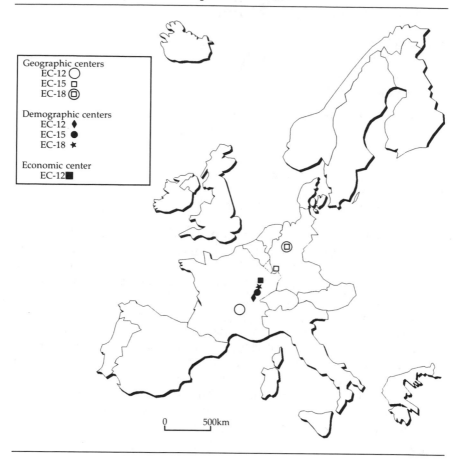

The geographic center of a 12-member EC will be near the city of Issoire, South of Clermont-Ferrand in the French Auvergne region. With the inclusion of Austria, Norway, and Sweden, the center would move 520 kilometers north—near the village of Consdorf in Eastern Luxembourg. If Finland, Switzerland, and Iceland join the EC, the center would move another 220 kilometers to the northeast, to near the village of Bigge, east of Dortmund in Germany's Arnsberg region.

Probably more significant is that the demographic center of the EC will be near the village of Arnay-le-Duc, 45 kilometers from Dijon in the French

Bourgogne region. If Europeans were to follow the Americans, who chose Washington, D.C. because of its central location at the time, Dijon could become the capital of a United States of Europe! In the event of a 15-member EC the demographic center would move even closer to Dijon, near the village of Moloy, and with 18 countries it would move to the village of Longeau, north of Dijon.

Northern European countries tend to be richer than their Southern neighbors. For instance, Denmark, Germany, and the Benelux states will have 27.8 percent of Europe's population but 35.2 percent of its GDP in 1990. The economic center will therefore be north of the demographic center, closer to the German border. Specifically, it will be near the village of Bologne in the French Champagne Ardennes region, about 100 kilometers north of Dijon.

As regulatory barriers within the EC crumble, firms (both inside and outside Europe) are making plans to seize new opportunities from what will become one of the largest, most stable, and wealthiest markets in the world. Managers need a new picture of this market; we have tried to provide it in this article. We have also compared the market's key attributes to those of the U.S. and Japan to give managers a global perspective. Although some multinationals have treated Europe as one market for some time, most corporations have had to deal with a collection of small markets bound by local technical and legal regulations. We emphasize the decreasing significance of national borders in devising strategies for the new, undivided market.

Each company must determine to what degree it can regard the expanded market as one entity. In line with global trends, we believe Euro-Consumers in general will continue to become more homogeneous. But the markets for some products and services will remain complex and local for some time.

The point is that managers at different companies must cut the market differently. Rather than look for one mass market or for consumers who fit old purchasing molds, they need to identify clusters of Euro-Consumers and adjust their strategies and operations to cater to these new groups.

There will be plenty of room for specialized niching. However, with advanced manufacturing and technology, managers will find it increasingly feasible to combine mass market strategies with customization.

Euro-Consumers will live in a new economic and demographic space. In fact, managers may have to redraw the map of Europe and design corporations around new strategic centers. In this way, they will be able to structure their organizations to take advantage of a unified Europe.

The integration of Europe is a complicated process and the implications of 1992 are not readily apparent. What we do know, though, is that Euro-Consumers will be a new and vital market and a great marketing challenge for the 90s.

REFERENCES

1. Gross Domestic Product expressed in current U.S. dollars gives a good estimate of a country's or region's purchasing power in the international market.
2. Five variables: cultural (language), geographic (latitude and longitude), demographic (age groups), and economic (income) were used to group the 173 EC-18 regions into six clusters using cluster analysis.
3. Centrographic analysis was used to measure centrality. Europe's centers of gravity were found by assigning x and y coordinates to each region of the EC. These two coordinates were then weighted according to the area, population, or GDP of the region.

The following article provides the views of a leading corporate consultant on the steps American firms must take to position themselves for operating in post-1992 Europe. Suggestions are made about strategy options available to four types of firms ranging from those that have no experience in Europe, including exporting, to U.S. based multinationals with well established operations in several European countries.

1992: MOVES AMERICANS MUST MAKE

by John F. Magee

Over the next few years, American companies, whether they are active in Europe today or not, will need to take constructive, thoughtful action to defend themselves against more aggressive competition from European companies and to exploit the opportunities an integrated European market has to offer.

Postwar Europe, composed of insular, protected national markets, has been stagnant economically compared with the United States and the Far East. European companies have lacked a home market of sufficient size to support the investments necessary to compete with aggressive Japanese and American competitors in what are clearly the industries of the future—electronics, information technology, biotechnology, and telecommunications. Indeed, the fragmentation of the European marketplace, with its multiplicity of regulations, economic conditions, cultural preferences, tensions, and jealousies, has made doing business in Europe a humbling experience.

Today there is a real possibility that this fragmented, chauvinistic Europe

John F. Magee is chairman of the board of directors of Arthur D. Little, Inc. Over the past three decades, his professional consulting assignments have taken him to Europe frequently.

may disappear and a dynamic, integrated market grow in its place. This development is projected to be good for Europe, and indeed many observers predict it will be good for the global economy. A renewed European economy, however, is also a real threat to those American and other non-European businesses that fail to react quickly and flexibly to a change as potentially profound—economically—as any in European history.

The need to free the European economy from self-imposed regulatory constraints has been seized by political leaders of the European economy as the rationale for a renewed push toward the post-World War II vision of a "common market." The Commission of the European Community issued its White Paper, *Completing the Internal Market,* in 1985. This document, the Commission's manifesto, called for the creation of a single market for products, services, finances, and labor in the 12-nation European Community by the end of 1992.

The force of the Commission's program—known as EC'92—has been reinforced by the enactment of the Single European Act, ratified by the parliaments of all EC member states and effective July 1, 1987. The act commits the member states to the target date of December 31, 1992 to complete the internal market, confirmed in the act as "an area without internal frontiers in which the free movement of goods, persons, services, and capital is ensured. . . ."

The year 1992 has thus come to symbolize the transformation of the European economy, though in fact it is the *program* called EC'92 that matters, not the somewhat arbitrary date. For that matter, no sudden, miraculous metamorphosis is likely to occur. There is confusion and disagreement among Europeans as to the exact scope and nature of the changes they want.

To achieve the vision of an integrated Europe, EC member states will have to transfer important elements of their national sovereignty to the EC as a whole. Never before have 12 nations voluntarily relinquished so much of their freedom to act independently, and doubts about the success of this transfer of power have raised important questions about the success of the entire experiment. No wonder so many American business executives are a bit puzzled by EC'92. Those with whom I have spoken ask questions like these: Will the single market be achieved? How long can we afford to wait to see how the European market will evolve? How will EC'92 affect particular industries and businesses? *No one* knows exactly what to expect. Yet the change is under way. Non-European companies must begin to act now, and they must act with continuing vigilance. The vision that Europeans hold for Europe is conflicted, so the form the single market will take is uncertain and the precise outlines of the future European business environment are still dim. But the energy and reality of substantial change are irrefutable. European companies know it and are acting on it; European business and political leaders are forcing the pace. If the outcome is anywhere near as radical as some Europeans hope, the American eagle and the so-called Asian dragons are about to meet a kind of European wolf pack.

The forces driving change in Europe are specific to each industry, and effective responses need to be specific to each company. The stongest forces—global in character but still industry specific—relate to changing markets, competition, and technology. Political forces are also at work. Some of these are responses to international pressures—for example, the need to create a home market large enough to permit the huge R&D investments necessary for global competition in new technologies. Other political pressures reflect the desire of specially protected groups to maintain their privileged positions—the trucking industry in Germany, for example. Still others come from social and environmental groups that want to use unification to extend improved social benefits and better environmental protection throughout the Community. All these forces will have their effect on the roughly 300 directives the European Commission expects to issue before the 1992 target date. Those directives, together with the decisions of the European Court of Justice, will shape the business environment for every company doing business in Europe.

Let me examine the probable impact of 1992 on American businesses by looking at the opportunities and potential threats it poses to four types of companies.

Company A is a U.S.-based multinational with well-established manufacturing and distribution operations in several European countries. Heinz, Johnson & Johnson, and several other makers of packaged consumer goods are companies of this kind.

Company B is a U.S. business with operations in one European country, perhaps as the result of an opportunistic acquisition, possibly in a protected local market such as medical supplies.

Company C exports manufactured goods to EC countries from an offshore location, in this case the United States.

Company D is part of an industry that has not actively exported to EC countries, either because the European markets were too fragmented or because their domestic producers were too well protected. Telecommunications equipment and truck components are two such industries.

COMPANY A: THE ESTABLISHED MULTINATIONAL

U.S. companies with broad bases in Europe face three challenges:

1. Learning to exploit the opportunities for improved productivity that lower regulatory barriers will bring. These opportunities include greater efficiencies of production and distribution, simplified organizations with lower costs, and more coherent marketing.

2. Meeting the challenge of European competitors—many of them local companies but some of them other multinationals—who are moving aggressively to consolidate and rationalize.
3. Dealing with customers, whether retail merchants or industrial manufacturers, who are themselves expanding, merging, and rationalizing in order to increase the efficiency of their own purchasing and marketing.

Addressing these challenges with an established, or even entrenched, organization will be difficult.

I have watched American companies in Europe go through cycles of development and maturity. When the Common Market was established by the Treaty of Rome in 1957, many American businesses rather naively assumed that Europe would become a relatively integrated marketplace like the United States. They tried to choose manufacturing locations and set up distribution networks much as they might have done in the United States—to serve a common market. They were disappointed to discover that Europe was not one market but many, with subtle and not-so-subtle barriers to multinational trade: regulations, transport barriers, national tastes, and cultural prejudices, to mention just a few.

As these companies grew in size and sophistication, most of them evolved into groups of unrelated national subsidiaries, each serving its own local market. Coordination—in manufacturing, marketing, logistics, or even finance—has been limited or nonexistent. This drift away from the notion of an integrated market was partly a reaction to European realities and partly a result of the kinds of acquisitions many U.S. companies made as a means of expanding. Local pressures called for local strategies. There was simply no incentive to struggle for a unified European structure.

So I'm intrigued to hear Europeans say that the American multinationals are ahead of European companies in making plans for the single European market. This mistaken impression seems to stem from two misapprehensions. First, that Americans still think of Europe as an entity, and so the idea of a single European market comes naturally to them. Second, that the presence of a U.S. multinational in several European countries presumes a pan-European business strategy. In my observation, Americans got over the pan-Europe misconception some time ago, and they are only now beginning to develop a European strategy, or even to move toward the formation of organizations *capable* of creating a European strategy.

It was only in the fall of 1988 that Coca-Cola announced a reorganization of its European, African, and Middle Eastern management to form a new focused team with responsibility for the European Community. Colgate-Palmolive, with manufacturing operations in nine EC countries, just recently appointed a pan-European management board. Heinz, probably one of the more European of U.S. companies, proclaimed in its annual report for 1988: "The potential for an integrated European market engages the Heinz imagination." Even IBM, considered by many Europeans the prototypical pan-European corporation, may have to develop a Europe-wide marketing program by industry to complement its nationally oriented sales organizations.

For the multinationals, the integrated European market is an opportunity. For example, the European Economic Interest Grouping is a new legal form that will facilitate the operation of a network of national subsidiaries as a single coherent business. An EEIG is not a "European company" or a form of joint venture. It is a contractual association—operating under the laws of one designated home country—that provides for the allocation of revenues and profits among association members in accordance with the terms they themselves lay down in the contract. The concept was first employed in the Airbus consortium, the Euromissile project; and the Carte Bleu banking system, and can greatly simplify the problems of operating a coordinated business in a variety of tax and legal jurisdictions. An EEIG formed by common subsidiaries of a single parent, each established in individual member states, can be used to coordinate and integrate the activities of the group.

In combination with new technologies and improved transportation, reduced barriers to trade can improve production, simplify logistics, and cut costs. The introduction of aseptic packaging systems, for instance, will increase shelf life and allow products to be shipped over greater distances. In itself, this development would mean very little, but in combination with the elimination of many regulatory barriers it permits consolidated production. For example, a large yogurt supplier with plants in France, where its product is not pasteurized today, and in the low countries where it is pasteurized, expects to centralize production in one place to serve both markets. Either product is now acceptable in both countries under the principle of "mutual recognition," which provides that—absent compelling health and safety risks— products manufactured in compliance with the standards of one EC country must be accepted for sale in every other EC country. The yogurt manufacturer has developed a common product and production process to supply both markets and the rest of the European Community as well.

Reduced barriers to information flow and the physical movement of goods reinforce the effects of reduced regulatory barriers. The battle over truck transportation is not over, but introduction of the so-called single administrative document has already simplified paperwork at border crossings and so drastically cut the time, and thus the cost, of moving products between countries. The European Commission is also committed to a Community-wide integrated telecommunications network. Better telecommunications will help make it possible to operate a network of production and distribution facilities as a single logistical system. It will also certainly have an effect on location decisions. In banking, for example, the processing operations necessary to support mass retail banking services will be centralized in low-cost locations, just as they have been in the United States.

Another example is Bayer, the German chemical company, which now produces chemicals in several EC countries. For years, Bayer has manufactured products in Spain, but only for the Spanish market. Now it plans to expand production in Spain for export to the rest of the EC. Foreign investment in Spain is already growing to take advantage of a skilled younger population with lower social costs and restraints, while in West Germany there has been a net loss of industrial investment since 1987. I expect a gradual shift of labor-intensive industry to southern Europe, and I think the odds favor a concentration in the northern countries of services and high value-added specialties, a movement similar to the migration of U.S. industry in the 1950s, 1960s, and 1970s. American companies too should think about the effect of an integrated European market on plant locations.

Skeptics point out that custom and local taste will inhibit the integration of markets. They are right to some extent. Customers in different European countries have shown distinctly different preferences in the design of appliances, for example. So some argue it is better to be dominant in one country than to have a comparable total volume consisting of a small share of national markets all across Europe, since the latter is clearly more expensive to maintain.

But it is dangerous to overestimate the force of local preference. I recall European friends arguing years ago that Europeans would not accept Coca-Cola, which later became the dominant soft-drink supplier throughout Europe. The forces pushing for pan-European markets—even in food products—are powerful. Many new products are introduced to children, whose preferences are less well defined than those of their parents. Travel is creating ethnic exchange in tastes. And new product concepts spread readily where local preferences are not established; examples include fast-food restaurants and instant (microwave) foods. Antoine Riboud, chairman of the French manufacturer B.S.N., summarized the evolution of European tastes succinctly: "My grandfather was local, my father was national, and I have to become European. . . . It is no longer true that you can remain local and survive."

COMPANY B: THE CORPORATION WITH ONE EUROPEAN SUBSIDIARY

An American company with a position in one local European market faces pretty much the same challenges that face most European businesses, especially the moderate-sized, private companies that dominate an economy like Germany's. The American subsidiary may have greater financial and technical resources than its locally owned counterparts, but the risks and the choices are similar.

The first risk is that when technical and regulatory barriers fall, multi-national players will very likely make use of their production and logistical economies and their stronger research and development capabilities to move into local markets and push aside the established local company. The second risk is that the mutual recognition of standards mandated by EC regulations may eliminate a company's protected niche.

Like its European counterparts, an American-owned subsidiary faced with these risks has several choices: expand, through acquisition or merger; form a strategic alliance such as joint venture or cooperation agreement; rationalize by turning a diversified local company into a focused multinational company; or sell out and withdraw.

Expansion, whether it occurs through acquisition or merger, necessarily involves a major commitment of capital and management effort. To judge by their tactics, European companies seem to differ sharply in their view of whether future competition will take place between strong pan-European companies or between strong national economies. While some concerns are pursuing a strategy of expansion across Europe, others are entering into expansionary mergers in order to consolidate local positions and defend their home turf. The banking industry provides examples of both approaches: Deutsche Bank has acquired the Italian branches of BankAmerica in order to penetrate the Italian middle market. On the other hand, the four principal Spanish banks have consolidated into two, the better to defend themselves against encroachment by the likes of Deutsche Bank. We can see both approaches in the insurance industry as well. The French government has authorized two of the largest French companies to merge, while the French Compagnie du Midi has purchased Equity & Law Life Assurance Society in Britain.

For the American concern that chooses acquisition, moderate-sized European companies do appear to be available for purchase. Lacking the resources to invest in the technology or marketing campaigns' that would enable them to compete on a European scale, many privately owned businesses have been put on the block. But the best expansion route to follow depends on the nature of a company's products and market. Despite the reduction of regulatory and technical barriers, traditional business ties may remain. In telecommunications, for example, the sale of traditional gear to national companies will stay under the strong influence of established commercial ties. The sale of equipment and software for new services such as automatic directory systems will be free of this type of constraint, as will the market for customer on-site equipment. In general, the greater the growth potential and the weaker the ties between supplier and customer, the greater the opportunity to expand outward into a multinational position.

A second approach open to the American company with a European subsidiary is to seek an alliance with some company in a related industry for joint R & D or cross-marketing of products. London's Hambros Bank is building a network of relationships with continental banks to extend its service market throughout Europe.

B.V. Safari, a Dutch manufacturer of dried animal foods, and Continentale de Conserves, a French maker of canned pet foods, have announced a wide-ranging agreement that illustrates well what alliances can accomplish. The two companies have roughly equal sales. Each will take one-third equity interest in the other. Each will have an exclusive right to market the product of both companies in it's own country. They will run a joint research and development unit and will form a jointly owned marketing company to sell the products of both companies in the rest of the EC.

A third approach is rationalization. Companies with diversified positions in a single country have the option of consolidating their activities to gain European scale in a more focused product line. For example, the British company Imperial Chemical Industries exchanged its polyethylene division for the polyvinyl chloride division of British Petroleum. ICI then joined its combined polyvinyl chloride business with that of the Italian company Enichem to create a business scaled for the global market. The Spanish petroleum products company CEPSA sold its carbon plant and tanker fleet to free up assets to build its petroleum distribution capability. Sanofi, a French company, sold positions in sectors like food products, where it was not sigicant, in order to focus on niches like food additives and cosmetics where it could be strong not just in Europe but in the world market.

A final option, of course, is to divest. Divestiture is a difficult decision for many companies to make, but it is preferable to the slow death that can result from failing to commit the resources needed to transform a local position to a European scale. BankAmerica made this choice in selling its Italian subsidiary. The rash of leveraged buyouts in the United States may generate a group of companies too heavily leveraged to invest in the potential of their European subsidiaries and too cash poor to ignore the value of those subsidiaries in an active seller's market.

COMPANY C: THE BUSINESS THAT EXPORTS TO EUROPE

U.S. companies that export to Europe have primarily two things to worry about: Will strengthening European competition aggravate the problems of maintaining market share from an overseas base. Will European protectionism crowd out offshore manufacturers?

As to the first set of problems, the issues and options facing a U.S. exporter to the EC are much the same ones facing Company B, with one

European subsidiary. Competition will intensify, European competitors will grow stronger, and the road to survival may involve acquisitions or new strategic alliances. U.S. exporters may also find their EC distributors consolidating or going into active competition with one another. Finally, unlike Company B, whose subsidiary is making its products within the EC, the U.S. exporter will enjoy none of the benefits of mutual recognition—the principle that products manufactured to acceptable standards in any one EC country can be sold in all. In other words, an exporter to the EC will not find Europe to be the same unified market that is available to a European-based competitor.

The second set of fears is generally grouped under the rubric "Fortress Europe"—the threat that a unified European Community will impose new constraints on importers. The threat of "Fortress Europe" is ambiguous and highly industry specific. It bears close examination.

One result of EC'92 could certainly be increased protectionism by the EC as a whole. Some observers firmly predict this result. As weaker member states seek to offset the loss of internal EC quotas or subsidies, they may argue for limits on competition from outside. At the same time, as EC members realize the size and power of the market they seek to create—in some cases at substantial pain to themselves—we can expect them to demand concessions from outsiders who want entry to the new European opportunity.

The European Community has already begun to articulate a so-called principle of reciprocity, which provides, in general, that the EC will give access to foreign suppliers on the same terms that the foreign country gives access to EC companies in the same industry. But exactly what this means is not yet clear.

Banking provides a typically muddled example. The generally accepted interpretations of reciprocity implies that for a foreign bank to operate in any EC nation, the bank's home country must provide access on the same terms to banks from all EC members. One big unanswered question has to do with differing regulations inside and outside the European Community. In Europe, for example, banks have substantially broader investment banking powers than they have in the United States. Does reciprocity imply that for U.S. banks to operate in European markets with full competitive powers European banks must have the same broad powers in the United States? Or does it simply require that European banks be free to operate in the United States with the same powers as their American competitors? The issue has not been decided, and dozens of similar questions in other industries remain to be resolved.

Some Europeans would like reciprocity to mean that if any one member state believes its suppliers are discriminated against by a foreign country, then the EC as a whole will take collective action. Conceivably, the reciprocity principle could even be used to limit access to the European market by a foreign-owned company located within the EC. This might result, for example, from a conclusion by the Commission that the parent's home country was limiting the ability of EC-based businesses to operate freely in its market. "Reciprocity" today remains a potential weapon for trade retaliation.

The European Commission and European political leadership intend to use the single market to support development of critical industries in the EC. The Community is clearly not willing to form a unified market to be exploited from abroad, as has happened in some U.S. industries. We can expect the Commission to search for ways to pursue the goal of Europe for Europeans.

High-definition television illustrates the commitment and some of the problems. The Japanese are probably closer than the Europeans to a workable HDTV technology, so Europe is intent on adopting standards that will exclude Japanese broadcast and receiver products. Will it work? Japanese manufacturers are pushing ahead with their own systems and products. By the time the European broadcasters agree on standards, the Japanese may well have developed technology that can be adapted to whatever standards the Europeans eventually adopt, which is what happened with conventional TV. Then too European suppliers of HDTV equipment may be forced to seek product sources in the Far East as a result of the loss of essential technical skills, like optics, to foreign competition over the last two decades.

Telecommunications is another area of concern for foreign manufacturers. The European Commission is obviously committed to a European telecommunications industry, which it sees as essential to the growth of key service industries like finance. Moreover, telecommunications looks like a growth industry. (European per capita investment in telecommunications is substantially below U.S. levels.) The Commission has no intention of letting foreign businesses crowd out European suppliers, regardless of economics. The draft EC directive on telecommunications procurement proposes not only that bids be rejected unless 50% of their value is derived from EC sources but that EC companies be preferred anyway, even if the 50% condition is met.

Clearly, U.S. exporters should take the prospect of self-interested protectionism seriously. Representatives of the EC such as Lord Cockfield, Willy de Clercq, and Andreas van Agt have been blunt: the benefits of EC'92 will be available to companies of nonmember countries only if they provide reciprocal opportunities. American exporters should begin now to plan and implement a strategy for maintaining access to the European single market.

Other than continuing with business as usual, there are three alternatives for such companies to consider.

1. A European branch. Remember that the EC may not accord local status to a business that simply assembles or packages imported components,

176

a concept it refers to disdainfully as a "screwdriver factory." France even objects to classifying British-built Nissans as European because they meet only the British standard of 50% local content rather than the French standard of 80%.

2. Selective acquisition. Hughes Aircraft, a unit of General Motors, agreed in April 1988 to buy Rediffusion Simulation in Britain as a way of gaining a secure position in the European market for military flight simulators.
3. Strategic alliance. In August 1988, Whirlpool formed a joint venture in appliances with Philips that will have an immediate 10% share of Europe's major appliance market and help Whirlpool compete in the Europe of the future.

COMPANY D: THE BUSINESS WITH NO INTEREST IN EUROPE

The message here is simple: Watch out!

Most businesses today compete globally for markets, technology, finances, or people. The thrust of the single market movement called EC'92 is to build a market base on which European companies can supply Europe with world-class products and from which they can compete globally with U.S., Japanese, and other competitors. U.S. companies that have focused exclusively—and sometimes quite comfortably—on their own home markets may suddenly discover aggressive competition from European corporations. Companies like GEC, Siemens, and Philips have already declared their intentions.

At the same time, EC'92 also offers opportunities for companies that have previously found Europe too fragmented to be interesting. The reduction of technical barriers and the consolidation of European companies will create new markets and customers with sufficient potential to attract American and Asian interests. In some industries, U.S. companies already have a hand up on the competition. For example, the deregulation of U.S. trucking and telecommunications has given American businesses several years' experience with innovative product and service concepts—experience that their European counterparts lack.

Some managers of U.S. companies in Europe hope secretly that EC'92 will not amount to much. They prefer the status quo and have allowed that preference to affect their thinking. The attitude of many American managers in Europe is nevertheless what one British acquaintance of mine calls "struthious." The word means ostrichlike. In his opinion, some of his colleagues in American-based companies have their heads buried firmly in the sand.

Europe is launched on a course of economic—and perhaps political—unification that will have profound implications. What the outcome will be and how long it will take are not yet clear. What is clear is that Europe has the makings of the world's largest integrated market, with buoyant growth potential, and that Europeans have shown a commitment to manage this potential for the benefit of Europe. By the time some struthious non-European companies pull their heads out of the sand and clarify their vision, they are likely to find strategic alliances already formed, regulations established, market access closed, and powerful new competitors in place.

6

Looking to the Future:
Some Alternative Scenarios

In this chapter, we provide a discussion of what may happen to the economic, political and military situation in Europe as a consequence of EC-1992. A number of scenarios are suggested and the forces working to bring about these scenarios are identified. The very nature of the market integration process is such that if it succeeds, as many want it to, it is certain to alter the economic and political landscape of Europe. The implications of these changes go far beyond Europe itself and will extend to fundamental geopolitical questions—questions such as (1) What will happen to the current superpowers and the bipolar nature of their relationship to which many credit the overall peace and stability that has existed since World War II? (2) Will ideological issues that have dominated the current superpower rivalry be replaced by purely economic ones and if so, how will disputes between emerging superpowers be resolved in the future? (3) If economics does supplant purely ideological concerns and the new twelve nation European Community market does become a strong competitor to the U.S. and Japan, will a three economic bloc-world be stable? (4) How will the East-West situation play out in Europe. Already both Western European and Eastern bloc leaders are talking about the re-unification of Europe. Is such a re-unification in the cards? (5) Will military alliances like NATO survive the changes that have been set in motion by EC-1992 and will Europe increasingly undertake its own foreign policy initiatives which may on occasion, be at odds with the position of what is presently considered the Western alliance of Japan, North America and Europe? (6) Will E.C. membership eventually increase and what are the forces working for or against such a

178

development? Besides EFTA countries, is there a likelihood of some Eastern bloc countries being admitted to the European Community? Hungary, for example, has already been mentioned as a possible candidate. (7) What will the effects of the increased industry concentration that is already underway all over the world, but which is being further encouraged by E.C.-1992, mean for the nature of competition in industries worldwide? Will there be a need for a supranational antitrust system and if so, how will this be constituted?

The above questions give an idea of the far reaching consequences that EC-1992 may have if the Single Market program succeeds and goes on to the level of full political and economic union as some have suggested. One observer[1] has even speculated that the long term concern for the United States will stem from the fact that Europe is trying to integrate internally to become more competitive while Japan may try to forge economic alliances with other Asian countries, leaving North America vulnerable since it is also the one that is saddled with the most developing country debt. At this point, the focus is more on the economic balance of power and many observers feel that future world conflicts will increasingly revolve around economic issues, but a political union in Europe that also takes more responsibility for its military defense is not unthinkable in the future.

What then, are some of the scenarios that we may suggest for Europe after 1992? In order to construct these scenarios, we will first consider a range of possible events in several critical areas of the E.C. integration process. These critical areas which are not completely independent of each other, will be crucial determinants of the shape that Europe will take in the future. The areas are, in order of chronological likelihood:

1. Success of Single Market System
2. Success of common currency/monetary system
3. Expansion of E.C. membership (This will be highly influenced by what happens in the economic/political liberalization process within the East Bloc)

We consider next a range of possible outcomes in each of the above three areas. Specifically,

Success of Single Market System

Failure   Limited   Full

It needs to be emphasized that the White Paper issued by the European Commission in 1985 and the ensuing events leading up to the 1992 deadline are not and have not been contingent on the adoption of a common currency system. Only the successful functioning of the EMS is envisaged at this time and it seems to us that further progress towards a European Central Bank, common currency and complete centralization of monetary and fiscal policy will in large measure depend on the success of the single market program. If the program, set for completion in 1992, achieves a great measure of success on that date or within a reasonable span of time after that date, then the forces working for a single currency and complete monetary union will be greatly strengthened. If, at the other extreme, the single market program gets bogged down and largely fails (it must be remembered that the most difficult directives of the White Paper have yet to be acted on), then it is likely that Europe will stay a fragmented 12-country group and even the degree of cooperation on trade and other matters that have already been achieved, may be threatened. A third possibility which is somewhere along the continuum of failure to success is, of course, that the single market program will be a limited success, and some will argue that the progress achieved so far has already ensured such a level of success. Business leaders and several key politicians in the twelve countries seem convinced that Europe has no choice at this time but to integrate and this fact alone should keep the integration process from unraveling. The degree of success is another matter and a lot will depend on how the events unfold between now and 1992. There is also an element of luck involved because the performance of the global economy, which has already enjoyed an unprecedented length of growth, will be crucial to determining the attitudes of politicians and the general public in Europe without whose enthusiasm, success will be hard to achieve.

If we assume that the single market program will be a success in the forseeable future, if not exactly on December 31, 1992, the next question is whether a common currency and monetary system is going to be adopted by the E.C. after the 1992 process is complete. Once again, there are three possible outcomes. On one extreme, it may be that the creation of a central bank, common currency and other aspects of economic policy will be considered too much of a loss of sovereignty by one or more of the E.C. countries and this nationalistic reaction will scuttle the whole process. It is our view that a successful conclusion of the single market program will ensure that such a complete failure will not occur on the monetary union/currency front. Also, as Lord Cockfield, Vice President of the European Commission has himself said,[2] the only thing an E.C. country loses by taking the final step towards a single currency is the facility of devaluation and that is hardly any loss at all when one thinks about it, because devaluation represents a failure by the country to take care of its economic affairs. At the other extreme, the adoption of a single currency and a move towards full monetary union may move so smoothly that the European Community is just a step away from both political and monetary union. In between the two extremes is the likelihood that a single currency and full union will not occur, but the countries will strengthen the EMS system while expanding the areas in which the ECU is used as a medium of exchange without fully abandoning their own individual currencies and central banks. In this situation, some degree of coordination may be initiated among the central banks in order to cushion wide currency swings and the economic shocks these may cause.

If we can assume that both the single market integration process and the full monetary union are successfully concluded, we may ask whether an expansion of the European Community is likely and if such an expansion occurs, how far could it go and what consequences would it have for the political and military future of Europe?

E.C. officials have often stated that no new members will be allowed into the European Community at least until 1992, and that the first priority is to get the single market integration completed successfully. Thereafter, members may be admitted and already one or more countries have either applied or expressed an interest in joining the European Community. There is no reason to believe that the question of E.C. admission for new countries is necessarily predicated on the single currency/monetary union issue, but we believe along with many others, that a truly successful European Community will have to have a full monetary union someday. Besides, it is unlikely that other countries will be as interested in joining the European Community if the single market integration process has itself been a failure. So, at one extreme we see no new members of the European Community if the earlier two steps in our scenario development have not been successful. At the other extreme, a successful European Community will be a strong attraction for potential new members and we expect that Austria, Norway and Turkey will be admitted relatively soon. Austria has already applied and Turkey has frequently expressed the wish to do so. As this process unfolds, a key question will be whether the political and economic reforms introduced in the East bloc will be successful because some East bloc members could also conceivably be admitted. Indeed, the European Community has already extended special trade preference status to Hungary and it is not inconceivable that Poland and Yugoslavia among others may be strong candidates for special treatment. This, of course, leaves one question unanswered. How will the entry of previously neutral countries (e.g. Austria which is bound by a 1955 neutrality treaty with the Soviet Union) and possibly even East bloc countries, affect the political and military posture of Europe. Clearly, it is a difficult question to answer because of its hypothetical nature and the fact that this scenario seems so remote from today's perspective. On the other hand, the forces drawing Europe away from the strong trans-Atlantic alliance with the United States have already been set in motion and indeed, EC-92 is itself an attempt by the European Community to assert its independence in the marketplace. So, it should be conceivable at the other ex-

treme of the scenario that a united Europe will emerge even if it stops short
of being a federal United States of Europe in the same sense as the United
States of America. Such comparisons with the United States are important
because they are frequently mentioned as the ideal towards which Europe
should strive. Of course, the United States was formed at an earlier time
before all of today's technological and industrial development and it would
be much harder to forge such an alliance today between developed countries
of Europe with their own different languages, cultures, etc. The important
point to note is that unification is possible without a full federal structure
to the Union. The military and defense question is a more interesting one.
Even in the presently constituted European Community, there is a country,
Ireland, which is not part of NATO. What will happen if many other non-
NATO members and possibly some Warsaw Pact members were to be admitted to the European Community? Already, the Soviet Union has reportedly expressed its disapproval to Austria on the latter's application for E.C.
membership. It would appear to us that at this extreme of the scenario when
the political/economic reforms in the East bloc have succeeded and the European Community has successfully completed its single market with a common currency and full monetary union, the thought of a common military
position among European countries should not seem so unlikely. The odds
against such a complete reunification of Europe are, however, so high that
our best guess is that only a limited union will occur in the European Community. In such a limited union, we see a central core of countries which
may be cohesive enough to have close coordination of economic, political
and military matters. Around this core would be countries which are willing
to accept close economic coordination including possibly a common currency. Finally, on the periphery would be other countries that are only interested in the free trade aspects of the relationship. In a sense, the EFTA
countries already enjoy considerable free trade with the European Community and other non-EFTA/non-E.C. countries may seek similar benefits.
One observer has recently suggested that the changes taking place in Hungary, Poland and elsewhere may actually be encouraged by the Soviet Union
in an attempt to Finlandize them and open a direct conduit for the Soviets
to establish the trade links with Western Europe which they so desperately
need. In our view, such a picture of Europe is highly probable and the only
certainty is that, increasingly, the relationship between the United States and
Europe will revolve around economic matters rather than military ones. In
this situation, Europe and the United States will be competitors more than
allies, and with the Pacific Rim countries' economic strength, a tripolar world
will result. History has seen no similar situation and therefore it is very
difficult to speculate on the stability of such a tripolar alignment of economic
power. A reasonable guess is that two of the economic powers will get closely
aligned against the third, but to speculate on what form such a rivalry will

have, takes us too far afield from the topic of this monograph, which was EC-92 and the events currently unfolding as the European Community tries to integrate its market.

ENDNOTES TO CHAPTER 6

1. Peter Passell, "Economic Scene—Old Games, New Rules," *The New York Times,* Wednesday, August 16, 1989, p. 28.
2. Lord Cockfield, "Beyond 1992—The Single European Economy," *European Affairs,* No. 4, 1988 Winter, p. 70.

Appendix
A

The following is adapted from "An Executive's Guide to EC-92: A Glossary of Ten Terms," *Business,* September–October, 1989.

AN EXECUTIVE'S GUIDE TO EC-92:
A GLOSSARY OF TWELVE TERMS

Introduction: Executives around the world are following closely the developments leading up to EC-92—the creation of a single European market set for 1992. The integration of the 12-member E.C. market is expected to allow the free movement of goods, services and factors of production across national borders within the European Community. This will lead to the creation of a single market with a population of 320 million and an economy of $4 trillion. It is generally assumed that the process of E.C. market integration which has been set in motion is irreversible, but there are several aspects of the process that are still unclear and unresolved. Since these aspects will have important implications for firms, the following glossary of terms is designed to inform executives about various facets of the EC-92 question and it is hoped that the discussion below will help executives to consider the important issues that surround the historic market integration process that is currently underway in Europe.

1. *WHITE PAPER:* The European Commission, which is the European Community's principal executive body, put out in 1985, a list of about 300 pieces of legislation which needed to be acted upon before the task of integrating the twelve national markets into a single market could be completed. This document has come to be known as the "White Paper" and it details all the physical, technical and fiscal barriers to the free movement of labor, capital goods and services which have to be removed. About a third of these proposals have already been approved by the E.C. Council of Ministers, which has representation from all 12 member states. Not surprisingly, many of the unresolved areas relate to issues such as harmonization of value-added and excise taxes across member states, public procurement policies, product standards and country of origin rules, quantitative quotas such as the Italian and French restrictions on automobile imports, etc.—issues that are likely to be the most difficult to resolve. The White Paper is, therefore, a document that executives need to understand fully because it represents a sort of scorecard against which to measure the progress of the EC-1992 process.

2. *SINGLE EUROPEAN ACT:* An act passed in mid-1987 by the European Council which is the main legislative body of the European Community. This act has made it easier for the E.C. Council of Ministers to act on directives and regulations initiated by the European Commission. Before this act, the Council of Ministers had to unanimously support a proposal before it could be adopted. The Single European Act makes it possible for the Council of Ministers to adopt a regulation or directive with a majority vote, though there are some areas such as tax matters, where a unanimous vote is still required. Given the divisive nature of many proposals that come to

the Council of Ministers for vote and the difficulty of achieving unanimity, the Act has clearly accelerated the process leading up to a truly integrated European Community Market.

3. *ECU:* The European Community has adopted a common currency known as the European Currency Unit (ECU) for transactions between member countries and other official transactions. The currency, however, is not the medium of exchange at the consumer level because each of the member countries continues to have its own individual currency that is quoted on the world exchange markets and is used for everyday transactions. The ECU is really a weighted average, or a composite unit based on the twelve individual country currencies which floats along with the world's currency market. There are strong nationalist sentiments among some member countries against the adoption of a single European currency for everyday transactions, because this would also imply the creation of a full scale European monetary union (see next topic), which they see as an erosion of their individual identities and national sovereignty.

4. *EUROPEAN MONETARY UNION:* Neither EC-92 nor any of the documents associated with it ("White Paper", "Single European Act", etc.) ever mentioned a full European Monetary Union and everything else that would entail—a common currency, an European Central Bank, etc. However, there are many in the European Community who feel that a complete market integration can only be completed with a full Monetary Union. The topic is, however, so sensitive among some countries and some European leaders that it is not considered a major objective in the near term. It is generally recognized that many elements of the market integration (common product standards, elimination of border controls, tax harmonization) can proceed without the creation of a monetary union, and any attempt to move towards a full monetary union will require revision of the original E.C. treaty. Mr. Jacques Delors, the E.C. Commission President, has issued a report identifying stages in the development of an European Monetary Union, but in the absence of a revision of the original treaty, only the first stage is likely to be possible. The first stage calls only for a coordination of the monetary and budgetary policies among E.C. member countries.

5. *"FORTRESS EUROPE":* a term used to refer to the fear of some companies outside the European Community that after 1992, the E.C. will erect a fortress around it to keep outside firms from having free access to the E.C. market. The fears of a Fortress Europe have taken on several aspects—a great fear among some firms from outside the European Community is that in public procurement, governments at all levels in the E.C. countries will favor local E.C. firms over outside firms in the awarding of contracts. Another concern has been that E.C. local content rules will discriminate against products of non-E.C. firms. There have already been cases, even within the European Community, of Nissan Bluebirds, for example, whose entry into

France from the United Kingdom was sought to be restricted on local content grounds. The United States is somewhat worried that similar problems may arise with say, the export to the European Community of Japanese automobiles made in the United States. A lot of the Japanese investment in E.C. automobile industry, much of it in the United Kingdom, has been in the form of "screwdriver factories," and many in the European Community express concerns about such operations. Ultimately, though, there is increasing talk in the European Community today, not of "Fortress Europe" but "Partner Europe" and companies, particularly from the United States, have little to fear because any protectionist action taken by the European Community is sure to meet with retaliatory action from the United States, and it is in the best interests of the European Community itself to avoid a fortress mentality. The only industry in which there is still considerable concern is financial services because E.C. documents frequently refer to reciprocity (see No. 10) in connection with this industry and the laws regulating the financial services industry differ so much between the United States and Europe that U.S. financial firms are afraid of how the concept of reciprocity may be applied to them.

6. *PRODUCT STANDARDS:* One of the most complicated tasks facing those charged with overseeing the integration of the E.C. market is the great variation in the standards set by the different E.C. member countries for a variety of products. For example, electrical sockets vary from one country to another and would therefore greatly hinder a manufacturer (E.C. or non-E.C.) from taking advantage of the larger E.C. market because economies of scale cannot be achieved when a uniform product standard across the European Community does not exist. Fortunately, some of the greatest movement on the EC-92 process has occurred in the area of setting common standards. The European Community has already adopted common standards in a number of industrial goods, and for gaseous emissions in passenger cars, toys, etc. Work is progressing on standards in a number of other product categories and overall, the issue of product standards should not be one to cause great concern to U.S. firms. Individual firms, in specific industries, will however have to follow the process closely and see if they can participate in the standard-setting exercise. Recently, for example, there was great concern expressed by both U.S. and Japanese companies, because the European Community had adopted a high definition television standard which was incompatible with that of both the United States and Japan.

7. *LOCAL CONTENT REQUIREMENTS:* Reference to this has already been made under 5 above. The European Community, besides stating that it may have to continue quantitative restrictions on the import of some products (e.g. automobiles) for a period of time while the E.C. firms adjust to the new conditions, has also specified local content requirements for a variety of products. The precise definition of "local-content" could be a prob-

lem. If the "amount of value added" is used to define local content, there can be problems for firms from outside the European Community which move to the Community with assembly operations. In such a situation, it may be determined that not enough value was added within the E.C. to meet the local content requirements. Again, Japanese automobile assembly operations may need to be particularly concerned about such a problem. The exact shape of local content requirements finally adopted by the European Community is likely to vary across industries and therefore all firms would be well advised to watch how the "local content" question develops in their respective industries.

8. *EUROBRANDS:* A topic of great interest to firms has been the question of what EC-92 means for their European marketing strategies in general, and their branding policies, in particular. Eurobrands refer to brands that are standardized across Europe. The existence of national boundaries which in turn, required the establishment of national subsidiaries often led to the proliferation of brands. With the integration of the market in 1992, a new opportunity will present itself for consumer product companies in particular, to use common branding and perhaps, other aspects of marketing strategy (e.g. advertising) across Europe. This can help reduce some of the marketing costs for the firm and also lead to a more coherent brand image in an expanded market which will likely see a greater mobility of people across national boundaries. Procter and Gamble is considering making Pampers a Pan European Brand, for example, and other companies like Colgate Palmolive are also looking at how they can make their European marketing strategies more standardized.

9. *TAX HARMONIZATION:* Perhaps the most difficult task facing the creation of a single European market is the harmonization of the various taxes across the E.C. countries which can vary greatly today. This applies to all forms of taxes (corporate, personal income, etc.) but from a marketing standpoint, the two most important ones to consider are the excise and value added taxes (VAT) which are levied on individual products. Value added taxes are a form of sales (consumption) tax that vary greatly across countries in the European Community today. This can lead to a wide variation in final retail prices between E.C. countries and a major task facing the E.C. commission is the harmonization of these taxes. Individual countries in the European Community are also dependent on VAT revenues to differing degrees and this will also have to be taken into account. France, for example, depends on VAT for more than half of its total tax revenue and any harmonization will have to consider means by which high VAT countries can deal with the reductions in VAT that harmonization will bring.

10. *RECIPROCITY:* This is a word that is frequently encountered with reference to the financial services industry in post-1992 Europe. However, the broad principle of reciprocity applies across all industries and basically refers to the fact that access will be provided to outside firms only to the

extent that the countries in which those firms are located give the same access to the foreign firms in that industry. Interestingly, the recent trade legislation passed in the United States called Super-301 has a similar objective and seeks to target those countries for retaliatory action which do not allow free access to their own markets. The reason reciprocity is encountered frequently in connection with the financial services industry in EC-92 is because the E.C. Commission has specifically mentioned access to that industry as being predicated on a reciprocal access to the insurance/banking sector of the foreign country. Many U.S. financial executives have been worried that such a rigid definition of reciprocity may hurt them because the laws relating to financial institutions in the U.S. (ex. Glass-Steagall Act) differ from those in the European Community and E.C. banks cannot be expected to have the same operating mode in the United States as they have in the home country. Another concern relating to reciprocity is that too many bilateral discussions of reciprocity issues may subvert the multilateral approach to trade negotiations in the world, which has been the cornerstone of GATT (General Agreement on Tariffs and Trade).

11. *SOCIAL DIMENSION:* A major part of the market integration process involves the harmonization of national statutes relating to labor laws, professional certification, conditions of employment and other such matters. If free mobility of labor, a major feature of any true common market, is to become a reality, these matters have to be addressed and discrepancies between laws in individual countries have to be reduced or eliminated. There are major differences currently between minimum wages in different countries and in the level of representation of labor in company management—in West Germany, for example, a representative of labor usually sits on the corporate board of public companies. The social dimension, like the monetary union issue is often a divisive one because it is seen as another example of the Community interfering in the sovereign and national policies of individual E.C. countries. At the same time, recognition of professional certification across countries, portability of pension and social security benefits, length of work week across countries and other such policies have to be addressed before the full intent of the White Paper can be achieved. To this end, the European Commission has issued a Social Charter detailing some steps that have to be taken to harmonize the disparate policies of the twelve member countries. The Social Charter is quite specific in some aspects—an E.C.-wide minimum wage and maximum work week have been set down—but also general enough in other aspects to allow individual countries to have some latitude in their deliberations on the social dimension. The latitude has been provided in recognition of the fact that some countries may not choose to participate in this important activity if it is seen that the E.C. administration in Brussels is unilaterally rewriting the employee relations statutes of member nations.

12. *GREENING OF EUROPE:* In many respects, the environmental

movement is much more visible on the other side of the Atlantic than it is in the United States. In the recent elections to the European Parliament held in June, 1989, significant gains were made by various environmentally oriented political parties and constituencies in many E.C. countries. This clear expression of the will of the people makes it imperative that environmental issues be kept at the forefront in the process leading to EC-92. It was perhaps no accident that environmental issues also dominated the deliberations of the Group of Seven during their July, 1989 summit. Memories of the Chernobyl nuclear power plant accident and the Swiss chemical plant incident are fresh in the minds of Europeans and as a result, environmental issues have been given top priority by the European Commission.

The Single European Act of 1987 introduced a specific Treaty basis for rules on the environment. A series of action programs on the environment have been undertaken by the European Community even before the Single European Act but the Act has added fresh impetus to the efforts. The current action program, due to run through 1992, covers a broad list of activities to combat pollution and protect the environment. Already, the European Community has adopted the most stringent restrictions on emissions of small cars even in the face of opposition and concerted lobbying by the E.C. auto manufacturers. These emission restrictions meet those in effect in the United States and should be easy for U.S. and Japanese manufacturers to meet. Other actions relating to the environment that have been taken include:

1. A ban on the use of chlorofluorocarbons (CFC's) in most applications by the end of 1990. The use of these compounds in refrigerators and aerosol spray cans will be completely banned by that date.
2. The E.C. Directorate General on the Environment is also drawing up a proposal for the creation of a voluntary "ecological label" which manufacturers can place on their non-polluting products.

As stated before, current environmental regulations in the European Community are frequently not as stringent as those in the United States but the vigorous environmental movement now evident in the European Community will ensure that as the market integration progresses, manufacturers will have to pay increasing attention to environmental matters. Manufacturers are therefore well advised to voluntarily adopt the strictest environmental standards in all their activities so as to forestall any punitive action against them. BP, the British oil giant, for example, has decided to emphasize the green in its logo as a reflection, in part, of its environmental concern, though the green has been in its logo for a number of decades and initially had nothing to do with environmentalism, whatsoever. (Financial Times, 02/02/89).

Appendix
B

APPENDIX B

There has been so much written on the subject of EC-92 that a completely exhaustive bibliography of books, articles and reports in the popular press would constitute a book in itself. However, Cynthia C. Ryans, Professor of Library Administration at Kent State University has compiled specially for this monograph, an extensive bibliography that will provide the reader with a wealth of additional sources of information on EC-92.

SELECTED BIBLIOGRAPHY

A myriad of materials (books and periodicals) have been written on EC-92 and the list is mounting daily. The references provided here represent a sample of the better publications that have recently appeared, but should in no way be considered a "definitive" listing of E.C. works.

It is particularly important to note the publications where a number of EC-92 related articles have appeared. Some periodicals such as the *Economist,* the *Financial Times (London),* the *New York Times,* and the *Wall Street Journal,* are providing a daily or weekly up-date on EC-92 happenings. Among the books that have been written to date, the Cecchini and the Pelkmans books represent the "classics" and combine theory and practice. In addition, publications by the Conference Board, Ernst & Whinney, Peat Marwick, etc., provide very practical information on the subject.

By carefully reviewing the periodicals/books mentioned here, the corporate/academic reader can identify those publications that should be a part of their EC-92 library. A recent study I completed found that eleven periodicals had particularly heavy (and high quality) coverage of EC-92 issues. These include: *Business America, Economist, Europe, Euromoney, Across the Board, OECD Observer, European Journal of Marketing, Financial Times (London), International Management, McKinsey Quarterly,* and *Journal of Commerce.*

BOOKS

Balassa, Bela. *The Theory of Economic Integration.* Homewood, Ill.: Richard D. Irwin, Inc., 1961.

Bieber, Roland, et al., eds. *1992, One European Market?* Baden-Baden, Germany: Nomos, 1988.

Calingaert, Michael. *The 1992 Challenge From Europe.* Washington, D.C.: National Planning Association, 1988.

Cecchini, Paolo, et al. *The European Challenge, 1992.* Brookfield, Vt.: Gower, 1988.

Coffey, Peter. *Main Economic Policy Areas of the EEC, Towards 1992.* Dordrecht, The Netherlands: Kluwer Academic, 1988.

Davis, Evan, et al. *1992: Myths and Realities.* London: Centre for Business Strategy, London Business School, 1989.

Dudley, James W. *1992: Strategies for the Single Market.* London: Kogan Page Ltd., 1989.

The Elimination of Frontier Barriers and Fiscal Controls. Luxembourg: Office for Official Publications of the European Communities, 1988.

Emerson, Michael, et al. *The Economics of 1992.* New York: Oxford University Press, 1989.

Ernst & Whinney. *Europe 1992: The Single Market.* New York: Ernst & Whinney International, 1988.

Europe 1992. Paris: Presses Universitaires de France, 1989.

Europe 1992: Blueprint for Dictatorship. Wiesbaden: Executive Intelligence Review, 1988.

Europe 1992: Research on the "Cost of Non-Europe". Washington, D.C.: European Community Information Service, 1988.

Gleed, Richard, Andrew Baker and Andrew Blacknell. *Deloitte's 1992 Guide.* London: Butterworths, 1989.

Heseltine, Michael. *The Challenge of Europe.* London: Weidenfeld & Nicolson, 1989.

Howell, R. Patton. *Wars End, 1992: The Revolutionary New Thought in the European Community.* San Francisco, Saybrook, 1989.

King, Robert E. and Helena Tang. *International Macroeconomic Adjustment, 1987–1992.* Washington, D.C.: World Bank, 1989.

Mendes, A. J. Marques. *Economic Integration and Growth in Europe.* London: Croom Helm, 1987.

Morrison, Catherine. *1992: Leading Issues for European Companies.* New York: Conference Board, 1989.

1992: Single European Market. London: Euromonitor Publications, 1988.

Owen, Richard and Michael Dynes. *The Times Guide to 1992.* London: Times, 1989.

Peat Marwick. *1992: Your Passport to Europe.* New York: Peat Marwick, 1988.

Pelkmans, Jacques. *Market Integration in the European Community.* Boston: Martinus Nijhoff, 1984.

Servan-Schreiber, Jean Jacques. *The American Challenge.* New York: Atheneum, 1968.

Slot, P. J. and M. H. van der Woude. *Exploiting the Internal Market: Co-operation and Competition Toward 1992.* Boston: Kluwer Law and Taxation Publishers, 1988.

PERIODICALS

"An Action Plan." *Accountancy* (March 1987), pp. 159–160.

Anguiera, Marta Alfonso. "Harmonizing the World's Accounts," *New Accountant* (September 1989), pp. 11–14+.

Agnelli, Giovanni. "The Europe of 1992," *Foreign Affairs* (Fall 1989), pp. 61–70.

Armbruster, William. "EC Unification Expected to Aid US Exporters," *Journal of Commerce and Commercial* (April 21, 1989), pp. 1–2A.

Armbruster, William. "Plan to Profoundly Affect All Modes of Transport," *Journal of Commerce and Commercial* (April 21, 1989), pp. 1–2A.

Arnold, Tim, John Hooper and Iain Sanderson. "Three Brits Take on 'Unified Europe': What Will 1992 Mean for Sales Promotion?" *Adweek's Marketing Week* (April 3, 1989), pp. P24–25.

Balladur, Edouard. "Investments in Europe," *European Affairs* (Winter 1988), pp. 107–111.

Barnum, Cynthia and Natasha Wolniansky. "A Dress Rehearsal for Europe 1992," *Management Review* (March 1989), pp. 56–58.

Barrett, Matthew. "1992: A New Chapter for Europe," *Euromoney* (September 1988), pp. SS2–5.

Barrett, Matthew. "1992: One for All?" *Euromoney* (September 1988), pp. SS10–12.

Barrett, Matthew. "1992: Yes, But Will It Work," *Euromoney* (September 1988), pp. SS6–9.

Barzini, Luigi. "North vs. South," *International Management* (May 1989), pp. 20–26.

Beguillard, Roberto and Kevin Keegan. "Site Selection in Europe: Planning for '92 Begins Now," *The Journal of European Business* (September–October 1989), pp. 24–29.

Belden, E. Marvin. "Be Ready for 1992," *Business America* (August 1, 1988), pp. 14–16.

Bellanger, Serge. "Toward an Integrated European Banking System: 1992 and Beyond," *The Bankers Magazine* (July–September 1988), pp. 54–59.

Bertrand, Kate. "Scrambling for 1992," *Business Marketing* (February 1989), pp. 49–50.

Bhatt, Gina. "Europe 1992: The Quest for Economic Integration," *Finance & Development* (June 1989), pp. 40–42.

Blanden, Michael. "Toward a New Alliance," *The Banker* (March 1989), pp. 29–31.

Brusea, R. "The European Age" *Financial World* 157 (August 9, 1988), p. 98.

Bruynes, Cees. "Europe in 1992 and Beyond: Philips Looks to the Future," *Europe* (October 1988), pp. 18–19.

Buchan, David. "Building From a Disputed Blueprint," *Financial Times* (July 10, 1989), p. 10.

Buchan, David. "EC 'Set for Two Years of Strong Growth'," *Financial Times* (February 23, 1989), p. 2.

Buchan, David. "New Iron Lady Ventures Onto EC's Tax-Setting Battleground," *Financial Times* (April 17, 1989), p. 6.

Calingaert, Michael. "Information and Influence in 1992," *Association Management* (May 1989), pp. 72–78.

Canna, E. "1992: A Europe Without Frontiers," *American Shipper* 30 (July 1988), pp. 40+.

Carrington, Tim. "Europe's Left Fears 1992 Will Cost Jobs," *The Wall Street Journal* (March 16, 1989), p. A12.

Carson, Ian and Nigel Gibson. "The Return of Peugeot's Punch," *Eurobusiness* (June 1989), pp. 29–31.

Chesnoff, Richard Z. and Julie Wolf. "No Fences Make Good Markets," *U.S. News and World Report* (February 29, 1988), pp. 40–42.

Cockfield, Lord. "Beyond 1992—The Single European Economy," *European Affairs* (Winter 1988), pp. 66–74.

Comes, Frank J., Jonathan Kapstein, John Templeman and Elizabeth Weiner. "Reshaping Europe: 1992 and Beyond," *Business Week* (December 12, 1988), pp. 48–51.

Cooke, Patrick W. and Donald R. Mackay. "The New EC Approach to Harmonization of Standards and Certification," *Business America* (August 1, 1988), pp. 8–9.

Copacino, William C. "Preparing for 1992," *Traffic Management* (January 1989), p. 33.

Cote, Kevin. "European Advertisers Prepare for 1992," *Europe* (September 1988), pp. 18–19.

Cote, Kevin. "Uncertain Future Plagues Marketers Planning for 1992," *Advertising Age* (June 5, 1989), p. 1+.

Cox, Tony. "The EEC Single Market: Who Wins, Who Loses?" *European Chemical News* (September 5, 1988), pp. 18–19.

Crawford, Robert. "The Bottom Line About 1992," *The International Executive* (July–August 1989), pp. 6–7.

Cunniff, John. "Is Europe Ready to Fight or Cooperate," *Marketing News* (July 31, 1989), p. 4.

Dancing to the Tune of 1992," *World Property* (March 1989), p. 19.

De Bony, Elizabeth. "E.C. Is Prying Open Its Telecommunications Market," *Europe* (April 1989), pp. 18–19.

De Nicolais, Gene. "The Fashion and Apparel Sectors Are Becoming Leading Forces in the Rush to Globalize," *Europe* (June 1989), pp. 19–20.

De Toledo, Roberto Pompeu. "The Road to 1992," *World Press Review* (January 1989), pp. 15–16.

Denman, Roy. "Are You Waiting for 1992?" *Industry Week* (May 1, 1989), pp. S2–3.

Denman, Roy. "1992 EEC Economic Unification Won't Harm U.S. Exporters," *Daily News Record* (December 28, 1988), p. 6.

Dickman, S. "OECD Urges Changes for 1992," *Nature* (March 2, 1989), p. 7.

Dickson, Tim. "Americans Put New Accent on EC," *Financial Times* (July 10, 1989), p. 4.

"Divide and Regulate," *The Economist* (August 19, 1989), p. 53.

Dixon, Hugo. "Bad Connections Hamper the Freeing of European Telecoms," *Financial Times* (May 22, 1989), p. 4.

Donath, Bob. "A 'Seat At the Table'," *Business Marketing* (April 1989), p. 4.

Douglas, Susan P. and Yoram Wind. "The Myth of Globalization," *The Columbia Journal of World Business* (Winter 1987), pp. 19–29.

Drucker, Peter. "Strategies for Survival in Europe in 1992," *McKinsey Quarterly* (Autumn 1988), pp. 41–45.

Dulude, Richard. "Poised for Unification: Corning Crystallizes Its Global Strategy," *The Journal of European Business* (September–October 1989), pp. 17–19.

Dumaine, B. "Buying a Euro-Stake That Will Thrive on the Happenings of 1992," *Forbes* (January 30, 1989), pp. 37–38.

Duncan, Tom. "Europe: A Test Market for Global Media," *Marketing & Media Decisions* (April 1989), p. 128.

"EC and COMECON Relations," *European Affairs* (Winter 1988), pp. 99–105.

Egan, Jack. "A Genuine Common Market?" *U.S. News and World Report* (November 7, 1988), p. 96.

Eisberg, Neil. "Dow Plans $1.5bm Budget to Meet 1992 Challenge," *European Chemical News* (March 13, 1989), p. 21.

Emmrich, Stuart. "Consolidation Isn't Easy," *Business Month* (August 1989), p. 34.

Etheridge, J. "Interest Rate on the Rise," *Datamation* (March 1, 1989), pp. 30–31.

"Eurofuture v Europhoria," *Economist* (May 14, 1988), pp. 14–15.

"Europe 1992," *Accountancy* 102 (August 1988), pp. 73–90.

"Europe 1992," *Retail and Distribution Management* (November–December 1922), pp. 4–5.

"Europe Without Borders: Answers to Some Questions," *Europe* (October 1988), pp. 15–17.

"The European Community's Program for a Single Market in 1992," *Department of State Bulletin* (January 1989), pp. 23–28.

"European Retailing Faces the Future," *Chain Store Age Executive* (March 1989), pp. 18–19.

"A European Revolution," *MacLeans* (December 5, 1988), pp. 43–45.

"European Unification—1992," *Marketing News* (October 10, 1988), p. 12.

"European Unification—1992 Challenges U.S. Export Packaging," *Marketing News* (October 10, 1988), p. 12.

Evans, John. "US Bankers Attack European Policy: Changes Requested in Post 1992 Reciprocity Test," *American Banker* (April 10, 1989), p. 6.

Fahey, Allison. "Building for 1992," *Advertising Age* (October 9, 1989), pp. S-4, S-16.

Fallows, James. "Containing Japan," *The Atlantic Monthly* (May 1989), pp. 40–51.

Flint, Jerry. "Don't Tread on Us—Please," *Forbes* (June 12, 1989), p. 92.

Fraser, Ian. "Aiming to Be All Things Everywhere," *Eurobusiness* (June 1989), pp. 15+.

Free, Brant W. "The EC Single Internal Market: Implications for U.S. Service Industries," *Business America* (August 1, 1988), pp. 10–11.

Friberg, Eric G. "1992: Moves Europeans Are Making," *Harvard Business Review* (May–June 1989), pp. 85–89.

Fukukawa, Shinji. "The Role of the Japanese Economy, in a Changing Western World," *European Affairs* (Winter 1988), pp. 143–150.

Fusi, Deborah. "Global Economic Development Community Embracing Europe's Move to a Border-Free Market By 1992," *Site Selection* (February 1989), p. 261.

Gelb, Norman. "Countdown to European Unity," *New Leader* (March 21, 1988), pp. 6–7.

Gelb, Norman. "Europe Without Frontiers," *New Leader* (January 9, 1989), pp. 7–8.

Glage, Wolfgang. "The High Cost of Dismissals and Layoffs in Europe," *The Journal of European Business* (September–October 1989), pp. 30–33.

Goddeson, N. "Rates of Exchange" *Management Today* (September 1988), p. 168.

Graff, Don. "The Gateway to Europe," *World Trade* (Fall 1989), pp. 75, 82, 84.

Graham, W. Gordon. "The Shadow of 1992," *Publishers Weekly* (December 23, 1988), pp. 24–26.

Green, Robert T. "Potential Export Markets and Sources of Foreign Direct Investment," *Texas Business Review* (April 1989), p. 4.

Hamel, Gary. "Making European Firms Fit to Compete?" *Eurobusiness* (June 1989), pp. 8–14.

Herrhausen, Alfred and L. C. Lothar Spath. "Europe in the World Economy," *The McKinsey Quarterly* (Winter 1989), pp. 2–15.

198

Hester, Edward J. "As Europe Prepares for 1992, Insurors Plot Their Strategies," *Risk Management* (September 1989), pp. 20–25.

Higgins, James M. and Tims Santalainen. "Strategies for Europe 1992," *Business Horizons* (July–August 1989), pp. 54–58.

Hill, Julie Skur. "Euro, Pacific Spending Spree: Ad Budgets for '89 Lag in U.S." *Advertising Age* (April 10, 1989), pp. 4–5.

Hoffmann, Stanley. "The European Community and 1992," *Foreign Affairs* (Fall 1989), pp. 27–47.

Holstein, W. J. "Should Small US Exporters Take the Big Plunge?" *Business Week* (December 12, 1988), pp. 64–65.

Hood, Neil and Stephen Young. "Inward Investment and the EC: UK Evidence On Corporate Integration Strategies," *Journal of Common Market Studies* (December 1987), pp. 193–205.

Hormats, Robert D. "Redefining Europe and the Atlantic Link," *Foreign Affairs* (Fall 1989), pp. 71–91.

"How to Spoil 1992," *Economist* (June 4, 1988), pp. 16–17.

Howard, Donald G. and John K. Ryans, Jr. "Advertising Executives' Perceptions of Satellite TV's Potential Impact on the European Market," *European Journal of Marketing* (1989), pp. 22–30.

Hunter, Mark. "How to Get Your Way With the EC," *Business Month* (August 1989), pp. 42–44.

Kamm, Thomas and Philip Revzin. "Takeovers Aren't Likely to Sweep Europe," *The Wall Street Journal* (August 7, 1989), p. A14.

Kastil, Peter. "Europe's Safe for American Hondas," *The Wall Street Journal* (September 1, 1989), p. 2.

Keatings, Giles. "Towards a Free Market Approach to EMU," *Financial Times* (September 1, 1989), p. 17.

Keen, Michael. "Pareto-Improving Indirect Tax Harmonisation," *European Economic Review* (January 1989), pp. 1–11.

"Key to 1992," *Economist* (July 25, 1987), p. 13.

Kindel, Stephen. "Europe's Baby Boomers Clamor for American Luxury Goods," *The Journal of European Business* (September–October 1989), pp. 20–23.

Kirkland, R. I. "Outsiders' Guide to Europe in 1992," *Fortune* (October 24, 1988), pp. 121–124.

Koekkoek, Ad. "The Competitive Position of the EC in Hi-Tech," *Weltwirctschaftliches Archiv* (1987), pp. 157–168.

Krause, Axel. "1992's Impact on American Business Accelerates," *Europe* (June 1989), pp. 14–15.

Krugman, Paul. "EFTA and 1992," *EFTA Bulletin* (July 9, 1988), p. 21.

Kuttner, R. "The US Should Applaud the Coming of Europe . . . ," *Business Week* (July 11, 1988), p. 16.

Lamb, Denis. "EC Project 1992: The Dynamics of Change," *Department of State Bulletin* (February 1989), pp. 31–35.

Lamoriello, F. "Completing the Internal Market By 1992," *Business America* (August 1, 1988), pp. 4–6.

Lane, David. "Foreigners Gulp Down Some Tasty Tidbits," *Financial Times* (June 21, 1989), p. 6.

Laurent, Pierre-Henri. "The European Community: Twelve Becoming One," *Current History* (November 1988), pp. 357–360.

Lawdy, D. "Do Unto Others," *U.S. News and World Report* (September 12, 1988), pp. 55–58.

Lawler, Drew. "The Father of '1992'," *World Trade* (Fall 1989), pp. 32, 34, 70.

Leadbeater, Charles. "Transnationals Key Force in Economic Integration," *Financial Times* (September 15, 1988), p. 3.

Lee, Susan. "An Impossible Dream," *Forbes* (July 25, 1988), pp. 78–83.

Levitt, Theodore. "The Globalization of Markets," *Harvard Business Review* (May–June 1983), pp. 92–102.

Lewis, Peter. "Toward a Unified Europe," *MacLeans* (June 6, 1988), p. 41.

Linehan, Donald J. "Lessons from Europe 1992," *International Advertiser* (August–September 1989), pp. 17–19.

Liscio, J. "Europe 1992: A Truly Common Market?" *Barrons* (October 3, 1988), pp. 8–9+.

Loro, Laura. "Ads Across the Atlantic," *Advertising Age* (June 5, 1989), p. 51.

Lucaire, L. Edward. "Europe 1992: No Turning Back," *International Advertiser* (November–December 1988), pp. 13+.

McBurnie, Tony. "1992: The Realties of Single European Marketing," *Quarterly Review of Marketing* (April 1989), pp. 18–19.

McClenahen, John S. "Europe 1992: The Challenge to U.S.," *Industry Week* (April 3, 1989), pp. 78–82.

McClenahen, John S. "Europe's 1992 Challenge" *Industry Week* (July 4, 1988), pp. 16–17.

Macrae, Norman. "As 1992 Nears, Europe's Food Giants Battle for Dominance," *Business Month* (August 1989), pp. 21–23.

Macrae, Norman. "Holland Suffers From an Acute Case of Eurosclerosis," *Business Month* (March 1989), pp. 30–31.

Macrae, Norman. "1992 and All That: A Common Market in Name Alone," *Business Month* (June 1988), pp. 22–23.

Magee, John F. "1992: Moves Americans Must Make," *Harvard Business Review* (May–June 1989), pp. 78–84.

Maier, Harry. "Perestroika and East-West Relations," *European Affairs* (Winter 1988), pp. 22–25.

"Marketing the UK's Retail Revolution Post 1992," *Quarterly Review of Marketing* (Autumn 1988), pp. 1–4.

Martin, Lynda and James Rider. "1992 Opening Up Europe," *Euromoney* (September 1988), pp. SS20–22.

Maskal, Brian S. "Unprepared for '92," *Industry Week* (April 3, 1989), pp. 87–88.

Mead, Richard. "Europe 1992: The Single Market," *Management Accounting* (August 1989), pp. 25–27.

Melcher, Richard A., Gregory L. Miles, et. al. "Will the New Europe Cut U.S. Giant Down to Size?" *Business Week* (December 12, 1988), pp. 54–56.

Metzer, Andre. "Europe 1992: Opportunities Await Small Businesses," *Transportation and Distribution* (February 1989), pp. 26–29.

200

Meyer, Michael. "Storming 'Fortress Europe'", *Newsweek* (November 7, 1988), p. 82.

Milmo, Sean. "Are You Ready for 1992?" *Business Marketing* (September 1988), pp. 66–69.

Mitchell, David. "1992: The Implications for Management, *Long Range Planning* (February 1989), pp. 32–40.

Molyneux, Paul. "Big Fist, Little Fist," *The Banker* (January 1989), pp. 38–39.

"The Month in Europe," *Eurobusiness* (June 1989), pp. 44+.

Murray, Tom. "From European to Pan-European," *Business Month* (August 1989), pp. 35–37.

Murrow, David. "Various Paths Take Publishers to '92 Ad Opportunities," *Advertising Age* (June 5, 1989), p. 50.

"1992," *Economist* (July 9, 1988), pp. S1–S20.

"1992: A Load of Old Hype?" *Asian Finance* (May 15, 1989), p. 73.

"1992: Supplying Electronics to 320 Million Europeans," *Electronic Business* (September 15, 1988), pp. 16–18.

"1992 and All That," Publishers Weekly (February 3, 1989), pp. 21–28.

"1992 in a Global Context," *Multinational Business* (August 1988), pp. 1–7.

"1992 Winners and Losers," *Multinational Business* (August 1988), pp. 38–41.

Norman, Peter. "Success Turns to Uncertainty," *Financial Times* (March 13, 1989), p. 21.

Northart, Leo J. "Japan's Euro Watch," *International Advertiser* (November–December 1988), pp. 10–12.

O'Connor, Robert. "Europe's Oil Firms Face Challenge of Unified Market," *Oil Daily* (April 3, 1989), pp. 1–2.

Orr, Bill. "Fortress Europe?" *ABA Banking Journal* (April 1989), pp. 68–70.

Painton, Frederick. "Toward Real Community?" *Time* (April 18, 1988), pp. 54–55.

Patterson, Timothy D. "Globalization—With a Southern Accent," *World* (1989), pp. 16–27.

Perrin-Pelletier, Francois. "1992: A European Market for Cars?" *Long Range Planning* (June 1988), pp. 27–33.

Porter, Janet. "Rotterdam Prepared for 1992, Plans to Double Box Capacity," *Journal of Commerce and Commercial* (April 24, 1989), p. 10B.

Pyykkonen, Martin and Santhanam C. Shekar. "Europe Inc.: Exploiting the Window of Opportunity," *The Journal of European Business*. (September–October 1989), pp. 6–16.

Quinlan, Martin. "West Europe: Companies Braced for 1992 Changes," *Petroleum Economist* (January 1989), pp. 9–11.

Raphel, Murray. "End of the World Is Coming in 1992," *Direct Marketing* (November 1988), pp. 103–104.

Reichel, Jurgen. "How Can Marketing Be Successfully Standardised for the European Market?" *European Journal of Marketing* (1989), pp. 60–66.

Richard, Ivor. "How to Make the Most of the Community," *Euromoney* (September 1988), pp. SS26–29.

Riemer, Blanca, Joyce Heard, and Thane Peterson. "Laying the Foundation for a Great Wall of Europe," *Business Week* (August 1, 1988), pp. 40–41.

Rogalski, Heather. "When the Standard Is European," *Northeast International Business* (July 1989), pp. 17+.

Rosenbloom, Arthur H. "Buying Into Europe," *The International Executive* (July–August 1989), pp. 23–27.

Russell, John. "A Single European Market for Insurance: Fact or Fiction?" *The Journal of European Business* (September–October 1989), pp. 34–37.

Sansbury, Tim. "Will Integration Boost Coal Trade?" *Journal of Commerce and Commercial* (April 20, 1989), pp. 1–2A.

Seipp, Walter. "Is There a Place for Americans in Post 1992 Europe?" *American Banker* (February 3, 1989), pp. 10–11.

Senigallia, Silvio F. "One Europe Indivisible?" *New Leader* (January 23, 1989), pp. 5–6.

"Shape of Things to Come," *The Banker* (September 1988), pp. 31–34.

Sher, Paul D. "Countdown to 1992: Introduction to the Single Market," *Site Selection* (February 1989), pp. 263–264.

Simmonds, Andy. "1992—a Force for Change in Corporate Reporting?" *Accountant's Magazine* (January 1989), pp. 16–17.

Singh, S. Nihal. "From Market to Community," *World Press Review* (January 1989), p. 14.

Specht, Marina. "Southern Europe Heats Up for '92," *Advertising Age* (June 5, 1989), p. 47.

Stone, Nan. "The Globalization of Europe: An Interview With Wisse Dekker," *Harvard Business Review* (May–June 1989), pp. 90–95.

"Storming the World's Biggest Market," *Business Tokyo* (Summer 89), pp. 41–42.

Straetz, Robert. "U.S. Exporters Should Find That Benefits of 'Europe 1992' Program Will Outweigh Problems," *Business America* (May 22, 1989), pp. 10–11.

Sullivan, S. "Who's Afraid of 1992?" *Newsweek* (October 31, 1988), pp. 32–34.

Tate, P. "With Europe's Market Unity Comes IS Urgency," *Datamation* (March 1, 1989), pp. 28–32.

Taverne, Dick. "1992: The View From Outside," *Euromoney* (September 1988), pp. SS14–16.

Taylor, Robert. "Danes Finally Come to Terms With EC." *Financial Times* (June 7, 1989).

Taylor, Robert. "Looming EC Deadline Prompts EFTA Rethink," *Financial Times* (March 14, 1989), p. 4.

"Telecommunications in Europe-The Challenge of Change," *European Affairs* (Winter 1988), pp. 78–98.

"They've Designed the Future and It Might Just Work," *Economist* (February 13, 1988), pp. 45–46.

Thimm, Alfred L. "Europe 1992—Opportunity or Threat for U.S. Business," *California Management Review* (Winter 1989), pp. 54–75.

Thompson, Donald N. "Buyouts and Buyins: Europe's 1992 Shows the Big Way for Free Trade," *Business Quarterly* (Winter 1989), pp. 42–46.

Thompson, Roger. "EC92," *Nation's Business* (June 1989), pp. 18–24.

Thompson, Sandra J. "The Making of an Internal Market Directive: The European Community's Legislative Process," *Business America* (August 1, 1988), p. 12.

Tigner, B. "Home-Country Rule: The Catalyst for 1992 That Makes Us All Equal," *International Management* (September 1988), p. 16.

"The Time to Forge Ties Is Now, Not After 1992," *American Metal Market* (April 11, 1989), p. 14.

"To 1992," *Economist* (April 23, 1988), pp. 52–53.

Toll, Erich E. "Hamburg Predicts '92 Unity May Slow Port's Nordic Trade," *Journal of Commerce and Commercial* (April 24, 1989), p. 10B.

"Tomorrow's Europe," *Economist* (April 25, 1987), pp. 49–50.

Tully, Shawn. "Europe Gets Ready for 1992," *Fortune* (February 1, 1988), pp. 81–84.

"U.S. Business Should Prepare Now for EC 1992," *Business America* (October 24, 1988), pp. 12–16.

"United Kingdom: Positioning Itself to Profit in 1992," *Expansion Management* (May/June 1989), pp. 29+.

Vandermerwe, Sandra. "Strategies for a Pan European Market," *Long Range Planning* (June 1989), pp. 45–53.

Vandermerwe, Sandra and Marc-Andre L'Huillier. "Euro-Consumers in 1992," *Business Horizons* (January–February 1989), pp. 34–40.

Verity, C. William. "U.S. Business Needs to Prepare Now for Europe's Single Internal Market," *Business America* (August 1, 1988), pp. 2–3.

Vernon, Raymond. "Can the US Negotiate for Trade Equality?" *Harvard Business Review* (May–June 1989), pp. 96–103.

"The View From the Boiler Room," *Economist* (May 14, 1988), p. 52.

Vranitzky, Franz. "Austria at the Doorstep," *European Affairs* (Winter 1988), pp. 49–54.

Wallace, Alan. "Europe 1992: Old World, New Market," *Business Age* (June 1989), pp. 22–26.

Wallenberg, Peter. "Submit the Single Market to Global Forces," *European Affairs* (Winter 1988), pp. 116–119.

Watson, Richard. "1992: There's More to Tax Than Martelange," *Euromoney* (September 1988), pp. SS17–19.

Weinberger, Casper W. "The Common Market—Friend or Foe?" *Forbes* (March 6, 1989), p. 31.

Weinberger, Casper W. "1992 Is Closer Than We Think," *Forbes* (April 17, 1989), p. 33.

Wentz, Laurel. "1992 to Breed Global Brands," *Advertising Age* (April 24, 1989), p. 44.

Werber, Marilyn. "Japan, Europe 1992 Seen As Challenges to US," *American Metal Market* (April 7, 1989), p. 2.

Wijnand, George. "Try to Put Yourself in His Place," *European Affairs* (Winter 1988), pp. 112–115.

William, Francis. "An Uneasy Truce," *Eurobusiness* (June 1989), pp. 24–27.

"Working for a Unified Europe By 1992," *Communication World* (December 1988), pp. 27–28.

Zampaglione, Arturo. "A Family Business Takes the World By Storm," *Europe* (June 1989), p. 21.